IPR, Biosafety and Bioethics

IPR, Biosafety and Bioethics

Deepa Goel

Assistant Professor
IMS Engineering College
Ghaziabad

Shomini Parashar

Assistant Professor
IMS Engineering College
Ghaziabad

Pearson

Assistant Editor–Acquisitions: Jigyasa Bhatia
Associate Editor–Production: M.R. Ramesh

ISBN 978-81-317-7470-0

First Impression

Published by Pearson India Education Services Pvt. Ltd, CIN: U72200TN2005PTC057128.

Head Office: 1st Floor, Berger Tower, Plot No. C-001A/2, Sector 16B, Noida - 201 301, Uttar Pradesh, India.

Registered Office: 6th Floor, Tower A, Unit A and B, International Tech Park, CapitaLand Chennai, 200 Feet Radial Road,Zamin Pallavaram, Old Pallavaram Chennai – 600117, Tamil Nadu, India

Website: in.pearson.com; Email: companysecretary.india@pearson.com

Digitally printed in India by Trinity Academy for Corporate Training Ltd, New Delhi in the year of 2026

Contents

Preface xi
Acknowledgements xiii
About the Authors xiv

Chapter 1 Meaning and Justification of Patenting an Invention 1

Introduction to Intellectual Property Rights 1
Concept of IPR 2
Designs 10
Trademarks™ 11
Trade Secret (TS) 12
Domain Names 13
Geographical Indications 13
Copyright© 14
Chapter Summary 19
Multiple Choice Questions 20
Review Questions 20

Chapter 2 History and Evolution of Patent Law 21

Evolution of Patent Laws 21
History of Indian Patent System 22
International Conventions and Treaties 27
Patent Laws in Other Countries 39
Chapter Summary 45
Multiple Choice Questions 46
Review Questions 46

Chapter 3 Classification of Patents 47

Classification of Patents in India 47
Classification of Patents by WIPO 48
Categories of Patent 50
Special Patents 50
Patenting Biological Products 57
Chapter Summary 60
Multiple Choice Questions 61
Review Questions 61

Chapter 4 Grant of Patent and Patenting Authorities 62

Invention 62
Eligibility Criteria 62
Patentable Inventions in India and Abroad 63
Non-Patentable Inventions in India and Abroad 66
Patent Office 70
Patent Authorities 72
Chapter Summary 81
Multiple Choice Questions 82
Review Questions 83

Chapter 5 Patent Owner: Rights and Duties 84

Ownership of Patent 84
Rights of Patent Holder and Co-owners 85
Duties of Patent Holder and Co-owners 86
Transfer of Patent Rights 87
Limitations of Patent Rights 90
Restoration of Patents 92
Infringement of Patent Rights and Offences 92
Actions Against Infringement: Remedies/Relief 94
Patent Agent 99
Chapter Summary 100
Multiple Choice Questions 101
Review Questions 101

Chapter 6 Protection of Plant Varieties and Farmers' Rights Act, 2001 102

Methods of Protection of Plant and Plant Products 102
Essentialities of Plant Protection 106
Plant Variety Protection and Farmer's Right Act 106
UPOV Convention (Plant Varieties) 1961 113
Chapter Summary 114
Multiple Choice Questions 115
Review Questions 115

Chapter 7 Patent Law: Present Scenario 116

Patent and Economy 116
Patent Management 118
Patent Growth 119
Patenting in Life Forms 119
Biodiversity and IPR 121

Bioinformatics Patenting 122
Gene Patenting 124
New Patent Regime 126
Chapter Summary 127
Multiple Choice Questions 128
Review Questions 128

Chapter 8 Introduction to Biosafety 129

Overview of Biosafety 129
Risk Assessment 130
Cartagena Protocol on Biosafety 132
Capacity Building 133
Chapter Summary 137
Multiple Choice Questions 137
Review Questions 137

Chapter 9 GMOs: Concerns and Challenges 138

Introduction 138
Transgenic Technology 138
Gene Flow 143
Future Opportunities and Challenges 148
Chapter Summary 149
Multiple Choice Questions 149
Review Questions 149

Chapter 10 National and International Regulatory Mechanism for GMO 150

Introduction 150
International Regulatory Bodies 151
National Regulatory Bodies 153
Regulatory Measures for Biosafety 159
Biosafety Guidelines in India Evolved by DBT 160
Prevention Food Adulteration Act, Food and Safety Standard Bill and Seed Policy 161
Rules for the Manufacture and Storage of Hazardous Microorganism and GMO 163
Biosafety Management 164
Chapter Summary 165
Multiple Choice Questions 166
Review Questions 166

Chapter 11 Biosafety of Genetically Engineered Products 167

Genetically Engineered Products and Recombinant DNA Technology 167
Risk Assessment of RDT Products 168
Regulating Recombinant DNA Technology 168
Permit for Movement and Import of GMOs 169
Some of the Products Developed from RDT and Their Biosafety Issues 169
Biosafety in Gene Therapy 171
Ecological Safety Assessment of Recombinant Organisms 172
Chapter Summary 173
Multiple Choice Questions 174
Review Questions 174

Chapter 12 Allergenicity: Assessment of Genetically Modified Food 175

Introduction 175
Food Allergy 175
Allergens and GMOs 177
Chapter Summary 180
Multiple Choice Questions 180
Review Questions 181

Chapter 13 Introduction to Bioethics 182

Bioethics and Its Scope 182
Different Approaches to Ethics 183
Biological Weapons and Their Social and Ethical Implications 194
Chapter Summary 195
Multiple Choice Questions 195
Review Questions 196

Chapter 14 NGOs for Biosafety and Bioethics 197

Introduction to NGOs 197
Public Sector Organizations 198
Private Sector Organizations 198
National NGOs 199
Media 200
Important Roles that NGOs Play 200
Chapter Summary 201
Multiple Choice Questions 201
Review Questions 201

Chapter 15 Web-based Information of Biosafety on GMO 202

Introduction 202
Biosafety Database 203
Chapter Summary *205*
Review Questions *205*

Chapter 16 Good Laboratory Biosafety Practices 206

Importance of Good Laboratory Practices 206
General Good Laboratory Practices 212
Multiple Choice Questions *212*
Review Questions *212*

Chapter 17 Case Studies in IPR and Biosafety 214

Diamond vs Chakraborty Case (1980) 214
Dimminaco A.G. Case (2002) 215
Neem Patent Case 215
Turmeric Patent Case 215
Asgrow Seed Co. vs Winterboer Case 216
Harward College vs Canada Case 216
Delta Pineland Co. vs the Sinker's Corporation Case 217
Myriad's Case on Gene Patenting 217
Bt Brinjal 218
Bt Cotton 220
Golden Rice 221

Glossary 225
Related Websites 229
References 230
Index 231

Preface

Biotechnology, the discipline that has taken centre stage in the 21st century, is now creating products for all spheres of life such as human health care, industrial processing, environmental bioremediation, food and agriculture. Biotechnological advances give researchers the power to change the characteristics of a living organism by transferring the genetic information from one organism to another, thus exploring new frontiers and effecting novel inventions in the process. After the creation of Dolly, the first successfully cloned sheep in early 1997, the advances in genetic engineering have gained global attention. Biotechnology includes areas of development of transgenic crops, structural and functional genomics, development of new drugs and bio-molecules, both in plant and animal sciences and other diverse sources that could provide us with vital breakthrough in both quality and quantity to achieve improvements in a sustainable manner.

New developments in biotechnology carry legal implications and many are clouded by ethical controversies. Research in this sophisticated area requires huge monetary investments and dedication of time. Institutes, companies and research centres investing in such research are looking to protect their investments; as a result, the patent process has become important in the field of biotechnology. Intellectual property is abstract but the rights that protect it are real. The knowledge of intellectual property rights (IPR) is essential for all students who work in this area. They should know how their work should be protected and what benefits they can draw out of their intellectual property. They should be aware of the ways in which they can contribute to the name and fame of their institute/organization and, broadly, to their country. We understand that biotechnology processes and products thereof in diverse areas have great promises for agriculture, medicine and other industrial applications. However, ironically, many of the economic and medical advantages associated with the genetic modification of plants and animals are considered to be biologically disadvantageous. Many organizations and people are hesitant to accept genetically modified produce for personal, philosophical religious and bioethical reasons.

There can be huge benefits from transgenic crops if they are handled properly, keeping biosafety and bioethical concerns in mind before they are commercialized. Biosafety and bioethics relate to the safe application of biotechnology to the environment, human and animal health. India has framed the rules for regulatory activities involving the use of genetically engineered organisms (GEO) and their products in 1989. The use of GEO addresses the issues that may have adverse effects on the conservation and sustainable use of biological diversity, taking into account the risk to human health and trans-boundary movements. These biosafety protocols have been designed all over the world for the sustainable development of biological diversity.

This book provides a broad coverage of IPR, Biosafety and Bioethics. The contents of this book are developed to create an awareness in students about intellectual property, to foster a better understanding of the rights associated with intellectual property, to discuss biosafety and bioethical concerns of modern society, to motivate research and development and ultimately, to instil in them a personal respect for IPR in a way that changes their perception about copied content and work.

Presently, very few books are available on IPR, Biosafety and Bioethics that are student-friendly. The course contents of this book are in accordance with the syllabi of graduate and post graduate students (B.Tech., M.Tech., B.Sc. and M.Sc.) of Indian universities and are written in a simple language to ensure that the concepts are well understood by the student-reader.

Deepa Goel
Shomini Parashar

Acknowledgements

During the course of writing this book, I was fortunate enough to get help and guidance from a large number of people. It is my pleasure to acknowledge them though it is still an inadequate gesture in appreciation of their contributions.

At the outset, I express my profound gratitude to my late grandfather, Shri. Ram Sahay Ji, and my late uncle, Shri. Ramniwas Gupta Ji, who inspired me constantly to devote time and effort in active pursuit of scientific rigour and academic excellence.

I am obliged to my friend and colleague, Mamoon Rashid, for his suggestions and my friend and co-author, Shomini Parashar, who was always available with her elegant ideas during our brainstorming sessions relating to this book.

Thanks are due to my past and current students at IMS Engineering College, Ghaziabad; my interaction them helped me shape my thoughts on the subject.

I am also thankful to my husband, Puneet, who helped me with the proof reading of the chapters of this book, and to my family members for their constant support and encouragement.

Deepa Goel

Writing a book is an arduous task. A small idea that sprouted, gradually took shape as a book. I have a long list of people to thank for their helpful comments and suggestions.

I would like to express my gratitude to the many people who helped me obtain factual materials, all those who provided support, talked things over, read, wrote, offered comments, allowed me to quote their remarks and assisted me in editing, proofreading and designing the book.

I am indebted to my colleague, Mamoon Rashid, for reviewing the chapters and enabling me to publish this book, and my friend, Dr Keerti Gupta, for supporting me throughout the process. I have a long association with my collegue and friend, Dr. Deepa Goel, who is also my co-author. I thank her for always sharing and solving the problems we had faced while writing the book.

Above all, I thank my husband, Subhash, and the rest of my family for their support and encouragement to take up this task.

Shomini Parashar

About the Authors

Dr Deepa Goel is Assistant Professor at the Department of Biotechnology in IMS Engineering College, Ghaziabad. She received her postgraduate degree in Biotechnology from Banasthali Vidyapith, Rajasthan, and her PhD from Delhi University, Delhi. Her core area of interest is the development of transgenic plants with elite traits.

Ms Shomini Parashar is Assistant Professor at the Department of Biotechnology in IMS Engineering College, Ghaziabad. A postgraduate in Microbiology from Gurukul Kangri Vishwavidyalya, Haridwar, she has also received an MPhil degree in Bioinformatics. She is currently pursuing active research for her PhD at Mahamaya Technical University, Noida. Her core area of interest is screening of microbes with novel traits that are useful to mankind.

1

Meaning and Justification of Patenting an Invention

Chapter Objectives

This chapter introduces the concept, definition and types of Intellectual Property Rights (IPR). Intellectual property is an intangible property that a person can hold. Before filing a patent, it is important to know the three essential prerequisites of the Indian Patent Act, which are novelty, inventive step and industrial applicability. The chapter describes briefly the different types of intellectual properties, namely patent, design, trademark, copyright and trade secrets. It also differentiates among the four major forms of intellectual properties.

INTRODUCTION TO INTELLECTUAL PROPERTY RIGHTS

The capability of the brain to think and imagine something innovative or novel is known as 'intellect'. When someone possesses such an intellect, which can be used to invent something for the benefit of the masses, then the invention becomes his property, for which he can possess all the rights to use it the way he likes. There are various types of intellectual properties that are intangible in nature: patents, trademark, copyright and trade secrets. Intellectual property is just like any other form of property a person can possess in the form of movable and immovable assets. However, unlike other forms, its origin is intellectual. Such properties are associated with rights, which are given to the person who created the intellectual property. If a person invents a machine which is a unique design on crockery, then he is eligible for various patents. He can file a patent for such a machine design. The method of making that machine and the product obtained from the machine can also be considered as his intellectual property. If everything falls under the patentability criteria and the inventor wishes, he can be given all the rights to hold the monopoly of that machine or the product produced by the machine.

Invention and creativity are two major aspects that give benefits and help in the economic development of the nation. Protection of such creativity and invention is very important. Intellectual property is an indicator of the economic growth of the country and needs to be protected in order to prevent the trans-boundary movement of novel inventions. It implies a grant from the sovereign power, securing the invention for a limited period of time from making, using and selling by others. The central concept behind 'patent law' is the protection of intellectual property, without which anyone can have free access to copy new and innovative processes, treatments, formulas and secrets from the original inventor. This deprives the rights of the real inventor.

Moreover, it is also important to motivate the inventors so that there is always a regular inflow of innovative ideas for performing further research and development, and this motivation can be achieved by patents.

The term 'patent' is derived from the Latin word *literae patentes*, which means an 'open letter'. The Crown in England used to grant a right to an individual by writing a document with the seal of King or Queen. Such grants were known as 'letters patent'. This was a letter which was rolled up and not sealed. Nowadays, the word patent is used as a synonym to the monopoly right associated with the invention. In French *Brevet* (Latin, meaning brief letters) is the document that grants right or privilege for an identified invention.

Thus, patents dating back several years in different forms are legal rights, which are granted for new inventions based on scientific and technical knowledge. It does not permit the inventor to commercialize the invention and prevents others from using and benefitting out of the patented invention. The patent protects the first producer or inventor of an article against manufacturing, using or selling the article without his/her consent. It should also be clear that the patent is not granted for an idea or principle as such, but can be granted for an article or the process of making an article by applying an idea. A common misconception about the patent right is that it gives an inventor absolute right to exploit the invention but it is not so. The exploitation of the right also depends on whether others have patent, which overlap with the subject matter of the invention. It also depends on other existing laws, such as those concerning health and safety. The basic patent right provided under trade-related aspects of intellectual property rights (TRIPs) agreement is that the patent holder has the legal right to prevent others from making, using or selling the new invention for a limited period of time, with a number of exceptions, which we will study in the following chapters. It, however, does not provide information on whether the product is safe for the customer or not.

CONCEPT OF IPR

Invention can be seen throughout Nature and is a well-recognized phenomenon that can be seen in birds and other animals in the construction of their dwelling places with intricacy. For example, the tailorbird constructs a well-weaved nest, bees construct honeycombs and the spider constructs its web, each of which are unique in their style. They all do it without any risk of appropriation of the invention of one species by another. Infringements are done by man alone and so an invention requires protection from unauthorized copying or commercial exploitation, which hampers the rights and profit of the real inventor.

The most significant feature of an invention is that it must be useful, novel and unobvious. It is a contract between an inventor and the government where the government grants a limited monopoly right to the inventor excluding others from using, selling or manufacturing that particular invention. But it has the condition that the details of the invention have to be disclosed by the inventor in the application for filing the patent. Thus, the whole of the patent can be thought of as a contract between the inventor and the state. Both of them bring consideration to that contract.

Under this social contract, a person applying for the patent brings consideration in terms of fees and finally after getting the patent gets consideration as royalty. The inventor is given the exclusive rights to prevent others from using, selling or manufacturing the patented invention/article for a fixed period of time and as a result gets the reward for disclosing his invention to the public. Ultimately, it can be concluded that the patent is not only a patentee's consideration but also a consideration of the state as well the country. It is not possible to separate the patent and the state.

Forms of Intellectual Property Rights

Intellectual property (IP) could be called a gift to mankind. By using this, special abstract innate gift creations and innovations that are beneficial to mankind can be designed. But it is also important

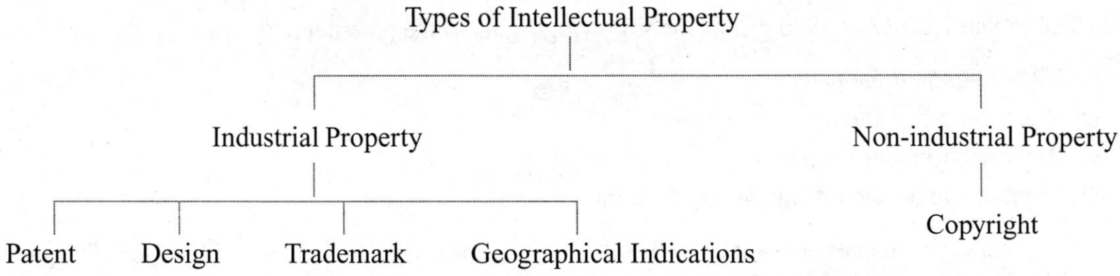

Figure 1.1 *Types of Intellectual Property*

to safeguard the misuse of such inventions and protect the rights of the inventor. As it is common knowledge that any property, moveable or immovable, is to be legally protected in order to prevent it from getting stolen, similarly the rights in the intellectual property created need also to be protected to prevent it from infringement. There can be various kinds of innovations based on research, ideas and thoughts, graphics, designs and the way of writing a logo, and many more.

The different forms of intellectual properties are shown in Figure 1.1. Patents, designs, trademarks, copyright and geographical indications, follow their own rights and term of protection. Patents are for new inventions, which are solutions to scientific and technical problems. Industrial designs are aesthetic creations determining the appearance of industrial products. Trademarks are useful to the consumer for the identification of the product manufacturer. Copyrights are the rights given for literary works, artistic works, software, etc. We would be discussing them in detail in this chapter.

Patents

Patent is an open letter. Patent is the grant of legal rights, privilege, property or authority for new inventions employing scientific and technical knowledge. A patent is issued by the government to give the inventor exclusive rights for a limited period or 'term' (20 years for patent) for their innovation. The subject of patent, which involves scientific and legal issues, is relatively complicated as compared with the other types of intellectual property like designs, trademarks and copyrights. It involves inventions which are new, useful, industrially applicable and non-obvious with an exhaustive list of non-patentable inventions. Some important examples of patents are calculator, television, elevator, radio, anaesthetic drugs, diesel engine, sewing machine, typewriter, motion picture, air conditioner and computer.

In India, currently, the Patents Act 1970 and the corresponding rules govern the grant of patents. Indian Parliament has made several comprehensive amendments to the Patents Act 1970 in 1999, 2002, 2005 and 2006. Patent Rules 2003 were amended in 2005 and again in 2006. Some of the important features of both the 2005 and 2006 rules are the introduction of reduced timelines and a fee structure based on specification size and number of claims, in addition to a basic fee. The amendment in 2005 has major implications on the introduction of product patent protection for food, pharmaceutical and chemical inventions (agrochemicals) and examination of the 'mail box' applications. This was done under the TRIPs obligation to introduce product patenting in these sectors, latest by 1 January, 2005. Until, then only process patents were allowed in India. As on date, India is fully compliant with its international obligations under the TRIPs agreement.

The Indian Patent Act 1970 grants the following rights to the patentee:

- Right to exploit the patent
- Right to license and assign the patent
- Right to surrender the patent
- Right to sue for the infringement of patent.

The patent system does not protect each and every inventor who conceives an invention. The patent is granted based on the right on first disclosure of an invention. Whosoever tries to hinder the rights of the patentee suffers from remedies available for the infringement. There are legal remedies or punishments available for the patentee like interlocutory or interim injunction, damages or account of profits or permanent injunction.

Prerequisites for a patent

Patent is an invention that is novel, useful and industrially productive and which is so valuable that it requires protection from infringement. It is also important to know that every invention is not patentable. In the forthcoming chapters, non-patentable inventions, the inventions for which patents cannot be provided, are covered. For patentability, there are only three prerequisites according to the Section 2 (1)(ac) of the Indian Patent Act, which are as follows:

1. An invention must be *novel.*
2. An invention should have an *inventive step.*
3. An invention should be capable of *industrial application.*

According to the US patent law, Section 101 of the US Patent Act, inventions are patentable when they fulfil the criteria of

- novelty,
- usefulness and
- non-obviousness.

Novelty means that the invention should be new or innovative, i.e. it should not be available to the public earlier. According to the Indian Patent Act 1970 (Section 2(1)(j)), the word 'invention' has been defined after several amendments as 'a new product or process involving an inventive step and capable of industrial application'. An invention must be an inventor's own discovery. It can be either an improvement on existing articles or methods or even a small functional improvement. For example, a design patent protects the improved appearance of the product while a utility patent protects the functional improvement to the existing product or a process. But if the difference between the pre-existing and the new product or process is not sufficient enough, it will not get the patent. If the inventor or anyone else has publicly disclosed the claimed subject matter of the invention more than one year before the filing date of the patent application, then such an invention will be barred from receiving a patent.

Usefulness is another requirement to apply for patents. The invention should have some industrial applicability and provide benefit to the masses.

Non-obviousness of patents is considered if the inventor gets an unexpected outcome from the combination of known prior art elements with their known characteristics. For example, combining the molecules that comprise 'minoxidil' resulted in maintaining good blood pressure but if by using the same medicine, hair growth occurs, which was unexpected, it is the non-obvious and patentable combination of molecules. Non-obviousness and inventive steps are the two terms that reflect a same general patentability requirement present in most patent laws, according to which an invention, in order to be patentable, should be sufficiently inventive or non-obvious. US patent law requires an invention to be non-obvious while European and Indian patent laws require an invention to involve an inventive step. Though this may seem at first to be essentially the same, there are important differences.

In Europe, the examiner determines the differences between the invention and the prior art. If there is no difference, the invention is not novel. But if there are differences, the examiner determines what technical problem is solved by adding these elements to the prior art system. If no technical problem is found, it is considered that the invention docs not involve an inventive step. While in the USA, the examiner checks the obviousness of the combination of the novel elements without looking for the solution of a technical problem.

Nature of patent

Patent is of two different types. On one hand, it acts as an intangible property and holds all the rights that can be applicable for a property, while on the other hand, it acts as a document which is concerned with details of the invention and legal formalities.

(a) **Patent as a form of property:** It is considered as a piece of personal property and possesses all the characteristics of any other type of property (movable/immovable). Like any other business commodity, it may be bought, sold, mortgaged or licensed. It can also be bequeathed or passed to the heirs of a diseased patentee. Therefore, anyone can make money out of his/her intellectual property by treating it as a property. Thus, patent right is a tradable commodity which results in profiting the inventor commercially. Unlike any other property, the term of protection of such intellectual property is limited. The inventor loses all his or her rights on the property after the patent expires. The justification given is that the inventors are rewarded for their time, work and risk of capital by the grant of limited, though strong monopoly.

(b) **Patent as a form of document:** Patent is a document issued by the statutory authority to the patentee who enables him/her to possess legal rights for his/her invention. The patentee is authorized to commercially exploit the invention. This document is the most important document submitted by the applicant. It is a technical as well as legal document. The document must contain the description of the invention, and claims along with the drawings and figures required to explain the invention. The document consists of several forms, some of which are mandatory while some are optional. These forms collect the information regarding the inventor's detail, the details of the invention, power of attorney, statement and undertaking under Section 8.

The following documents are required to be filed at the Indian patent office:

- Form 26 (letter of authorization) on Indian Stamp Paper duly signed by the inventor(s) assignee/applicant in our favour
- Certified copy of the priority documents
- International search report, if any
- Preliminary search report, if any
- Proof of right.

The form contains the application number, date of filing the application, the name and address of the applicant or the inventors, agent and address for service, classification of the invention, field of search, title abstract, etc. The document specifies that the patent is protected from imitation by others. The document is composed of parts like

- specification/description,
- claim and
- grant.

(a) **Specification:** The process of obtaining the grant of a patent begins with the preparation of a specification describing the invention. The specification implies the complete description of the invention and is filed at a patent office for examination. Ultimately, a patent for the invention described in the application is either granted or refused.

The specification and claim are published as a single document, which is available to the public at a minimal charge from the patent office. The description must disclose the invention sufficiently enough so that any person skilled in the particular branch of learning will be able to reproduce the same result. It should give a narrative description of the subject and should explain how the invention is carried out. The specifications are of the following two kinds:

- *Provisional*: A provisional specification does not completely disclose the invention; it is taken to claim the priority date of an invention when the invention needs time to develop further.
- *Complete*: In complete specification, the document should contain the detailed description of invention along with the drawings and claims. Also the description regarding prior art is included.

The patent specification must be filled in a specific format. The format contains the following headings:

- *Title*: It should mention the name of the invention which denotes in general terms the technical field of the invention.
- *Field of invention*: It should clearly describe in few sentences the broad area or the field of invention.
- *Description of current techniques*: It should describe in brief the current systems or methods used related to the inventions.
- *Problem with the current system or method*: It should describe the shortcoming of the current system, technique or methods like poor performance, inaccuracy of results, cost, problems in manufacturing due to the current process etc.
- *Proposed solution*: It should explain its advantages over the current system. The main features of the inventions' description must be given. It includes the essential as well as preferred features. The essential features are those which solve the existing problems, whereas the preferred features add on to the performance of the invention.
- *Explain solution in detail with at least one example*: The inventor has to provide clear and full technical details of the invention at the time of filling the application. The details pertaining to the invention must be included in the description because after filing the application, the inventor is not allowed to add any technical information. Patent specification allows adding sketches, flow charts, and diagrams, which help in understanding the invention clearly.

- *Alternative techniques or modifications*: It should also explain the alternative techniques or modifications or additions.
- *Wider use or development of a solution*: It should also mention the wider use or applications of the invention, which can help in producing the solution for the problem with enormous results.
- *Outline of advantages*: If the advantages were not mentioned under the above headings then, its preferred features should be specified at the end of the description. It is equally important to describe the disadvantages of the invention, if any.

(b) **Claim:** A patent claim is defined as the extent of monopoly right which an applicant holds. It is that part of the document which may not be practiced by others. Inventors may claim a part or all of that which is described in the specification. The claim generally can cover the following:

A product: The claim covers a product with all its uses and also those uses which are yet to be discovered. For example, a novel drug which was patented for the cure of cancer was later found to cure heart disease; the patent will cover this new use also.

A use: The claim covers only the specific use of a product. Unlike the above said drug, the claim will protect only its use to cure cancer and not its new use to cure heart disease. In some countries, new uses of existing inventions are patentable. If the patent of the existing invention is still alive, then the owner of the new use of the invention will have to acquire license from the current patentee in order to exploit his new invention.

A process: The claim will protect the process of manufacturing the product but will not protect the product manufactured by that process.

A product by a process: The claim will protect only those products which are manufactured by the process described by the patent application. Therefore, it would cover the drug, but when made by a specified process.

(c) **Grant:** The grant is filed at the patent office and is not published. It is the signed document and is the agreement that grants patent rights to the inventor.

After completing the documents, they are submitted either online at the website https://www.ipindiaonline.gov.in/on_line/ or alternatively, the true copies or hard copies can be submitted to the patent office. There are four patent offices for each territory where patents can be filed. Table 1.1 gives details such as the address of the patent offices with their respective territorial jurisdiction.

After the applicant identifies the patent office, he or she should file the patent application along with the requisite documents as discussed earlier. The following is an overview of some of the forms that have to be submitted.

Form 1—Application for Grant of Patent

As the name suggests, this form is an application for grant of patent in India. In this form, the applicant furnishes the information, such as name and address of the inventor(s), name and address of the applicant(s), information corresponding to prior patent applications relating to the current

Table 1.1 *Patent Offices in India*

Office	Address	Territorial Jurisdiction
New Delhi	Intellectual Property Office, Intellectual Property Office Building, Plot No. 32, Sector 14, Dwarka, New Delhi -110075. E-mail: delhi-patent@nic.in	The states of Haryana, Himachal Pradesh, Jammu and Kashmir, Punjab, Rajasthan, Uttar Pradesh, Uttaranchal, Delhi and the Union Territory of Chandigarh
Chennai	Intellectual Property Office, Intellectual Property Office Building, G.S.T. Road, Guindy, Chennai - 600032. E-mail: chennai-patent@nic.in	The states of Andhra Pradesh, Karnataka, Kerala, Tamil Nadu and the Union Territories of Pondicherry and Lakshadweep
Mumbai	Intellectual Property Office, Boudhik Sampada Bhawan, Near Antop Hill Post Office, S.M. Road,Antop Hill, Mumbai - 400 037. E-mail: mumbai-patent@nic.in	The states of Maharashtra, Gujarat, Madhya Pradesh, Goa and Chhattisgarh and the Union Territories of Daman and Diu & Dadra and Nagar Haveli
Kolkata	Intellectual Property Office, Intellectual Property Office Building, CP-2 Sector V, Salt Lake City, Kolkata - 700091. E-mail: kolkata-patent@nic.in	The rest of India

invention, which is filed by the applicant or any authorized entity, and some declarations, along with other information.

Form 2—Provisional/Complete Specification

This form furnishes the patent specification. The patent specification can be provisional or a complete patent specification depending of the type of patent application (provisional or complete). The specification particularly describes the invention and the manner in which it was performed. Its details were explained earlier.

Form 3—Statement and Undertaking under Section 8

Form 3 is used to furnish information/actions relating to patent applications filed in other countries for the current invention. Additionally, any information relating to the rights corresponding to the present patent application has to be furnished. Further, Form 3 is used to undertake that the applicant will keep the patent office informed in writing if he files the patent outside India.

Form 5—Declaration as to Inventorship

This application is used to declare that the inventors of the subject matter ought to be protected using the current patent application.

Form 9—Request for Publication

If this form is not filed, then the patent specification will be published by the patent office after 18 months from the priority date (filing of the first patent application for the current subject matter). On the other hand, by filing this form, the applicant generally gets his specification published within

1 week of filing this form. It should also be noted that the patent rights start from the date of publication of the patent application (enforceable after grant of patent).

Form 18—Request for Examination of Application for Patent

This form can be filed within 48 months from the priority date. The patent office does not consider the patent application for examination unless this form is filed. Therefore, to expedite the patenting process, Forms 9 and 18 should be filed as early as possible.

Scope of Patenting

The scope of the patent is very wide. One can imagine that a patent for a completely new type of 'engine' would have a very broad scope, whereas a patent for an improvement in one component of that engine might be quite limited in scope. Patent policies encourage innovation, investment in research and development, disclosure of information and help problem-solving by inventions that benefit a mass of people.

Patent laws are territorial, and therefore, a separate patent must be obtained in each country. Indian patent office protects only the inventions filed in India. The scope of patent protection shall be determined by the claims, and the claims can be determined on the basis of specifications such as description and drawings. The field of patenting is very open and wide. Patents can be filed for technical work in all the branches of science and technology (from basic to applied). However, it is still an emerging field that needs to be explored.

Purpose and Advantages of Patent Laws

The main objective of the patent law is to protect the patent (meaning the invention) and encourage the development of new technology and industry for the economic growth and development of the nation. In the absence of such protection laws, the inventors would conceal their research work. As a result, the society would remain deprived of the benefits of the invention. Thus, these laws are very important and required for encouraging the inventor and growth of the nation as well. Moreover, the inventor will be interested in disclosing the details of his invention only when he is rewarded and not otherwise.

Therefore, the major purpose of the patent laws are the following:

- To encourage the researchers for making inventions or the subsequent innovative work that can be practically useful to the society.
- To enhance the economic growth of the community and of the nation as a whole. This can be done by granting patent protection.

World Trade Organization (WTO) and TRIPs agreement have increased the importance of the patents around the world. Consequently, it encouraged the establishment of the industries, which in turn improved the existing industries and increased employment opportunities. Motivation is very much required in the field of research, as most of the inventions are the result of extended and expensive research and development. Therefore, return on investments need to be accelerated and financial risk reduced. The patent grants the inventor certain specific advantages, which are as follows:

- It encourages the inventor to attempt innovation in research.
- It induces commercialization of the initial inventions that would otherwise have limited commercial value.
- It imparts incentives, rewards or royalty in monetary terms for their technical innovations.

- It does not compel the inventor to file a patent for his invention under the law. Although the government encourages the disclosure of the invention for the benefit of the country, yet, he can keep it secret.
- It provides that the inventor can transfer or assign or license the patent for his invention to others on payment of fees or royalty.
- It protects the invention from imitation and infringement. If the inventor fails to file a patent for his invention and suffers from pilferage or infringement, he will not be entitled to any legal remedy available to a patentee. There will always be a risk that any competitor might get the same invention patented and sue the original inventor on the grounds of infringement.
- It encourages wider use and licensing of the innovative work rather than relying on secrecy.
- It forces the exposure of alternative designs and methods of making of the patented product, which ultimately helps in the technological growth of the industry (for example, pharmaceutical industry is more into it).

DESIGNS

According to Design Act 2000, 'design' means only the features of shape, configuration, pattern, ornament or composition of lines or colours applied to any article whether in two-dimensional, three-dimensional or in both forms by any industrial process or means, whether manual, mechanical or chemical, separate or combined, which in the finished article appeal to the eye and are judged solely by the eye. But it does not include any mode or principle of construction or anything, which is in substance a mere mechanical device and does not include any trademark as defined in clause (v) of sub-section (1) of Section 2 of the Trade and Merchandise Marks Act 1958 or property mark as defined in Section 479 of the Indian Penal Code or any artistic work as defined in clause (c) of Section 2 of the Copyright Act 1957. The Design Act 2000 has undergone two amendments till now: one in 2001 and the other in 2008.

A design, in order to secure legal protection, must consist of a shape which is three-dimensional or of a pattern which is two-dimensional and the shape or pattern must be applied to an article or articles. The basic requirement for the protection of design is that it should be novel and have some individual character and originality. It is immaterial whether it is registered because design is an additional category of patent. The design patent protects only the appearance of an article, but not its structural or functional features. An example of design is the shape and design of sunglasses, pencils (cross-section: triangular, circular, hexagonal, etc.), water bottles, soft drink or hard drink bottles (Coke, Pepsi, Kingfisher, etc.), vacuum flasks, shapes of mugs and cups, pin holders, etc.

Designs are considered to be independent. The designs of two apparently unrelated articles like a pair of shoes and a door handle are claimed in separate applications. For related articles, the design can be considered as distinct if they possess different shapes and appearances. To qualify for the design, the subject must conform to the following features:

- it must have ornamental or aesthetic aspects of a useful article,
- it must have a definite shape, pattern or colour combination and
- it should be reproducible by industrial means (otherwise creation work of art like painting is copyrightable).

The design can also function as a trademark if it is embodied in an article. Only colour by itself does not form the subject matter of the design. Combinations of known designs without any significant distinguishable changes or designs which comprise or contain scandalous or obscene matter are not registered under the Act.

The term of copyright in design under the Act is 10 years from the date of registration. It can be extended up to 5 years. Thus, the maximum period of copyright in design is 15 years.

The registration of design grants the following rights:

- Right to exclusive use of the design
- Right to protect the design from piracy.

The judicial remedies are also available for the infringement of design like damages and injunction.

TRADEMARKS™

A trademark is a visual symbol in the form of a word, name symbol or device that is used to denote the product or goods in trade. It distinguishes the goods in trade market from the goods manufactured by others in the trade. In other words, a trademark enables a customer to distinguish the products of one manufacturer from that of others. When properly advertised, the mark becomes an effective instrument and attracts customers by its brand name. By its proper use, the trademark acquires goodwill by the customers also. Goodwill and reputation of the company is essential in the competitive market. A trademark, through its widespread and extensive use in public, becomes popular and eventually results in acquiring an exclusive legal right by its owner on the mark. It helps in developing brand strategies and builds consumers loyalty. It can also be a valuable asset to the business which can be either sold or licensed.

Indian Trademarks Act 1999 came into force on 15 September 2003. India has taken steps towards fulfilling its international obligations. As a result, the Indian trademark law has now become fully compatible with the international standards laid down in the TRIPs Agreement. The new Act primarily consolidates and amends the old Trade and Merchandise Marks Act 1958 and provides for better protection of goods and services.

The essential criterion for securing a trademark registration is its distinctiveness and non-deceptiveness. The Trademark Act 1999 defines it as a mark capable of being represented graphically, capable of distinguishing goods and may include shape of goods, their packing and combination of colours. The other features of the trademark are as follows:

- It should be preferably an invented word.
- It should be easy to pronounce and remember.
- It should be short.

The trademark may include a device, brand heading, label, ticket, name, signature, word letter or numeral or any such combination. But the registration fails in case the following happen:

- It is likely to deceive or cause confusion among the people.
- It is merely the combination of two words or similar words.
- It is likely to hurt religious sentiments.
- It is an official seal or emblem of a country.
- It is the name of any UN organization.
- It is a commonly used actual name of a product with adjectives as prefix or suffix (e.g. best paint).

There are two terms, Trademark ™ and Registered Trademark (®), which differ from one another minutely in a way that trademark is unofficial registration while registered trademark is an official permission to make use of the trademark with its legal protection. Any new product with a distinctive and unique name can be considered to be trademarked. A company can put out a new line of cricket bats called 'champions', for example, complete with a graphic of a player. The graphic and the name 'champions' would be considered a trademark, and the company can put the ™ designation on it immediately. A registered trademark is an official registration with the Trademark Office. A trademark (™) may be in the process of becoming registered or it may never be officially registered at all. Anyone who claims rights in a mark can use the ™ (trademark) or SM (service mark) designation with the mark to alert the public of the claim. It is not necessary to have a registration, or even a pending application, to use these designations. The claim may or may not be valid. But the registration symbol (®) may only be used when the mark is registered.

The term of a trademark registration is for a period of 10 years. The renewal of trademark is also possible for a further period of 10 years. Unlike patents, copyrights or industrial design, the trademark rights can last indefinitely if the owner continues to use the mark. However, if a registered trademark is not renewed, it is liable to be removed from the register. In case of unauthorized use of the trademark or its imitation by the other company, two types of remedies are available to the owner of the trademark:

- 'An action for infringement' (in case of a registered trademark)
- 'An action for passing off' (in the case of an unregistered trademark).

The basic difference between an infringement action and an action for passing off is that the former is a statutory remedy and the latter is a common law remedy.

Registration of trademark confers the following rights:

- Exclusive right to use the trademark in relation to those goods and services
- Right to file a suit for infringement.

The proprietor of the trademark can avail the remedies like injunction, damages and accounts of profit.

TRADE SECRET (TS)

Trade secret is one of the methods of protecting intellectual property as secret. It is used to describe confidential information relating to trade and commerce. It is the legal term used for confidential business information. It can be a closely guarded secret related to a process. But certain conditions must be fulfilled for any information to be a trade secret, which are as follows:

- The information must not be generally known or readily ascertainable through proper means, i.e. it should not be available by obvious means.
- The information must have independent economic value due to its secrecy. For example, KFC is famous for its chicken recipes, which is a secret.
- The trade secret holder must use reasonable measures under the circumstances to protect the secrecy of the information.

Trade secret may consist of any formula, a pattern, a physical device, an idea, a process of manufacturing an article or food, etc. For example, the formula for preparing a soft drink, recipes, marketing strategies, manufacturing techniques, computer algorithms and an invention for which no patent application has been filed yet. Unlike patents, trade secrets are protected without registration, i.e. trade secrets are protected without any procedural formalities. Consequently, a trade secret can be protected for an unlimited period of time. If a trade secret is well protected, there is no definite term of protection. It can be protected for any length of time. For example, Coke's formula is considered to be one of the best well-protected trade secrets. The protection lasts as long as the information is kept confidential.

It has several advantages and disadvantages. The advantage is that there is no defined term of protection and it is recommended if anyone can manage to keep the process or formulation as secret, while the disadvantage is that any trade secret that could be discovered by 'reverse engineering' cannot be protected and care must be constantly exercised to ensure confidentiality.

DOMAIN NAMES

A domain name is used for an Internet protocol (IP) address, which can be viewed by typing in the domain name allocated for it, i.e. www.greenasia.in. The name chosen should be unique and not similar to an existing name. The main domain name is called the second level name while the last part is called top level domain. For instance, 'greenasia' is second level name and '.in' is the top level domain.

With the advent of Internet, companies with similar names can be searched with ease, which was difficult earlier. So two companies of similar names can now come into contact which they couldn't before. A domain such as Expedia.com® is registered and protected as a trademark because the owner provides services through the website. Google, eBay and Amazon are all domains turned famous trademarks because their owners not only registered the term as a domain, but chose a term that could also be distinctive for trademark purposes.

Companies invest huge amount of money in developing and promoting the website and thereafter not getting the website registered can prove to be fatal, as in the case of amazonnetworks.com, which dealt in computer services and had not registered its domain name as a trademark, sued later by amazon.com, a registered trademark domain name, which sold only books initially. Thus, it is now expedient for a domain name applicant to not only get domain registration but also protect it as a trademark later on for the goods and services provided by the website.

The domain names must be unique. Under the trademark registration system, there can be a multitude of identical trademarks coexisting in the register. For example, they can be used and registered for different goods or services or used and registered in different territories. But only one of all the proprietors that own the identical trademark can register and use the corresponding domain name. There are a number of proprietors who use the same trademark STERLING, but for different goods and services. Only one of them would be allowed to register the domain name sterling.co.za in South Africa. It requires renewal every year.

GEOGRAPHICAL INDICATIONS

Geographical indications (GIs) are a class of intellectual property used to identify goods as originating in a particular territory of a country, a region or locality in that territory. The product/goods are identified by its quality, reputation or other characteristics which attributes to its geographical origin. The geographical indications of goods (Registration and Protection Act 1999) can be registered and protected by geographical indications in India. The TRIPs agreement requires the member countries to enact legislation for the protection of geographical indications. An office for the registration of the geographical indication in India has been opened at Chennai, which is under the Office of the Controller General of Patents, Designs & Trade Marks.

Every region has its claim to fame. India is also best known for mangoes, tea, oranges, etc. by its geographical indications. Some of the examples of GI are Darjeeling tea, Kanchipuram silk sarees, Alphonso mangoes, Nagpur oranges, Kolhapuri chappals, Bikaneri bhujia, Agra ka petha, Basmati rice, etc.

The GIs is an indication if

- it originates from a definite geographical territory,
- it is used to identify agricultural, natural or manufactured goods,
- such goods are produced, processed or prepared within that territory and
- it has a special quality or reputation or other characteristics.

It has several advantages. It motivates the producers to export their goods outside the territory and promotes economic prosperity of producers in a geographical territory and it also prevents unauthorized use of a registered geographical indication by others. It generates revenue for the growth of the territory or the state and also for the country. The growth of geographical indications is a gradual process, which results due to the perfect combination of nature and skills of man and is transferred from generation to generation. Geographical indications are different from trademark. The former denotes the identity of goods having special characteristics originating from a definite territory, whereas the latter is a sign or mark of goods or services, which differs from one entrepreneur to another. Thus, trademarks identify a product with a company or brand, whereas GI identify a product with a particular territory.

The wines from 'Champagne' region of France are the best example; its copyright protects and prevents others from using the word 'Champagne' for English wine. Even the name Champagne is not allowed for shampoo or perfume, as customers may get confused and believe that the product to have originated from France.

COPYRIGHT©

The word 'copyright' means copier of words according to Oxford dictionary. According to the Copyright Act 1957, copyright means the exclusive right to do or authorize others to do certain acts in relation to literary, dramatic or musical work; artistic work; cinematograph film or sound recording.

It refers to laws that regulate the utility of the work done by the creator, such as an artist or an author. The regulation of the work includes copying, distributing, altering and displaying creative, literary and other types of work. Unless otherwise stated in a contract, the author or creator of a work retains the copyright. It is indicated by the symbol ©. But for a copyright to apply to a work, it must be an original idea that is put to use. The idea alone cannot be protected by copyright, but it should be physically presented in the form of a written novel or poetry so that it could be covered under copyright law. Copyright is a proprietary right and comes into existence as soon as the work is created. In early days, the concept of copyright had its origin under the Common Law. Subsequently, it came to be governed by the statutory laws of each country. The main criterion for the copyright registration is its originality.

The term of copyright in literary, dramatic, musical or artistic work published during the lifetime of the author runs until 60 years from his death.

India has a very strong and comprehensive copyright law based on Indian Copyright Act 1957, which was amended several times in 1981, 1984, 1992, 1994 and 1999 (with effect from 15 January 2000). The 1994 Amendment was made in response to technological changes in the means of communications like broadcasting and telecasting and the emergence of new technology like computer software while 1999 Amendments have made the Copyright Act fully compatible with TRIPs Agreement and fully reflects Berne Convention. The amended law has made provisions for the first time to protect performers' rights as envisaged in the Rome Convention. With these amendments, the Indian copyright law has become one of the most modern copyright laws in the world.

The Indian Copyright Act is valid only within the borders of the country. In order to secure protection for Indian works in foreign countries, India has become a member of the following international conventions on copyright and other related rights and the copyright works of the countries mentioned in the International Copyright Order are also protected in India just like Indian works:

- Berne Convention for the Protection of Literary and Artistic Works.
- Universal Copyright Convention.
- Convention for the Protection of Producers of Phonograms against Unauthorized Duplication of their Phonograms.
- Multilateral Convention for the Avoidance of Double Taxation of Copyright Royalties.
- Trade Related Aspects of Intellectual Property Rights (TRIPs) Agreement.

Indian Copyright Act protects the following works of human intellect:

1. Literary works, which include
   – Story, plays, poem, novel, etc.
   – Maintenance/Instruction manuals
   – Published edition of works
2. Artistic works, which include
   – Works of fine arts: painting, sculptures; drawing, diagrams, cartoons, map, chart,
   – Photographs, engraving
   – Cinematograph film
3. Dramatic works, which include
   – Recitation
   – Choreographic work
   – Dumb show
   – Acting
4. Computer programs
5. Electronic databases
6. Compilation work, which includes
   – Directories, who is who, Tambola ticket booklet
7. Letters: formal and informal, e.g. letter to newspaper editors
8. Exam question paper (if assigned through contract)
9. Questionnaire for data collection
10. Research thesis and dissertation

The following rights are conferred to the copyright holder:

- The right to assign or license the copyright
- The right to stop others from exploiting the work of the author without his consent
- The right to exploit his work for economic benefit in the form of royalty or lump sum payment
- Moral rights: rights of publication, right to maintain the integrity to prevent alteration and other actions, which may damage the author's honour or reputation and right to claim authorship of the work.

Other related or neighbouring rights are as follows:

- Performers' right
- Sound recordings
- Broadcastings rights

Author's Right

The 'Author' here means

- in relation to a literary or dramatic work, the author of the work;
- in relation to a musical work, the composer;
- in relation to an artistic work other than a photograph, the artist;
- in relation to a photograph, the person taking the photograph;
- in relation to a cinematograph or sound recording or the producer; and
- in relation to any literary, dramatic, musical or artistic work, which is computer-generated, the person who causes the work to be created.

Performer's Right

As per the Indian Copyright Act, a 'performer' includes an actor, singer, musician, dancer, acrobat, juggler, conjurer, snake charmer, a person delivering a lecture or any other person who makes a performance. 'Performance' in relation to performer's right means any visual presentation made live by one or more performers. The performer's rights exist for 25 years.

A performer can enjoy the following rights on his/her performance:

- Right to make a sound recording or visual recording of the performance
- Right to reproduce the sound recording or visual recording of the performance
- Right to broadcast the performance
- Right to communicate the performance to the public.

Broadcasting Rights

'Broadcast' means communication with the public. The term of protection for broadcaster's rights is 25 years. There are certain rights enjoyed by the broadcasting organization related to broadcast, which are as follows:

- Right to make any sound recording or visual recording of the broadcast
- Right to make any reproduction of such sound recording or visual recording

- Right to re-broadcast the broadcast
- Right to cause the broadcast to be heard or seen by the public on payment of any charges
- Right to sell or hire the broadcast to the public
- Right to offer the broadcast for sale or hire, any sound recording or visual recording of the broadcast.

Exclusions of Copyright

To get the protection of copyright, a work must be original. There are some exclusions of copyright. Copyright does not apply to historical facts, translation of the original work without the consent of original owner, title of books and cartoons, pocket diaries and calendars. Copyright does not ordinarily protect titles by themselves or names, short word combinations, slogans, short phrases, methods, plots or factual information. Copyright does not protect ideas or concepts, criticism or review, reporting current events, performance by an amateur club or society if the performance is given to a non-paying audience. The law allows the use of a work without permission of the owner of the copyright, for the purpose of research or private study, as well as use of works in library, schools and the legislature.

There is a difference between copyright and patent in that the copyright covers only the expression of the idea, whereas a patent stops others from extracting that clever idea. Idea of software is protected by copyright not by patent. Copyright protects the rights of the authors from unauthorized copying. It is the right in literary property. The author is assigned for a specific period the sole and exclusive privilege of multiplying copies of the same and publishing and selling them. Moreover, patent is awarded country-wise and the copyright is given worldwide. The term of patent is 20 years while the term of copyright is more than 60 years.

Copyright Societies

A copyright society is a registered collective administration society under Section 33 of the Copyright Act 1957. A copyright society can issue or grant licences in respect of any work in which copyright exists, collect fees in pursuance of such licences, distribute such fees among owners of copyright after making deductions for the administrative expenses.

The following are the registered copyright societies in India:

- Society for Copyright Regulation of Indian Producers for Film and Television (SCRIPT), 135 Continental Building, Dr. A.B. Road, Worli, Mumbai 400 018 (for cinematograph and television films).
- The Indian Performing Right Society Limited (IPRS), 208, Golden Chambers, 2nd Floor, New Andheri Link Road, Andheri (W), Mumbai 400 058 (for musical works).
- Phonographic Performance Limited (PPL), Flame Proof Equipment Building, B.39, Off New Link Road, Andheri (West), Mumbai 400 053 (for sound recordings).

Acquisition of copyright is automatic and it does not require any formality. However, facilities exist for getting the work registered in the Register of Copyrights maintained in the Copyright Office of the Department of Education. The copyright office is headed by a Registrar of Copyrights. Certificate of registration of copyright can be achieved by the owner, which can be presented as evidence in a court of law with reference to dispute relating to ownership of copyright.

For the registration of the copyright, the application for registration is to be made on Form IV as prescribed in the first schedule to the Rules; separate applications should be made for registration of different work; every application should be accompanied by the requisite fee prescribed in the second schedule to the Rules; the applications should be signed by the applicant or the advocate in whose favour a Power of Attorney has been executed. The Power of Attorney signed by the party and accepted by the advocate should also be enclosed.

Copyright Infringement

Copyright owners have the right to control the reproduction of their work, including the right to receive payment for that reproduction. An author has the power to grant or sell those rights to others, like publishers or recording companies while illegally using one's copyright is called infringement. Some commonly known acts involving infringement of copyright are infringing a particular copyrightable article for sale or hire or selling or letting it for hire, public exhibition of infringing copies by way of trade and importation of infringing copies into India. A copyright owner can take legal action against any person who infringes the copyright in the work.

The copyright owner is entitled to remedies by way of injunctions, damages and accounts. The District Court concerned has the jurisdiction in civil suits regarding copyright infringement. Any person who knowingly infringes or abets the infringement of the copyright in any work commits criminal offence under Section 63 of the Copyright Act. The minimum punishment for infringement of copyright is imprisonment for 6 months with the minimum fine of Rs. 50,000. In the case of a second and subsequent conviction, the minimum punishment is imprisonment for 1 year with a fine of Rs. 1 lakh.

Table 1.2 categorizes and summarizes different intellectual properties on their essential features.

Table 1.2 *Summary of Different Intellectual Properties*

S. No.	Categories for Protection	Patent (The Indian Patents Act 1970)	Copyright (The Copyright Act 1957)	Trademark (The Trademarks Act 1999)	Designs (The Designs Act 2000)
1	Subject matter of protection	Invention: Product, process (protect how something works)	Literary works, artistic works, musical works, dramatic works, sound recordings, cinematograph films (protects expression of ideas)	Reputation and goodwill in goods and services (protect reputation of a company)	Shapes, configurations, pattern, ornamental or compositions of lines, colors (protect how something looks)
2	Criteria for protection	Novelty, Utility, Non-obviousness	Originality, creativity	Distinctiveness, Non-descriptiveness	New or original, appealing to the eye and fixation on an article
3	Term of protection	20 years from the date of filing the application	Life of author + 60 years from the date of creation of the work	10 years from the date of registration + renewal each year for a period of 10 years	10 years from the date of registration + one renewal for a period of 5 years
4	Jurisdiction	Country-wise	Worldwide	Country-wise	Country-wise

CHAPTER SUMMARY

Intellectual property rights are intangible rights received by the inventor for his/her invention. Invention and creativity are two major aspects that give benefits and help in the economic development of the nation. According to the Section 2 (1) (ac) of the Indian Patent Act 1970, patentability requires novelty, inventive step in an invention and industrial applicability. There are various types of intellectual properties which are intangible, namely patents, trademark, copyright and trade secrets.

There are four patent offices, in New Delhi, Mumbai, Kolkata and Chennai. The major purpose of the patent laws are to encourage the researchers for creating inventions or the subsequent innovative work that can be practically useful to the society, to enhance the economic growth of the community and of the nation as a whole. The different forms of intellectual properties are patents, designs, trademarks, copyrights and geographical indications, which follow their own rights and term of protection.

Patent is the grant of legal rights, privilege, property or authority for new inventions employing scientific and technical knowledge. The Indian Patent Act 1970 grants several rights to the patentee like right to exploit the patent, right to license and assign the patent, right to surrender the patent and right to sue for the infringement of patent. Design means only the features of shape, configuration, pattern, ornament or composition of lines or colours applied to any article whether in two-dimensional, three dimensional or in both forms. The Design Act 2000 grants the rights like right to exclusive use of the design and the right to protect the design from piracy.

A trademark is a visual symbol in the form of a word, name symbol or device that is used to denote the product or goods in trade. Registration of trademark under Indian Trademarks Act 1999 confers the rights like exclusive right to use the trademark in relation to those goods and services and the right to file a suit for infringement. Trade secret is one of the methods of protecting intellectual property as a secret. It is used to describe confidential information relating to trade and commerce. It has several advantages and disadvantages. A domain name is used for an Internet protocol (IP) address, which can be viewed by typing in the domain name allocated for it. The domain names must be unique. Geographical indications are a class of intellectual property which is used to identify goods as originating in a particular territory of a country, a region or locality in that territory. It motivates the producers to export their goods outside the territory and promotes economic prosperity of producers in a geographical territory.

Copyright means the exclusive right to do or authorize others to do certain acts in relation to literary, dramatic or musical work; artistic work; cinematograph film or sound recording. The term of copyright in literary, dramatic, musical or artistic work published during the lifetime of the author runs until 60 years from his death. Several rights are conferred to the copyright holder like the right to assign or license the copyright, the right to stop others from exploiting the work of the author without his consent, the right to exploit his work for economic benefit and moral rights. The other related rights are performers' right, sound recordings and broadcastings rights.

MULTIPLE CHOICE QUESTIONS

1. The term of copyright is
   (i) 20 years
   (ii) 60 years
   (iii) 60 years after the death of the owner
   (iv) 10 years
2. The Indian Patent Act was not amended in the year
   (i) 1970 (ii) 1977
   (iii) 1999 (iv) 2006
3. Which intellectual property has indefinite term of protection?
   (i) Trademark
   (ii) Trade secret
   (iii) Design
   (iv) Geographical indication
4. Which of the following is applicable worldwide?
   (i) Patent (ii) Copyright
   (iii) Design (iv) Trademark
5. The following sign is associated with a company's name
   (i) © (ii) TS
   (iii) ® (iv) SM

REVIEW QUESTIONS

1. Define patent. What are the documents required for filling a patent application?
2. What do you understand by IPR? What are the various governing laws in India for IPR?
3. Differentiate the Indian Patent Act 1970 from its latest amendments.
4. What is the difference between copyright and patents?
5. Define invention. How is invention explained in the patent specification during filing of the patent?

2

History and Evolution of Patent Law

Chapter Objectives

As we have studied the importance of intellectual property rights, we know that this form of property plays an important role in the technological progress of the country. This is the reason why different countries have different patent laws. The patent laws have witnessed revolutionary changes across the world in the past several decades. In this chapter we will study the concept of origin of patents, evolution of patent laws, Indian patent laws with several amendments, international conventions, treaties and legislative framework, and the patent laws prevailing in various other countries. The chapter also summarizes the difference between patent laws of other countries with reference to IPL (Indian Patent Laws) and US laws.

EVOLUTION OF PATENT LAWS

The origin of patent is obscure but it is generally considered to have evolved in Italy in 1474 when Republic of Venice issued a patent for a period of 10 years. The first Italian patent was actually awarded by the Republic of Florence in 1421. Evidence also indicates that there existed something like patents in ancient Greek cities. Some 500 B.C., in the Greek city named Sybaris, annual culinary/cookery competitions were conducted and the winner was given the exclusive rights to prepare the dish for the entire year. Encouragement was given to all those who discover a new luxury item and the profit arising from such discovery was secured to the inventor for the whole year. UK however has longest tradition of patent in the world, which can be traced back to the 15th century. Patents in England were granted in the form of 'Letters Patent', which were issued by the sovereign to inventors who petitioned and acquired the patents. An example of such first letter patent is the patent granted by Henry VI to one Flemish-born John of Utynam in 1449 for developing a method of making stained glass, which was required for the windows of Eton College. The term of the patent was 20 years.

In France, King Henry II introduced the concept of publishing the invention with its complete specification in the year 1555. The patents were granted by monarchy and the parliament of Paris. Gradually, the modern patent system was created in 1791. Earlier, the patents were granted without the examination since the inventor's right was considered to be natural and original one. Further, several revisions were made to the patent laws in 1844, 1860, 1902 and further on. The Australian system of granting the patent is based on the British laws. 'IP Australia' is the Australian government agency responsible for administering patents.

However, in United States, Samuel Winslow of North America was the first one to get the patent in 1641for a new process of making salt. The 1836 United States Patent Act was arguably the first modern patent law. It required the examination of the all applications by the government patent office for the search of novelty and usefulness in them. Although, this law did not discriminate between US and foreign inventors with respect to the examination or the extent of rights granted, yet the foreign applicants had to pay much higher fees.

Some European countries managed without a patent law till much of the 19th century. Switzerland had a patent system only from 1799 to 1802, not re-establishing it until 1888. Netherlands prohibited patents from 1869 until 1912. Most countries that experienced Industrial Revolution during 19th century had patent systems. It very likely became clear that patent system stimulated the development and dispersal of new technologies, which in turn established the foundation of rapid industrial development.

HISTORY OF INDIAN PATENT SYSTEM

The first patent law in India was passed about 146 years back, which received the assent of the Governor General (GG) on 28 February 1856, one year before the first war of Indian independence in 1857. The concept of novelty and the grounds for revocation under the patent law has remained unchanged since 1856. The provisions which were not found in the Indian Patent Act 1970 are as follows:

- The term of patent could not be extended by Governor General (GG).
- The importers were also treated as an inventor subject to know-how and practices within a specified period.
- There was no provision for provisional specification.
- Inventions used by the inventor were not considered to be for public use.

The patent system of India is designed in such a way that it encourages technological innovation by granting for a limited period of time the monopoly rights to the inventor for disclosing their invention which is beneficial to the mankind.

The first law in India related to patents was the Act VI of 1856. The objective of this legislation was to encourage new and useful inventions and to induce inventors to disclose secret of their inventions. The Act was subsequently repealed by Act IX of 1857 since, it had been enacted without the approval of the sovereign.

Fresh law for granting 'exclusive privileges' was introduced in the Act XV of 1859.

In 1872, the Act of 1859 was consolidated to provide protection relating to designs. It was renamed as The Patterns and Designs Protection Act under Act XIII of 1872.

The Act of 1872 was further amended in 1883 to introduce a provision to protect novelty of the invention.

In 1888, new legislation was introduced to consolidate and amend the law relating to invention and designs in conformity with the amendments made in the UK law.

The Indian Patents and Designs Act 1911 replaced all the previous Acts. For the first time, this Act brought patent administration under the management of Controller of Patents. The Act was further amended in 1920 to enter into mutual arrangements with UK and other countries for securing priority. Provisions were made relating to the grant of secret patents, patent of addition, use of invention by government, powers of the Controller to rectify register of patent and increase of term of the patent.

In 1945, an amendment was made to provide for the filing of provisional specification and submission of complete specification within 9 months.

In 1949, the Government of India constituted a committee under the Chairmanship of Justice (Dr.) Bakshi Tek Chand, a retired Judge of Lahore High Court, to review the patent rules and regulations in India in order to ensure the implementation of the patent system in the interest of the nation.

- The committee submitted its interim report on 4 August 1949 with recommendations for prevention of misuse of patent right in India and suggested amendments. The committee also observed that the Patents Act should contain clear indication to ensure that food and medicine and surgical and curative devices are made available to the public at the cheapest price, which should be made proportionate with the reasonable compensation to the patentee.
- Based on the above recommendation of the Committee, the 1911 Act was amended in 1950 in relation to working of inventions and compulsory license/revocation. Other provisions were related to endorsement of the patent with the words 'license of right' on an application by the Government so that the Controller could grant licenses.
- In 1952 (Act LXX of 1952) an amendment was made to provide compulsory license in relation to patents in respect of food and medicines, insecticide, germicide or fungicide and a process for producing substance or any invention relating to surgical or curative devices.
- In 1957, the Government of India appointed Justice N. Rajagopala Ayyangar Committee to suggest necessary changes in the patent law. The report was submitted in September 1959 by the Committee, which comprised of two parts. The first part dealt with general aspects of the Patent Law along with evils of the patent system and solution with recommendations in regards to the law and the second part gave detailed note on several clauses of the lapsed bills 1953. This report recommended major changes in the law, which formed the basis of the introduction of the Patent Bill 1965.
- This amended bill was introduced in the Lok Sabha on 21 September 1965, which, however, lapsed. In 1967, an amended bill was introduced, which was referred to a Joint Parliamentary Committee and on the final recommendation of the Committee, the Patents Act 1970 was passed.
- This Patent Act 1970 replaced the 1911 Act so far as the patents law was concerned. However, the Act 1911 was continued to be applicable to designs. Most of the provisions of the 1970 Act were brought into force on 20 April 1972 with the publication of the Patents Rules, 1972.
- The Patents Act 1970 remained in force for about 24 years without any change till December 1994 with further amendments in 1999, 2002, 2005 and 2006.

A brief history of the Indian patent acts is shown in the Table 2.1.

Indian Patent Act 1970

The salient features of the Patents Act 1970, which was in force for 24 years are as follows:

1. The law elaborated the definition of "invention" to mean any new and useful
   (a) Art, process, method or manner of manufacture;
   (b) Machine, apparatus or other article;
   (c) Substance produced by manufacture; and includes any new and useful improvement of any of them, and an alleged invention.
2. No product patents was given for the substances intended for use as food, drugs, medicines or any product produced by any chemical processes.
3. The term of the process patent in respect of food, medicine and drug is for 5 years from the date of sealing of patent or 7 years from date of patent, whichever is shorter.
4. The law explained that certain inventions are considered as non-patentable inventions.
5. The law required mandatory furnishing of information and undertaking, regarding foreign application.

Table 2.1 *History of Indian Patent System*

Year of Act	Patent Law
1858	The Act VI of 1856 on protection of inventions based on the British patent law of 1852. Certain exclusive privileges granted to inventors of new manufacturers for a period of 14 years.
1859	The Act VI was modified as Act XV; patent monopolies called exclusive privileges (making, selling and using inventions in India and authorizing others to do so for 14 years from date of filing specification).
1872	The Patents and Designs Protection Act was enacted
1883	The Protection of Inventions Act was enacted
1888	The Act was consolidated as the Inventions and Designs Act.
1911	The Indian Patents and Designs Act was enacted
1972	The Patents Act (Act 39 of 1970) came into force on 20 April 1972
1999	The Patents (Amendment) Act, 1999 came into force on 26 March
2002	The Patents (Amendment) Act 2002 came into force from 20 May 2003
2005	The Patents (Amendment) Act 2005 effective from 1 January 2005

6. There was adoption of absolute novelty criteria in case of publication.
7. There was an expansion of the grounds for opposition to the grant of a patent.
8. It illustrated the exemption of certain categories of prior publication, prior communication and prior use from anticipation.
9. The laws illustrated secrecy directions relating to inventions relevant for defence purposes.
10. The law provided provision for the use of inventions for government purpose, research or instruction to pupils.
11. There was reduction in the term of process patents regarding the substances capable of being used as food or as medicine or drugs.
12. There was an enlargement of the grounds for revocation of a patent.
13. The law marked the provision for non-working patents as grounds for compulsory licences, licences of right and revocation of patents.
14. The law included additional powers of the Central government to use an invention for purposes of government including government undertakings.
15. The law had the provision of making restrictive conditions in licence agreements/contract as void for the prevention of abuse of patent rights.
16. The law had the provision for appeal to High Court on certain decisions of the Controller.
17. The law had the provision for opening several branches of the Patent Office.
18. The patent can be revoked at any point of time in the interest of the public.

Amendments to the Patent Act 1970

First Amendment

The Patents Act 1970 remained in force for about 24 years without any change till December 1994. An ordinance effecting certain changes in the Act was issued on 31 December 1994, which ceased to operate after six months. Subsequently, another ordinance was issued in 1999. This ordinance was consequently replaced by the Patents (Amendment) Act 1999 that was brought into force retrospectively from 1 January 1995. The amended Act provided for filing the product patent application in the areas of pharmaceuticals drugs and agro chemicals, as such patents were not allowed earlier. However, such applications were to be examined only after 31 December 1994.

Second Amendment

The second amendment to the 1970 Act was made through the Patents (Amendment) Act 2002 (Act 38 of 2002). This Act came into force on 20 May 2003 with the introduction of the new Patent Rules, 2003 by replacing the earlier Patents Rules, 1972.

The salient features of the Patents (Amendment) Act 2002 were as follows:

1. Non-patentable inventions were further codified. Section 2(1)(j) of Patent (Amendment) Act 2002 defines the term 'invention' as 'a new product or process involving an inventive step and capable of industrial application' where 'inventive step' means a unique feature.
2. The term of patent was extended to 20 years for all technologies. This term is calculated from the date of filing of the application. Earlier, the term of patent for method or process of manufacture of substance (e.g. food, medicines, drugs etc.) was 5 years from the date of the sealing of the patent, or 7 years from the date of patent, whichever period is shorter and in respect of any other invention, 14 years from the date of the patent.
3. The date of every patent will be the date of filing the application for patent. While, according to The Patent Act 1970, the date of patent was the date of filing of complete specification. This date of patent is very important in order to determine the term of parent.
4. Provisions were made for reversal of *burden of proof* on the defendant, in case of process patents infringement.
5. Provisions were made to issue compulsory licences in order to meet public health.
6. The provision of licence of right was deleted.
7. Introduction of system of deferred examination. This means the Controller will not initiate examination of the application. Examination of an application will now be taken up only upon request by applicant. The request is to be made within 48 months from the application filing date.
8. It emphasized on mandatory publication of applications after 18 months from the date of filing the application.
9. It included the provision for process patent for micro-organisms.
10. Appellate Board was established. This Appellate Board hears and decides appeals of the decision of the Controller. This board is above the Controller in hierarchy and the headquarters of the Appeal Board is in Chennai.
11. The time for filing the request for restoration of the lapsed patent (Section 60) was extended from 1 year to 18 months.

12. It incorporated the provision for parallel import of patented products at lowest international prices. Parallel import is the import of patented commodity from anywhere in the world where it is cheaper, even though it is patented here. A parallel import is a mechanism that helps in price control.
13. Provision was made for exemption from infringement proceedings for use of a patented invention for obtaining regulatory approval for a product based on that patented invention.
14. It included the provision to protect biodiversity and traditional knowledge.

Third Amendment

The third amendment to the Patents Act 1970 was introduced through the Patents (Amendment) Ordinance, 2004 on 1 January 2005. This ordinance was later replaced by the Patents (Amendment) Act 2005 on 4 April 2005, which was brought into force from 1 January 2005.

The salient features of the Patents (Amendment) Act 2005 amendment were as follows:

1. It extended the product patents to all the fields of technology including food, drugs, chemicals and micro-organisms.
2. The provisions relating to exclusive marketing rights (EMRs) were deleted.
3. Introduction of a provision for enabling grant of compulsory licence for export of medicines to countries which have insufficient or no manufacturing capacity to meet emergent public health situations.
4. It had modification in the provisions relating to opposition procedures having both pre-grant and post-grant opposition in the Patent Office.
5. Strengthening the provisions relating to national security to guard against patenting abroad of dual use technologies.
6. Rationalization of provisions relating to timelines with a view to introducing flexibility and reducing the processing time for patent application.

The Patent (Amendment) Rules, 2006, with a view to ensuring time-bound disposal of patent applications, has prescribed definitive time frames for various activities by the Patent Offices.

A patent application now has to be referred to an Examiner within 1 month of a request for its examination. Further, the Controller will now be required to take a decision on the report of the Examiner within 1 month of its submission and the First Examination Report has also to be issued within 6 months of the date of request for examination of a patent application. The time for granting permission to file patents abroad has also been reduced from 3 months to just 21 days.

Patent applications are now to be compulsorily published within 1 month after expiry of the statutory period of 18 months and, in case of request for an early publication, the application is to be published within 1 month from the date of request. This step will introduce an element of certainty regarding the date of publication, which was previously not available. Further, the timelines available for applicants and the public have also been extended in the following manner:

- Making a request for examination has been extended from 36 to 48 months.
- Filing a pre-grant opposition extended from 3 to 6 months.
- Filing reply to pre-grant opposition extended from 1 to 3 months.
- Meeting the requirements of the First Examination Report increased from 6 to 12 months.

Table 2.2 *Rules Before and After the 2006 Amendment to Indian Patent Act 1970*

S. No.	Rules Before Amendment	Rules After Amendment
1	Controller refers the application to the Examiner	Controller refers the application to the Examiner within 1 month from date of publication or 1 month from request for examination whichever is later.
2	Request for examination to be made within 36 months from date of priority or from date of filing application	Request for examination to be made within 48 months from date of priority or from date of filing application.
3	The first examination report has to be worked out within 6 months from the date of issue of the report.	The first examination report has to be worked out within 12 months from the date of issue of the report.
4	A pre-grant opposition to be filed within 3 months from the date of publication for the application or before the grant of patent.	A pre-grant opposition to be filed within 6 months from the date of publication of the application or before the grant of patent.
5	Reply to pre-grant opposition to be filed within 1 month from date of notice of opposition.	Reply to pre-grant opposition to be filed within 3 months from date of notice of opposition.
6	Official fees to be paid in cash or bank draft or cheque.	Official fees can also be paid electronically.
7	3 months were required by the controller to grant the permission for filing the patent abroad from the date of request.	21 days were required by the controller to grant the permission for filing the patent abroad from the date of request.

Changes have also been made to make the patent rules user-friendly.

1. The working of the Patent Offices has also been decentralized completely. All patent activities can now be carried on by all the patent offices (Delhi, Mumbai, Kolkata and Chennai). Earlier, certain patent activities could be carried out only by the Head Office (Patent Office at Kolkata).
2. Fees to the Patent Office can now be paid electronically.

Table 2.2 shows the rules before and after this amendment.

INTERNATIONAL CONVENTIONS AND TREATIES

India is a member of World Intellectual Property Organization (WIPO), an international organization responsible for the promotion and protection of intellectual property throughout the world. With respect to patents, India is a member of several international organizations and treaties as follows:

- World Intellectual Property Organization (WIPO)
- World Trade Organization (WTO) with effect from 1 January 1995
- Paris Convention (for the protection of industrial property) with effect from 7 December1998

- Patent Cooperation Treaty (PCT) with effect from 7 December 1998
- Budapest Treaty with effect from 17 December 2001.

World Intellectual Property Organization

The World Intellectual Property Organization (WIPO) is a specialized agency of the United Nations which is dedicated to ensuring that the rights of creators and owners of intellectual property are protected worldwide. It is of the view that the inventors and authors should be rewarded for their ingenuity. It is responsible for the administration of various multilateral treaties dealing with the legal and administrative aspects of intellectual property.

The roots of this organization can be traced back to 1833 with the birth of Paris Convention for the protection of industrial property. It was the first major international treaty formed to help the inventors of one country to obtain protection in other countries for their creation or invention. The Paris Convention was signed in 1883 for the first time by only 11 countries and entered into force in 1834. It set up the basic standards for the protection of intellectual property rights. The convention allows the granting of the patent for the innovation in technology including biotechnology, trade promotion among the member countries and protection of industrial property, which includes industrial patents, utility models, industrial designs, trademarks, indications of source of appellations of origin and repression of unfair competition. The patents under the convention included different types of industrial patents such as patents of importation, patents of improvement, patent of addition, etc., which is recognized by the laws of member countries.

The important features of the convention are as follows:

- National treatment
- Parallel importation
- Right of priority
- Independence of patents
- Protection against false indication and unfair competition.

However, the main objective of the convention is to give protection for obtaining, maintaining and enforcing the industrial property of the member nations. The member nations of the Paris Convention have the advantages that they alone can be the members of various international conventions and treaties such as the following:

- Patent Cooperation Treaty (PCT for centralized international application procedure for grant of patent at national as well as regional level)
- Budapest Treaty (Deposit treaty)
- UPOV (Union for Protection of New Varieties of Plants)
- Madrid Agreement (for repression of false or deceptive indications of source on goods)
- Madrid Protocol (regarding registration of marks)
- Hague Agreement (concerning deposit of industrial designs).

In 1886, copyright entered the international arena, with Berne Convention for the protection of literary and artistic works. Like the Paris Convention, the Berne Convention set up an international bureau to carry out administrative tasks.

In 1893, these two small bureaus united to form an international organization called the United International Bureaux (BIPRI, French acronym) for the protection of intellectual property with a staff of seven people, which was the predecessor of WIPO. Today WIPO is a dynamic entity with 184 member states, i.e. over 90% of the countries of the world are its members. BIPRI became WIPO later on, undergoing structural and administrative reforms. In 1974, WIPO became a specialized agency of the United Nations system of organization with a view to administer intellectual property matters recognized by the member states of the United Nations and expended its role. Through its member state and secretariat, WIPO seeks to

- provide services for international application for industrial property rights,
- exchange intellectual property information among member countries,
- provide legal and technical assistance to developing and other countries and
- resolve the private disputes on intellectual property and harmonizes the intellectual property (IP) laws and procedures.

WIPO was established by the convention of 14 July 1967, which entered into force in 1970. Since 1974, it has been a specialized agency administering a number of international unions or treaties in the area of intellectual property like Paris and Berne Conventions.

WIPO undertakes development cooperation for developing countries through advice, training and furnishing of documents. A similar agreement on cooperation between WIPO and WTO came into force on 1 January 1996. The agreement provides cooperation in the following areas:

- Technical knowledge
- Notification of and access to national laws and regulation
- Translation of national laws
- Implementation of procedures for the protection of national emblems.

The agreement between WIPO and WTO was concluded in December 1995. It provides assistance for legal and technical matters to the developing countries related to TRIPs agreement. Till date more than 134 countries have received its advice. WIPO's advice takes into account different situations in every country, given that member states have different legal systems and different political and cultural structures. In order to strengthen the TRIPs implementation process, during the last four years, WIPO has promoted the interaction among different stakeholders at the national level to include, for example, officials of law reform commissions, chambers of commerce and federation of industries, research and development institutions, parliamentarians, high-level officials of ministers of trade, agriculture, health, science and technology, culture, justice, environment and others.

World Trade Organization

World Trade Organization (WTO) is the successor organization to the General Agreement on Tariffs and Trade (GATT). GATT was signed in 1947, and came into force on 1 January 1948 signed by 23 states. It was amended in 1966 and lasted until 1993, when it was replaced by the WTO in 1995. It was required after the World War II to revitalize the world trade and encourage the countries to participate freely. It is one of the important agencies of the United Nations, which provides better and wider protection for the private patent holders of the developed nations than the Paris Convention.

GATT was the outcome of the failure of negotiating governments to create the International Trade Organization (ITO). It is a multilateral agreement regulating trade among about 150 countries. In its introductory section, the purpose of the GATT was explained as the 'substantial reduction of tariffs and other trade barriers and the elimination of preferences, on a reciprocal and mutually advantageous basis'. Under the GATT, eight rounds of negotiations took place to liberalize world trade. The last round was the Uruguay Round, which was completed on 15 December 1993.

The Uruguay Round began in 1986. It was the most ambitious round till date, hoping to expand the competence of the GATT to important new areas like services, capital, intellectual property, textile and agriculture. In this round, 123 countries took part, which led to the creation of WTO, through which the treaty was converted from a simple agreement to an administrative body. The round extended the range of trade negotiations, leading to major reductions in tariffs (approximately 40%) and agricultural subsidies, an agreement to allow full access to textiles and clothing from developing countries, and an extension of intellectual property rights. United States was the first developed nation to initiate a proposal for intellectual property rights in the Uruguay Round of GATT negotiations and submitted the proposal for a GATT agreement and Paris Convention for the protection of industrial intellectual property.

The other seven rounds held by GATT are as follows:

1. First round (Geneva Round) started in April 1947 and lasted for 7 months with the participation of 23 countries. The main focus was to achieve 45,000 reductions in bilateral tariffs covering 20% of world affecting $10 billion of trade.
2. The second round took place in 1949 in Annency, France, in which 13 countries participated and achieved 5,000 tariff concessions.
3. The third round was convened in Torquay, England in 1950, which lasted for 8 months, with 38 countries taking part in it. It received 8,700 reductions in bilateral tariffs covering a new range of goods.
4. The fourth round returned to Geneva in 1955 and lasted until May 1956 with the participation of 26 countries resulting in $2.5 billion tariff reduction.
5. The fifth round of negotiations again took place in Geneva (Dillion Round) during 1960–62. The talk was named after the US treasury secretary and former undersecretary of state, Douglas Dillion, who first proposed the talks. This round saw 26 countries participating in it, resulting in $4.9 billion tariff concession of world trade. It also yielded discussion relating to the creation of the European Economic Community (EEC).
6. The sixth round is the Kennedy Round, which took place from 1964 to 1967. With 62 countries participating in this round, there was tariff reduction of $40 billion of world trade. It also covered the subject 'anti-dumping'. In economics, the word 'dumping' is used in the context of international trade. It occurs when manufacturers export a product to another country at a price either below the price charged in its home market, or in quantities that cannot be explained through normal market competition. This is often referred to as selling at less than 'fair value'. Under the WTO Agreement, dumping is condemned (but is not prohibited) if it causes or threatens to cause material injury to a domestic industry in the importing country.
7. The seventh round was held in Tokyo, and began in 1973 and ended in 1979 with the participation of 102 countries. It covered the subjects like tariffs, non-tariff measures and 'framework' agreements. The round achieved the tariff reductions worth more than $300 billion.

In 1995, WTO was established, which replaced the GATT. There were three rounds under WTO:

- Seattle Round (1999)
- Doha Round (2001)
- Cancun Round (2003).

WTO intends to supervise and liberalize international trade, and officially commenced on 1 January 1995. The organization dealt with trade regulation among the member countries. It had 157 members (till 2012) of which 117 are developing countries. The headquarters of WTO is at Geneva, Switzerland. Its activities are supported by a secretariat of some 700 staff, led by the WTO Director General. There are three official languages of WTO: English, French and Spanish. Decisions are generally taken by consensus of the entire membership representing more than 97% of the world's population. The highest institutional body is the Ministerial Conference, which meets roughly once in every two years. Below this is the General Council, which normally consists of ambassadors and heads of delegation in Geneva, but sometimes officials sent from members' capitals are also included, which meets several times a year in the Geneva headquarters. The General Council acts as Trade Policy Review Body and the Dispute Settlement Body.

The Goods Council, Services Council and Intellectual Property (TRIPs) Council report to the General Council. There are other specialized committees, working groups and working parties which deal with the individual agreements and other areas such as the environment, development, membership applications and regional trade agreements.

WTO's principal rule book for trade in goods is GATT. It includes some 30,000 pages consisting of about 30 agreements and separate commitments (called schedules) made by individual members in specific areas such as lower customs duty rates and services market-opening. Through these agreements, WTO members operate a non-discriminatory trading system that spells out their rights and their obligations. Each country receives guarantees that its exports will be treated fairly and consistently in other countries' markets. Same rules apply for the imports into its market. The system also gives developing countries some flexibility in implementing their commitments.

WTO has several benefits like the system helps in promoting peace, helps in dispute settlement, makes rules that make life easier for all, conducts freer trade that cuts the costs of living, provides more choice of products and qualities, income that is due is raised and governments are shielded from lobbying. Moreover, the system encourages good government.

More specifically, its main objective is to help trade flow smoothly, freely, fairly and predictably at the international level. International trade is beneficial to all the countries and their citizens. It is a fact that trade leads to growth, which in turn promotes national development and reduces poverty. The following are its activities:

- Negotiation to reduce or eradicate hindrances in trade (e.g. import tariffs and other barriers to trade) and agreeing on rules that govern the conduct of internal trade (anti-dumping, subsidies, product standards etc.)
- Administrating and monitoring the application of WTO trade agreement rules in goods, trade in services, IPR
- Reviewing the trade-related policies of WTO members as well as ensuring transparency in regional and bilateral trade agreement
- Settling disputes among its members regarding interpretation and application of the trade agreement
- Educating public about WTO, its mission and its activities
- Conducting economic research
- Assisting the accession (process of becoming a member) of some 20 non-member countries
- Building capacity of developing country government officials in international trade matters
- Assisting developing countries in trade policy issues, through technical assistance and training programmes

- Cooperating with other international organization
- Provising detailed information on biotechnology, genetically modified (GM) food, and their business
- Dealing with the ethical issues in business
- Helping in smooth and easy conduction of trade at international levels.

WTO Treaties

The following treaties are enforced by the WTO:

- General Agreement on Tariffs and Trade (GATT)
- General Agreement on Trade and Services (GATS)
- Agreement on Technical Barriers to Trade (TBT)
- Agreement on Government Procurement (AGP)
- Agreement on the Application of Sanitary and Phytosanitary Measures (SPS)
- Agreement on Trade-Related Aspects of Intellectual Property Rights (TRIPs)
- Agreement on Trade-Related Investment Measures STRIMs)
- Agreement on Agriculture (AOA)

Doha Round

In November 2001, divergences between developing and developed countries led to a compromise on the declaration on the TRIPs Agreement and public health. It was the Doha Round, which is the latest round of trade negotiations among the WTO members in which 142 countries participated and the aim of the round is to achieve major reform of the international trading system through the introduction of lower trade barriers and revised trade rules. This was the joint effort of India, Brazil and 55 African countries and all the 142 countries supported the view that governments are free to take all necessary measures in order to protect the public health. WTO accepted the view that patents should not hinder the public health protection. Public health WTO's priority; this was a boon to India. It covered about 21 areas of trade. The round is also known semi-officially as the Doha Development Agenda as its fundamental objective was to improve the trading prospects of developing countries. The following areas were covered in the round:

1. Implementation-related issues and concerns
2. Agriculture
3. Services
4. Market access (for non-agriculture products)
5. Intellectual property: trade-related aspects
6. Relationship between trade and investment
7. Interaction between trade and competition policy
8. Transparency in government procurement
9. Trade facilitation
10. Anti-dumping
11. Subsidies
12. Regional trade agreements

13. Dispute settlement
14. Trade and environment
15. E-commerce
16. Small economies
17. Trade, debt and finance
18. Trade and technology transfer
19. Technical cooperation
20. Least-developed countries (LDCs)
21. Special and differential treatment for developing countries

Doha declaration comprises of the declaration on TRIPs Agreement and public health, and decision on implementation-related issues and concerns, includes elaboration of the timetables for current negotiations on agriculture, and services or negotiations related to other issues.

The TRIPs Agreement

WIPO already existed before the establishment of the WTO or the Paris Convention, which was established for the protection of industrial property (e.g. patents, industrial designs etc.) and the Berne Convention, which was established for the protection of literary and artistic works (i.e. copyright). But some areas were either not covered by these conventions or had inadequate protection standards. Therefore, TRIPs agreement came into being, which added significant number of new or higher standards.

The TRIPS Agreement, which came into effect on 1 January 1995 is to date the most comprehensive multilateral agreement on intellectual property. It provides standards for the full range of intellectual property rights and also the enforcement of those standards both internally and through legal and administrative actions.

The areas of intellectual property covered are as follows:

- Copyright and related rights (i.e. the rights of performers, producers of sound recordings and broadcasting organizations)
- Trademarks including service marks
- Geographical indications including appellations of origin
- Industrial designs
- Patents including the protection of new varieties of plants
- Layout designs of integrated circuits
- Undisclosed information including trade secrets and test data.

The TRIPs agreement extended its protection scope to such technological areas as pharmaceutical products and computer software, which were previously unprotected in many countries. The general timetable for implementing the TRIPs agreement is 1 year for industrialized countries; 5 years for developing countries and countries shifting from centrally planned economies; and 10 years for least-developed countries.

The agreement covers five broad issues:

- Application of basic principles of the trading system and other international intellectual property agreements.
- Methods used for the adequate protection of intellectual property rights.

- Enforcement of those rights sufficiently and adequately in their own territories.
- Settling of disputes on intellectual property rights between members of the WTO.
- Special transitional arrangements during the period when the new system is being introduced.

The TRIPS agreement has three basic features such as the following.

1. *Standards*: In respect of each of the main areas of intellectual property covered by the TRIPs Agreement, the Agreement sets out the minimum standards of protection that has to be provided by each member country. Each of the main elements of protection is defined, namely the subject matter to be protected, the rights to be conferred and permissible exceptions to those rights, and the minimum duration of protection. It allows countries to set their own standards, but it also says that regulations must be based on science. They should be applied only to the extent necessary to protect human, animal or plant life or health. And they should not arbitrarily or unjustifiably discriminate between countries where identical or similar conditions prevail. Member countries are encouraged to use international standards, guidelines and recommendations and if they do so, the probability to be challenged legally in a WTO dispute decreases. However, members may use measures which result in higher standards if there is scientific justification. The agreement still allows countries to use different standards and different methods of inspecting products. If the measure of health protection level of an exporting country is equivalent to that of the importing country, then the importing country is expected to accept the exporting country's standards and methods.

   The main TRIPs standards, relating to pharmaceuticals, that countries must include in their patent law are as follows:

   - Availability of patents for both pharmaceutical products and processes inventions that are new, involve an inventive step (i.e. non-obvious) and are capable of industrial application (or useful)
   - Protection of the product directly obtained using a patented process
   - Availability of procedures at national level to enable patent owners to protect their rights against infringement.

   In addition, if exceptions to patent rights and compulsory licences are incorporated in patent legislation, they should be, respectively, limited and conditional to conform to the TRIPs Agreement.

2. *Enforcement*: It is important to have intellectual property laws but mere laws are not enough, they have to be enforced. This second feature deals with the internal methods or procedures for the enforcement of intellectual property rights. The Agreement lays down certain general principles applicable to all IPR enforcement procedures. In addition, it contains provisions on civil and administrative procedures and remedies, provisional measures, criminal procedures, so that right holders can effectively enforce their rights. The penalties for infringement are tough enough to discourage others from further violations. The procedures must be fair and equitable, and not unnecessarily complicated or costly. The agreement describes in detail how enforcement should be handled, including rules for obtaining evidence, provisional measures, injunctions, damages and other penalties. It says courts should have the right, under certain conditions, to order the disposal or destruction of pirated or counterfeit goods.

3. *Dispute settlement*: The Agreement makes disputes between WTO members in respect of TRIPs obligations subject to the WTO's dispute settlement procedures. There is a long list of issues that indicates the subjects of WTO disputes. Because there are often a number of ways to describe an issue, each dispute can appear under more than one heading. The issues are broadly classified under goods, intellectual property and services.

> The obligations under the agreement apply equally to all member countries, but developing countries will have a longer period to face them. Special transition arrangements operate in the situation where a developing country does not presently provide product patent protection in the area of pharmaceuticals.

Patents are very important regarding drugs and pharmaceutical industry. The reasons for the importance of patents in the pharmaceutical industry are as follows:

- The costs of pharmaceutical R&D are high.
- There is a disclosure requirement, at the time of registration.
- Imitation in this area is relatively easy; therefore, the patent is essential to protect the original invention.
- Pharmaceutical patents allow the company to make extra profits due to the monopoly rights which the patent confers. The company can charge a higher price and earn more than would have been possible in case of free competition.
- From these profits, R&D costs can be recovered.

TRIPs Principles

The TRIPs Agreement has a major role to play in harmonization of the norms and standards of intellectual property protection. It requires members to comply with a defined set of minimum standards for the protection of intellectual property rights covered in it.

Its basic principles are as follows:

- It makes it compulsory for the member countries to provide patents for products and processes in all fields of technology, subject to the tests of novelty, inventiveness and industrial use.
- It mandates patenting of 'micro-organisms', and microbiological and non-biological processes.
- The members are allowed to make only limited exclusions from patentability. The exclusions are allowed on the grounds of public order or morality, or in respect of protection extended to human, animal and plant life or health.
- It also gives option to the states for protecting new plant varieties through patents or through the effective *sui generis* system.
- It ensures that the protection and enforcement of intellectual property rights should contribute to the promotion of technological innovation for the mutual advantage of producers and users of technological knowledge and in a manner conducive to social and economic welfare.

Major Changes in Indian Patent System Post-TRIPs

Before the TRIPs Agreement, pharmaceutical patents and other intellectual property rights on drugs were not recognized in many developing countries (unlike many industrial countries). There were no international standards for patent protection; countries had varied regulations on IP protection depending on their own needs. In the pharmaceutical sector, some 40 countries did not provide patent protection for pharmaceutical products. Patents were simply not available for pharmaceutical inventions in these countries, which implied that no one could claim an intellectual property right on such products. As a result, copies of medicines protected by a patent in other countries were widely available, usually at a lower price than the original patented drug. The copies were either manufactured by local companies or imported, without having to ask the patent holders' permission. This practice has now come to an end. Copies of patented drugs will remain on the market but it will no longer be possible to manufacture and market copies of new patented medicines in those 40 countries, unless the

Table 2.3 *Changes in Indian Patent Laws Post-TRIPs Agreement*

S. No.	Indian Patent Act 1970	TRIPs Agreement	Patent Amendment Act
1	*Only process patent was granted (not the product patent) in food, chemicals and medicines or drugs*	*Included Process and well as Product patent in all fields of technology*	*Full implementation of TRIPs agreement 2005 (Patent Bill 2005)*
2	*Term of patent: 14 years; in case of chemicals and drugs, 5 to 7 years*	*Term of patent: 20 years*	*Conforms to TRIPS requirement (Patent Act 1999)*
3	*Compulsory licensing and licensing of drugs*	*Limited compulsory licensing, no license of right*	*Conforms to TRIPS requirement*
4	*Several areas were excluded from patents like the method of agriculture, surgical or therapeutic methods of treating humans, animals or plants in order to increase the economic value of products*	*Almost all fields of technology are patentable. Plant varieties and some areas of agriculture and biotechnology are excluded from patentability*	*Uses the exceptions allowed by TRIPs. Rejects the patents on living things, non-living substances occurring in nature, plants and animals*
5	*Government allowed to use patented invention to prevent scarcity*	*Very limited scope for governments to use patented inventions*	*Conforms to TRIPs requirement*

original manufacturer has chosen not to seek any patent protection there. Table 2.3 differentiates the changes in the patent law after the introduction of TRIPs in 1995.

Under the TRIPs Agreement, all WTO members are required to make patents available for pharmaceutical and biological inventions in their countries. Article 27.3(b) of TRIPs Agreement gives its members some freedom to exclude plants, animals and 'essentially biological processes' from patentability as genetically modified organisms and GM foods had created fears and uncertainty of its impact on health and the environment and have raised important ethical issues in different countries. However, it also states that micro-organisms and non-biological and micro-biological processes have to be patentable. The wording is deliberately ambiguous, in order to give countries some freedom to interpret this in their national legislation as they consider fit.

The TRIPs Agreement requires the WTO member states to introduce patent protection only to products that were invented after 1 January 1995, i.e. products for which a patent application has been filed in a WTO member state after 1995. This means that, in accordance with TRIPs, products already on the market cannot be given patent protection, because if they are already marketed, they are not new, and so do not meet the TRIPs conditions necessary to grant a patent. Therefore, only new drugs or new indications, formulations or processes invented after 1995 are patentable in all WTO member countries, or before a year, if priority is claimed.

The developing and least-developed countries not granting drug patents must have a system, often referred to as a 'mail-box' system, to store patent applications as from 1995 until the transitional period expires. At this time, the various patent applications waiting in the 'mail-box' will be examined according to the TRIPs standards and, if granted, the patent term, which starts from the filing date, will last for 20 years. The member countries have to meet some minimum standards; however, some WTO member countries may go for greater IP protection than required in the Agreement. For example, in Europe and the United States, pharmaceutical patents may be extended beyond 20 years, for up to 5 years, to compensate for the long delays in obtaining marketing approval for a drug. Such patent extensions vary from country to country since there is absence of international standards, depending on the date of marketing approval. However, the pharmaceutical patent cannot be extended beyond 15 years from the date of marketing approval in European countries, and 14 years in the United States.

Patent Cooperation Treaty

Patent Cooperation Treaty (PCT) is administered by WIPO, which gives rise to 'centralized international application procedure' for the grant of patent at national and regional levels. The treaty was signed on 19 June 1970 at Washington, amended on 28 September 1979 and on 3 February 1984. It was further modified on 3 October 2001.

The treaty makes it possible to seek patent protection for an invention simultaneously in many countries. The total number of PCT contracting states as on 7 September 2012 is 146 (also known as International Patent Cooperation Union). A majority of countries are signatories of the PCT including major industrialized countries like Argentina and Taiwan.

PCT application can be filed by anyone who is a national resident of the contracting state. An international patent application (PTC application) is filed at the receiving office (RO). The receiving office is the branch of PCT where the patent applications are filed. Nationals and residents of India are entitled to file international applications for patents under PCT at Patent Receiving Office, Delhi while for US applicants, the branch office is US patent office. Applicant from any contracting state may file an international patent application at the International Bureau in Geneva.

An Indian applicant can file a PCT international application in the following manner:

1. He can file the application in the Indian Patent Office, which acts as the Receiving Office. After filing a patent application in India, anytime before the expiry of 12 months from the date of filing, an international application can be filed in International Bureau of WIPO or in Indian Patent Office as Receiving Office. However, if the international filing is done within 6 weeks from the date of filing in India, this can be done only after taking the permission under Section 39 from the Indian Patent Office.
2. The application can also be filed directly in the International Bureau of WIPO after taking permission under Section 39 from the Indian Patent Office, claiming the priority of the previously filed Indian patent application along with the prescribed application fee. A certified copy of the Indian patent application may be filed with the international application within 16 months from the date of priority.

The patent application can be withdrawn if the inventor or the applicant desires. In such cases, international publication will not take place. PCT makes an international patent search and the search is carried out by one of the major patent offices appointed by the PCT assembly as an International Searching Authority (ISA). The international search report and the written opinion are communicated by the ISA to the applicant. PCT does not issue the patent directly but it helps in the process of filing the patent in foreign countries in the most efficient and cost-effective manner. The examination is based on preliminary international search report and is made by the most competent people of the International Preliminary Examination Authority.

Paris Convention opens a number of international conventions and treaties exclusively to its members. PCT is one of the international conventions apart from Budapest Treaty (for deposit of microorganism), UPOV (for the protection of new varieties of plant), Madrid Agreement (for repression of false or deceptive indication of source on goods) and Madrid Protocol (concerning deposit of industrial design).

Procedure

After due verification by the International Searching Authority, PCT issues a search report between 4 and 16 months from the date of priority filing. Based on the international search report, the applicant decides whether it would be worthwhile to seek national protection. If yes, then it is important to know in how many countries because it includes fee amount and other expanses to enter the national phase in each country. Many patent authorities rely on the international search report. In addition to the compulsory international search, one or more optional supplementary international searches may also be carried out by participating International Searching Authority upon the applicant's request.

The patent application is published by PCT after 18 months from the priority date of filing the application. The applicant makes demand or requests the PCT for 'International Preliminary Examination'. As a result the applicant gets an opportunity to amend the claims. Such applications remain in PCT system for another 10 months, which is advantageous to the applicant. Finally, at the 30th month from the filing date of the international application, the role of PCT comes to an end. In this way, the international phase ends and the international application enters the national and regional phase. If the entry into national or regional phase is not performed within the prescribed time limit, the international application generally ceases to have the effect of a national or regional application.

Salient Features

- This system is quite good and efficient only if foreign protection is desired in one or two member countries but if it is desired in too many countries, the applicant has to bear the huge cost, which includes separate filing fees and translation cost.
- The system provides much longer time for filing the patent application in member countries. The time available under Paris Convention for securing priority in other countries is 12 months from the date of initial filing, whereas under PCT, the time available could be 20 to 31 months.
- The inventor is also benefitted by the search report as it is the International Search Report.

The main advantage of the PCT procedure or international procedure is the possibility to delay the national or regional procedures, and the respective fees and translation costs along with unified filing procedure.

Budapest Treaty

The treaty for the international recognition of the deposit of microorganisms for the purpose of patent procedures was started at Budapest on 28 April 1977 and amended on 26 September 1980. The treaty is administered by the World Intellectual Property Organization (WIPO) and allows the deposit of microorganisms at the International Depositary Authority (IDA) for the purpose of patent procedure. The important requirement is that the invention should be described in detail to the public and this disclosure is normally achieved by means of a written description supplemented by drawings where necessary. Usually in order to meet the legal requirement of disclosure, patent application and patents must disclose in their description the subject matter of the invention clear and complete enough to be carried out by the person skilled in the art. However, some problems may arise for inventions involving the use of new microorganisms (i.e. whose information is not available to the public). For example, in case of an organism isolated from soil, can be improved by mutation and further selection, it would be impossible to describe the strain and its selection sufficiently to guarantee another person obtaining the same strain from soil himself. In such a case, the microorganism can be considered to be an essential part of the disclosure. Moreover, if the microorganism was not generally available to the public, the written details and disclosure of the invention might not be sufficient. This led to the recommendation that the written disclosure of an invention involving the use of a new microorganism must be supplemented by the deposit of the microorganisms in a recognized culture collection/institute like IMTECH in India. The culture collection would then make the microorganism available to the public according to the requirement.

Before 1970s, there was no uniform system of deposit, or there was no alternative but to deposit the same microorganism in several collections in different countries to guard against the possibility of any of their applications failing on the grounds of insufficient disclosure. Such practice was wasteful, time-consuming and expensive too and also resulted in applicants depositing the microorganism in every country in which they wished to file a patent application referring to that microorganism. In order to solve the problem of such multiple deposits, the UK government proposed, in 1973, that the World Intellectual Property Organization (WIPO) should study the possibilities of one deposit serving the purposes of all the deposits that would otherwise be needed. This proposal was adopted by the Governing Bodies of WIPO.

The treaty ensures that an applicant needs not to deposit the biological material in all the countries where he or she want to obtain patent. Deposition of the biological material can be made at one recognized institute only and this deposit will be recognized in all countries that have signed the Budapest Treaty. It helped in solving the difficulties which may arise in describing the nature of invention by setting up a series of International Depository Authorities (IDA) and recognition by all of the member countries in a single IDA. The treaty does not define the meaning of microorganisms but the range of materials able to be deposited under the Budapest treaty includes the following:

- Cells: bacteria, fungi, eukaryotic cell lines, plant spores.
- Genetic vectors (plasmids or bacteriophage vectors or viruses) containing a gene or DNA fragment.
- Purified nucleic acids.
- Naked DNA, RNA or plasmids.

The period of storage of deposited microorganisms may be 30 years or 5 years after the most recent request of sample, whichever is earlier. It protects microorganisms from loss or non-availability. Till 20 November 2012, there were 78 contracting states to the Budapest Treaty including the United States and Australia but now the European Patent Organization (EPO) has also formally declared its acceptance of the Treaty.

PATENT LAWS IN OTHER COUNTRIES

Patents are granted country-wise, so there are different patent laws in different countries. However, some basic features remain the same in every country. The laws in various countries are explained in a tabular form so as to get précise information with reference to US patent laws.

Patent Laws in Unites States

The United States Patent and Trademark Office (USPTO or Office) was established as an agency of the United States within the Department of Commerce. The role of the agency is to grant patents for the protection of inventions and to register trademarks. The Office promotes the industrial and technological progress of the nation through the preservation, classification and dissemination of patent information.

The US federal patent laws have existed since 1790 and were a short Act of seven sections entitled 'An act to promote the Progress of Useful Arts'. In 1793, rights to patents were confined to citizens of the United States. This small Act of 1793 was replaced by a slightly longer Act, which was drafted by Thomas Jefferson. But the 1793 Act was amended in 1800 to allow foreigners also who had been resident in the United States for two years to obtain patents, subject to them making an oath that the invention in question is not a prior knowledge in the United States or abroad. Since the 1870s and 1880s were a period in which many international organizations were created, the United States underwent several amendments till 2009, though the basic structure of the present law was adopted in 1952. As we have already discussed the Indian patent laws in detail, Table 2.4 differentiates between Indian and US patent laws.

Table 2.4 *Indian and United States Patent Laws*

S. No.	Indian Patent Act	United States Patent Act
1	Indian patent laws are strict.	US patent laws are liberal.
2	The Indian Patent Act quite elaborately describes the non-patentable inventions under Sections 3 and 4 (e.g. business model or computer program, isomers of the chemical compounds, mathematical models etc.)	US patent laws allows the grant of patent to anyone who invents or discovers any new and useful article or machine or process of manufacture or composition of matter or any new and useful improvement in the existing invention
3	Inventions related to the atomic energy are not patentable in India	Inventions related to the atomic energy are widely accepted in United States
4	Inventions that are contrary to the public order or morality are not granted patent (e.g. patent or novel design of guns etc.)	Inventions that are patentable and novel in design are allowed (e.g. patent or novel design of guns etc.)
5	Inventions which are mere arrangements of components are not granted patent even if it has utility (e.g. Swiss knife assembly)	Inventions which are arrangements of components is granted patent if it has some utility (e.g. Swiss knife assembly)
6	Indian patent laws grant patent on 'first-to-file' basis. Thus, the true inventor should file the patent application and challenge his/her invention.	US patent laws grant patent on 'first-to-invent' basis. Therefore the inventor should maintain the lab records, proof of dates of invention.
7	Indian patent law has pre-grant and post-grant opposition.	US patent law has the provision of post-grant opposition only.
8	Plants are not patentable in India	Plants are patentable in the United States
9	Software is not patentable in India; they are copyrightable.	Software is patentable in the United States
10	Patent agent should be Indian	Patent agent from other countries can also practice in United States
11	The application for filing the patent starts with Form no. 2 with all the documents related to the invention attached with it	The patent document is the first sheet with abstract, details of the invention, assignees, classification no. and important drawing of the invention.
12	If the inventor has published his invention before filing the patent, then he automatically loses all his rights in India.	If the inventor has published his invention, he will not lose his right to file the patent till one year.

Patent Laws in European Countries

The European Patent Organization (EPO) is an intergovernmental organization, set up on 7 October 1977 on the basis of the European Patent Convention (EPC) signed in Munich in 1973. It has two bodies, the European Patent Office and the Administrative Council, which supervise the official activities. The patent law is shaped by international agreements such as the WTO's TRIPs and the Patent Law Treaty (PLT). Presently, 38 states are the members of EPO and the applications for patents can be filed at the relevant national patent office or at the EPO while an international application may be filed under the Patent Cooperation Treaty (PCT), which can be later nationalized in the desired countries or at the EPO. Table 2.5 differentiates between European and US patent laws.

Table 2.5 *European and US Patent Laws*

S. No.	European Patent Act	US Patent Act
1	The first person to have filed the application will get the patent. Filing date is important.	The first person to invent will get the patent. This usually involves examining laboratory logbooks, establishing dates for prototypes, and so on. If the person who filed later is found to have invented earlier, he may be awarded the patent.
2	If the invention has become publicly available in any way, by the inventor or anyone else, before the filing of patent application, the application will be rejected (Article 54 EPC).	There is a one-year grace period (35 US Code Section 102), which means that the inventor can freely publish his invention without losing patent rights. This only applies for the United States.
3	Any one way of practicing the invention must be included in the application (Article 83 EPC), but it is not compulsory to state that this way is the best way, or a good way.	US patent law requires the inventor to include the best way to practice the invention in the patent application (35 US Code Section 112).
4	All patent applications are published 18 months after their filing date, unless they have been withdrawn.	Now in the United States, patent applications are published 18 months after their filing date, unless they have been withdrawn or they are filed with a non-publication request, stating that the application is for United States only (Earlier the patents were published only after grant)
5	The European Patent Convention is a treaty signed by 27 European countries. Patents under the EPC are granted by the European Patent Office (EPO) in Munich.	A US patent right is enforceable in the whole territory of the United States. It allows the patent holder to prevent anyone from making, using or selling the patented invention in the United States as the US patent law (35 US Code) is a federal statute.
6	The two most important patentable requirements in European patent law are that, an invention must be *novel* and involve an *inventive step* (Article 52 EPC). It clarifies that the invention has an inventive step if it solves a technical problem in a non-obvious way, which further introduces two extra requirements: it *must solve a problem* (no problem solved means no inventive step), and that *problem must be technical* (excludes solving economic problems).	US requirement that the invention must be *novel* and must be *non-obvious* (35 US Code Sections 102 and 103)

(continued)

Table 2.5 (*Continued*)

S. No.	European Patent Act	US Patent Act
7	European patents and applications typically (virtually always) contain two-part claims.	US patent applications (and patents) will almost always have one-part claims
8	The opposition can be filed within nine months after the grant of a patent; anyone can file an opposition with the EPO, with arguments and evidence. The patent holder and the opponent can then debate with each other. Finally, a decision is made by the EPO based on evidences and arguments.	It has a re-examination procedure where anyone can present reasons and evidence to the USPTO to challenge the validity of a granted patent. Here the patent holder only engages in a discussion with the USPTO examiner to establish the validity of the reasons and the challenger is not a part of these proceedings.
9	According to the European and UK Patent Offices, an invention with respect to software is patentable, if it makes a 'technical contribution' over the known art to solve the existing problem.	United States is more open to the patenting of software than other countries.

Patent Laws in China

China became the member of the WIPO in 1980 and of the Paris Convention for the Protection of Industrial Property Rights in 1985. China is also a member of Patent Cooperation Treaty (PCT) since 1994, and has ratified the agreement on TRIPs since 2001. In 1984, China enacted its first patent law granting patents for inventions, utility models and designs with a view to promote development in science and technology. However, the law provided little protection to pharmaceutical and chemical inventions. In 1992, China faced amendments to the 1984 Patent Law, in compliance with an agreement between China and the United States, i.e. memorandum of understanding (MOU) with a view to join the WTO. The 1992 Amendment in the Patent Law resulted in a provision for the protection of pharmaceutical and/or chemical inventions, and also microbiological products and processes, along with the extension of patent term to 20 years. The law also promoted and encouraged investment in biotechnology research and development, and increased the importation of chemical or pharmaceutical products to China.

In 2000, the Chinese Patent Law was amended again, which came into force on 1 July 2001. The amendments provide patent owners new substantive rights, such as rights of 'offer for sale', simplified patent application procedures and improved administrative and judicial enforcement procedures. Both India and China have similar national laws for IP, and have signed up to similar international conventions and treaties; there are differences on basic political, social and economic fronts, which strengthen their IP regimes.

However, the Chinese laws are different from US laws. Although, China is engaged in significant efforts to enact IP protection, it lacks effective enforcement of these laws, which is a long-standing problem. The first reason for this can be education and cultural trends. For centuries, Chinese believe that inventions and creativity belong to the society, and should be freely shared or owned by the Chinese government. Therefore, traditional Chinese culture is not ready to accept IP rights as private rights owned by a particular person; moreover the entire concept of IP protection is quite new for many Chinese and business entities. They are not aware of their IP rights and their need to seek protection for an invention; also many infringers do not know that their activities infringe other's private rights. Many Chinese lawyers and judges are also new to this field. Therefore, much work has to be done in enforcing and implementing the patent protection in China. Table 2.6 differentiates between Chinese and US patent laws.

Table 2.6 *Chinese and US Patent Laws*

S. No.	Chinese Patent Law	US Patent Law
1	The law provides 'first-to-file' principle, according to which a patent will be granted to the first applicants filing an application for it.	The law follows 'first-to-invent' principle, according to which a patent should be granted to a person who first develops an invention.
2	The invention that can be protected under the Chinese Patent Law must be novel, inventive, and must have practical applicability.	Any man-made thing under the sun is patentable, if it produces a useful, concrete and tangible result, rather than just being an abstract idea.
3	Chinese Patent Law recognizes utility model patents providing limited protection for improvements relating to shape or structure.	US Patent Law considers the equivalent as part of the design patent.
4	Software, business methods, methods of diagnosing or treating diseases, and many plant varieties are non-patentable in China.	Software and plant varieties are patentable in the United States.
5	A patent right includes both 'positive' and 'negative' rights. That means, a patentee not only has a right to prevent others from making, using or selling the invention protected by a valid patent, also the patentee has a right to make, use or sell his/her own invention.	A patent right includes only a 'negative' exclusive right to prevent others from making, selling or using the invention protected by a patent. However, the patent right does not give a patentee the right to make, sell or use his/her own invention
6	Chinese government has strict standards on granting compulsory licenses for the protection of valuable patents. Compulsory licences can be obtained under certain conditions and after the expiration of 3 years from the grant of the patent right.	No compulsory license is available under US Patent Law practice.
7	Chinese legal system is a civil law system that does not support case laws, and renders any decisions on legal opinions with laws, statutes, and regulations.	Patents and copyrights are based on federal laws

Patent Laws in Japan

Fukuzawa Yukichi, a Japanese author and teacher who was the founder of Keio University and was also regarded as one of the founders of modern Japan, introduced the concept of patent to Japan in his 1867 writings. After the Meiji Restoration, the modernization of Japan began. In the year 1871, an experimental patent system was implemented. The first substantial patent law in Japan was established by the Patent Monopoly Act on 18 April 1885. In 1954, the same day was declared as 'The Invention Day' by the Ministry of International Trade and Industry of Japan.

The first seven patents under the Patent Monopoly Act were granted on 14 August 1885. Hotta Zuisho obtained Japanese Patent No. 1 for an anticorrosive paint while Takabayashi Kenzo obtained

Patent No. 2, 3 and 4 for tea processing machines. The Patent Monopoly Act was replaced by the Patent Act in 1888; the Patent Act was replaced by the Patent Law of 1899, which was completely revised in 1909. After the Meiji era, the Patent Act was completely revised twice, in 1921 and 1959. Thus, the Japanese patent law was amended several times in 1959, especially regarding the opposition proceedings, the term of patent, and compliance with the Patent Cooperation Treaty (PCT) in relation to the novelty criteria.

Table 2.7 differentiates between Japanese and US patent laws.

Table 2.7 *Differences between Japanese and US Patent Laws*

S. No.	Japanese Patent Law	United States Patent Law
1	Japan follows first-to-file system.	US follow first-to-invent system.
2	An examination will be carried out only for the application for which the applicant or a third party has filed a request for examination (within 3 years) and paid the examination fees	Applications are examined in the order they were filed, unless the US Patent Office finds a compelling reason to do otherwise
3	An application can consist of more than one claim. There is no surcharge for multiple dependent claims. However, when filing a request for examination, the official fee is calculated based on the number of claims	A patent application can have only one claimed invention. If the examiner determines that there is more than one claimed invention in the application, he will request the inventor to restrict the application to only one claim.
4	An unusual feature of the Japanese patent system is that applications are not automatically examined. The applicant has 7 years from the filing date to file a request for examination.	Applications are examined in the order they were filed automatically.
5	Recent changes to Japanese patent law in 1996 included the move from a pre-grant patent opposition system (3 months to file opposition) to a post-grant opposition system (6 months to file opposition, but the patent is valid until declared otherwise)	There is a re-examination procedure, where anyone can present reasons and evidence to the USPTO to challenge the validity of a granted patent. It does not work the same as an opposition.
6	Japanese patent law says patent infringement is a crime. A person who has infringed a patent right must be engaged in penal servitude for at most 5 years, or must pay a fine of at most 5 million yen (Article 196).	Infringement is not a crime, and damages are not intended as a penalty.
7	If the invention has become publicly available in any way, by the inventor or anyone else, before the filing of patent application, the application will be rejected.	There is a 1-year grace period (35 US Code Section 102), which means that the inventor can freely publish his invention without losing patent rights.

CHAPTER SUMMARY

The patent laws have evolved from very early times and are generally considered to be evolved in Italy in 1474. Patents were also given by the Queen to motivate and protect the foreign engineers, which resulted in industrial development of the nation and brought Industrial Revolution in Italy in 1474. Different countries have varied ways of evolution of patent laws but the basic purpose to start the patenting system was to support the intellectual creativity and encourage invention which resulted in rapid industrialization. The modern patent system was created in 1791. Earlier, the patents were granted without the examination since the inventor's right was considered to be natural and original ones.

The first patent law in India was passed on 28 February 1856, which received the assent of the Governor General (GG) and the law went through several amendments till 2006. The provisions which were not found in the Indian Patent Act 1970 are as follows:

- The term of patent could not be extended by Governor General (GG).
- The importers were also treated as inventors subject to know-how and practices within a specified period.
- There was no provision for provisional specification.
- Inventions used by the inventor were not considered to be for public use.

Presently changes have also been made to make the patent rules user-friendly. The working of the Patent Office has also been decentralized completely. All patent activities can now be carried on by all the patent offices (Delhi, Mumbai, Kolkata and Chennai). Earlier certain patent activities could be carried out only by the Head Office (Patent Office at Kolkata) also the fees to the Patent Office can now be paid electronically. Patents have gained global recognition and the international treaties provide basic principles to grant the patent. India is a member of several international organizations and treaties like WIPO, WTO, Paris Convention, PCT and Budapest Treaty, which are responsible for the promotion and protection of intellectual property throughout the world.

WIPO is a specialized agency of the United Nations, dedicated to ensuring that the rights of creators and owners of intellectual property are protected worldwide. WTO is the successor organization to the GATT and is one of the important agencies of the United Nations, which provides better and wider protection for the private patent holders of the developed nations than the Paris Convention. The TRIPS Agreement, which came into effect on 1 January 1995, is to date the most comprehensive multilateral agreement on intellectual property. It provides standards for the full range of intellectual property rights and also the enforcement of those standards both internally and through legal and administrative actions. PCT is a treaty administered by WIPO, which gives rise to 'centralized international application procedure' for the grant of patent at national and regional level. PCT is open to the members of the Paris Convention and helps in filing the separate patent application in member countries. PCT is one of the international conventions apart from Budapest Treaty (for deposit of microorganism) UPOV (for the protection of new varieties of plant), Madrid Agreement (for repression of false or deceptive indication of source on goods), Madrid Protocol (concerning deposit of industrial design). The International Union for the Protection of New Varieties of Plants (UPOV) was established by the International Convention for the Protection of New Varieties of Plants and protects the rights of the plant breeders. To have the plant variety right, the plant should fulfil the requirement of novelty, distinctiveness, uniformity and stability. Budapest treaty is another treaty formed to deposit the microorganisms at the international depository authority like American Type Culture Collection (ATCC) and Microbial Type Culture Collection (MTCC).

Patents are granted country-wise, so there are different patent laws in different countries. However, some basic features remain same in every country. US patent laws are liberal while Indian patent laws are strict. The European Patent Convention is a treaty signed by 27 European countries. Patents under the EPC are granted by the European Patent Office (EPO) in Munich. Chinese patent law is very close to European and US patent laws with a few exceptions. The only problem that China is facing now is effective enforcement of its patent law and implementation. While in case of Japan, the procedure for grant of patents is to a very small extent similar to that of India.

MULTIPLE CHOICE QUESTIONS

1. The provisions to issue compulsory licences as made in the year
   (i) 2002 (ii) 2005
   (iii) 1970 (iv) 2006
2. Pre-grant and post-grant oppositions can be filed in the patent office after
   (i) 2002 amendment
   (ii) 2005 amendment
   (iii) 2006 amendment
   (iv) None
3. How many rounds are held by GATT?
   (i) 5 rounds
   (ii) 6 rounds
   (iii) 7 rounds
   (iv) 8 rounds
4. GATT was replaced by
   (i) TRIPs (ii) WIPO
   (iii) WTO (iv) None
5. Which country follows the first-to-invent principle?
   (i) Japan
   (ii) India
   (iii) United States
   (iv) China

REVIEW QUESTIONS

1. How many amendments were done to the Indian Patent Act 1970? Discuss.
2. Why countries become members of International conventions and treaties? Discuss the advantages.
3. What changes were seen in the Indian pharmaceutical sector after the TRIPs agreement?
4. What requirements can be fulfilled by the plant to obtain Plant Variety Right?
5. How are the Indian patent laws different from US patent laws?
6. What are the major points of difference between the US and UK patent laws? Discuss.

Classification of Patents

3

Chapter Objectives:

It is evident that patents are required in every field of technology and research. Therefore, patents are classified accordingly into various categories such as product patent, process patent, utility patent, etc. The patents are awarded for many disciplines such as software, electrical engineering, textile, pharmaceutical, food industry. Patents cover a vast area in biotechnological products, plant and microorganisms, which are also discussed in detail in this chapter.

The patent system in India is governed by the Patents Act 1970 and The Patents Rules 1972, which became effective from 20 April 1972. Subsequently the Patents Act 1970 was amended and became effective from 1 January, 1995. Further the Patents Rules, 1972 were also amended and came into effect from 2 June 1999. The patent system was established to protect the invention that can be a process of making a product or a product itself. Thus process and product are the two major categories of patent. The product patent gives exclusive right to the owner of the product and prevents the third person from using, making, offering to sell or importing the product in the country while the process patent gives exclusive rights to the holder to prevent the third person from using the process, which may lead to the formation of any product, offering to sell, selling or importing products that are made by the process along with the invention.

India is a member of several organizations which govern patents like World Intellectual Property Organization (WIPO), TRIPs Agreement under the World Trade Organization, Paris Convention (for the protection of industrial property), Patent Cooperation Treaty (PCT), and Budapest Treaty. Every organization has different criteria of classifying the patent and so is the case with patent classification in India. The term of the patent remains 20 years and the criteria of patentability are also same throughout. The criteria are that the invention should be novel, industrially useful and should have some inventive steps in the process. Patent grants specific and exclusive rights for the invention, which can either be a process or a product that provides new ways or techniques to solve existing problems.

CLASSIFICATION OF PATENTS IN INDIA

The need for classification of the patent occurred in order to organize and index the technical information contained in patent specification that details the description of the invention and defines contents such as title, abstract, description and claim. Such data helps in retrieving the patent documents to study a particular area of technology and to identify the novelty of an invention. In order to be patentable, the invention must be novel, useful and non-obvious. Patent classifications are maintained by the patent-granting authorities on their own classification schemes. The patent rights are territorial and India grants

Table 3.1 *Type of Patents Awarded in India*

S. No.	Types of Patent	Examples
1	*Product Patent*	
	(a) Substance	*Chemical compounds, enzymes, cell lines, plasmids, recombinant DNA, vector-host, microorganisms*
	(b) Composition of matter	*Mixture of substances; pharmaceutical composition, food stuffs, composition of fertilizers, lubricant composition*
	(c) Devices	*Mouse trap, ball-point pen, x-ray tube, fermenter, coffee machine*
2	*Process Patent*	
	(a) Manufacturing process	*Method of preparing a substance; preparation of a hybrid plasmid, gene cloning techniques, semi-synthetic penicillin or new azo dyes, downstream process of extraction of plant or animal product*
	(b) Method of execution	*Analytical or diagnostic methods of examination; freeze-drying*
	(c) Usefulness	*Use of a substance or composition for a particular purpose; utilization of herbicides for combating weeds.*
3	*Design Patent*	*Design and shape of articles like machine, bottles, vehicles etc...*

patent rights only within the Indian territory and not outside. The classification of patents in India is shown in Table 3.1.

A product patent consists of inventions that are in the form of tangible products like any substance (e.g. an enzyme, a chemical compound, or recombinant DNA) or composition of matter (e.g. composition of a drug or composition of fertilizer) or it can be a device or machine.

A process patent on the other hand is that awarded to the process of making of a product (method of preparing a hybrid plasmid, method of extraction of a compound) or a process of execution or for the usefulness of a compound in the process of preparation.

Design patents are assigned for the shape of an article.

CLASSIFICATION OF PATENTS BY WIPO

India is a member-state of Word Intellectual Property Organization (WIPO), an international organization responsible for the promotion of the protection of intellectual property throughout the world. According to WIPO, patents are classified as follows:

- Utility patent
- Design patent
- Plant patent.

Utility Patent

Utility patents are given based on usefulness of the invention. Every invention is innovative either in terms of product formation or the method of manufacturing the product. The utilitarian feature of an invention is the criterion for the grant of the patent. The patent provides protection in the way an article is used and works, i.e. it deals with the functionality of the patent. It is also known as 'petty patent', 'innovation patent', 'minor patent' or 'small patent' because its cost, threshold of examination and duration of protection is lesser than a standard patent. Unlike Standard patent, the Utility model provides protection for the duration of 6 or 10 years without renewal and extension possibilities. Such models are more suitable for inventions for small scale enterprises, which makes minor improvement of the existing inventions. Approximately 90% of the patent documents submitted recently to the PTO are for utility patents. Computer-related inventions that have short commercial life before they go obsolete requires patent monopoly for a short duration of time. Examples of utility patent include duplicate key making machines, coloured eye lens and, calculator cum calender cum timer cum weather reporter. Also biotechnology inventions such as isolation of gene sequences that need to be best protected for a short duration may be brought under a utility patent. The Patent Law in India does not provide registration for the Utility Patent model. The origin of this Utility model is U.S.Patent Law. However according to the Indian Patent amendment Act 2002, the subject matter of this patent, in the coming years, would include an apparatus/device or a method or process of making an invention. Any invention that is harmful to the environment is not included under utility patent. The utility patent has the following salient features:

- It is fast in order to protect the short commercial life of the invention.
- It is cheaper in terms of filing and maintenance of the patent invention.
- The examination procedure is less complex.
- It is for a shorter period of time.

Design Patent

The patent law allows patents to an invention that deals with the shape or ornamental feature of an article. Design patent protects the appearance of the article for 14 years from the date of filing the application but the conditions for design is that it should be novel and unique. The visual feature of the design is embodied in or applied to an article of manufacture. The application of design patent consists of a combination of configuration or shape of the article and surface ornamentation. An ornamental design may be embodied in the entire invention/article or only on a part of the invention. Design patents are a type of industrial design right. Ornamental designs of jewellery, furniture, beverage containers (coca cola, coke, Pepsi bottles etc.), and computer icons are a few examples of objects that are covered by design patents.

Plant Patent

A patent is granted by the government to an inventor who has invented or has discovered new and distinct varieties of plants except tuber-propagated plant or a plant found in uncultivated state. The term of plant patent granted is 20 years from the date of filing the application. It protects the inventor's right to exclude others from asexually reproducing, selling or using the reproduced plant. This protection is limited to living plants that express only one set of characteristics determined by its genotype through asexual reproduction, which otherwise cannot be made. It includes algae and micro fungi but not bacteria. For a plant variety to get protection, it must be novel, distinct, uniform, and stable. However, plants are protected in India by a special *sui generis system*. Plant patents do not require maintenance fees.

CATEGORIES OF PATENT

The patents can be classified into various broad categories. It can either be industrially applicable or not applicable in industries; it can either be for a product or for a process; it can be a utility patent focussing on the usefulness of an invention. These are briefly discussed below:

Industrial or Non-Industrial Patents

Basically, the patent is either industrial or non-industrial in nature. By industrial patents, we mean that the invention can be made or used in any kind of industry like agriculture, chemical, pharmaceutical, and many others. And it can be considered as industrially applicable if it is made or used in industry while for the grant of non-industrial patent, the invention is not necessarily be made or used in industry.

Product and Process Patent

The utility patents are divided into two categories: product patent and process patent. This type of patent provides protection to any invention that executes functions such as a new product or a process, which requires a periodic maintenance fees and its term is 20 years from the date of filing the application. The utility patent deals with processes, machines, manufacture or composition of matter and improvements, which are new and useful.

Utility Patent

Utility patent as discussed earlier protects an invention that provides a new and useful process, machine, manufacture, or composition of matter, or a new and useful improvement over the existing invention. The protection is provided to the functionality of the invention and must possess three requirements of usefulness, novelty, and non-obviousness. Utility patent is used in the United States to distinguish it from other types of patents (e.g. design patents). The term should not be confused with utility models, also known as 'petty patents,' granted by other countries.

Other categories of this patent are as follows:

- *Reissue Patent*: The patent is issued to correct an error in an already issued patent; it however will not affect the period of protection offered by the original patent.
- *Defensive Publication* (DEF): The patent is issued instead of a regular patent to offer limited protection, defensive in nature and prevent others from patenting an invention, design, or plant. Since 1986, the Statutory Invention Registration has replaced DEF.

SPECIAL PATENTS

Some special types of patents are those awarded for textile invention, electro-mechanical inventions, software products, food inventions, drugs, chemical items, and for living entities like plants and microbes as discussed below:

1. *Textile Invention*: The inventions related to textile manufacturing and textile machinery involving both process or product innovations are patentable. The inventions in textile technology can be related to areas like textile manufacturing, chemical processing, fibre science and technology, textile machines and dyes. Dyes are included in chemicals, so the process of making a dye is patentable under Sections 3 and 5 of the Indian Patent Act. The term of patent is 14 years from the date of patent filing.

2. *Electrical Invention*: Inventions in the area of electronics are related to the application like consumer electronics, communication systems, video technology, manufacturing, control devices, biomedical instrumentation, optical projection system, processing of video signals, washing machine and humidity sensors, etc. Though semiconductor products are not patentable but the process of making the semiconductor product is patentable under the provisions of the Indian Patent Act 1970. The term of such patent is 14 years.
3. *Software Patent*: The Indian Patent Act 1970 does not recognize software programs and computer data for granting patent. They are protected by Copyright Act of 1957 but now sophisticated computer programmes are being recognized as inventions and are entitled to patent protection in line with the emerging international trend. Computer software is generally protected under the copyright law but software as essential part of the hardware, when connected to hardware can be protected by patents, for example, UV spectrophotometer, automatic fermenters, etc. Software patent is granted for an invention based on computer-related innovation and is not permitted in many countries. Patenting in this field is extremely controversial and the reasons for some who are against this patent are as follows:
   - It is not clear whether the software patents encourage innovation or not.
   - It is difficult to generate the software patent product in large numbers.
   - Software products mostly do not result in huge profits than physical products.
   - The system of patenting diverts the intellectual bodies towards the patent processing instead of engaging in spending time for innovations.
   - The software is quickly superseded by its latest version and the term of patent being 20 years, the user is unable to make use of it for long.

   The software patent guidelines state that the claimed subject matter must provide some practical benefit in the area of technology. Till 1970, the USA did not grant patent to innovations in mathematical calculations made by the computer/software as they were with the view that patents are granted only to the processes, machines, articles of manufacture and compositions of matter. It did not include scientific truths and mathematical algorithms, but the situation changed gradually when US Supreme Court granted patent to inventions related to software in 1981. The invention described the technique of moulding rubber using mathematical algorithm and the algorithm got the patent.
4. *Patents in Food Industry*: Foods that are produced by combining traditional ingredients and using standard cooking or preparation techniques are unlikely to meet the patent requirements, but innovations in food technology often result in products that qualify as patentable inventions.

   Some new food products are innovative chemical compounds, such as artificial sweeteners and fat substitutes. Dozens of patents, many now expired, were filed around the sweetening agent sucralose and its production methods. Other inventions are modifications of known food components that improve the components' properties. For example, encapsulated fish oils increase its stability, introducing components (e.g., Probiotics or other biologically active agents) to enhance the nutritional value of food. Combining well-known ingredients in a special arrangement gained New Zealand ice-cream manufacturer 'Tip Top' a patent for the Memphis Meltdown, a triple-dipped ice cream with a layer of caramel, sandwiched between two layers of chocolate.

   In addition to the patentable qualities of new food products, valuable intellectual property may reside in food preparation methods. Although many methods are kept as trade secrets, patent protection is more suited to some commercial strategies, particularly where it may prove impossible to keep the method secret. Although a patent provides only a 20-year monopoly, the method need not be kept secret, making it easier to implement and license. In addition, competitors will infringe on a patent for a new method even if they have developed the method independently, whereas it may be impossible to prevent competitors from using a method if a trade secret becomes more widely known.

5. *Pharmaceutical Patents*: The pharmaceutical industry has grown logarithmically in India over the past three decades and has become one of the most flourishing sectors in India and the world as a whole. India ranks in the top 15 pharmaceutical manufacturing countries worldwide. Pharmaceutical inventions are based on integrated discoveries in the field of biology, chemistry, medicine, botany, and bioinformatics. The government of India has formulated policies in these sectors whose objectives is to provide incentives to research-based pharmaceutical companies for encouraging indigenous research and encourages new investments into the pharmaceutical industry and promote the introduction of new technologies and new drugs.

   The Patent Act 1970 was enacted with the objective of promoting industrial process development and to achieve fair equilibrium between private and public interest for promoting healthy competition and innovation in Indian industries. According to this Act, the requirements of the invention should satisfy the criteria of being new, useful and obvious. The Act of 1970 excluded pharmaceuticals and agrochemical products from the grant of patents. Thus, pharmaceutical products were not granted patents in India under the copyright laws. Hence there has been a rapid growth in the cheaper adaptation of a number of drugs to be used in the domestic market and manufacture of generic drugs on the expiration of the international patents for the international market. Process patent was granted in respect to preparation of drugs and medicines under the provisions of the Indian Patent Act 1970.

   According to the Patent Act 1970, drugs and medicines consisted of medicines for internal or external use of human beings or animals, substances used for mitigation or prevention of diseases or used in the diagnosis treatment, substances used to maintain public health or prevent epidemic diseases, chemical substances used as insecticides, fungicides, germicides, weedicides that help in protecting plants from infection, and the substances used as intermediates in the preparation of a drug or medicines. In India, patents were not granted for drugs as there was no such system for protecting them but the TRIPS agreement has placed an obligation on India to grant product patents to drugs by 2005. On the grant of patent protection, the firms that have patented their drugs may either export their drugs to India or may produce them in India through license to firms. According to the terms of the TRIPS agreement, the pharmaceutical patents have to undergo rigorous testing and should be approved before put to market for sale. The Indian drug industry has benefitted a lot through WTO and TRIPS agreement. When the term of the patent expires, the drug becomes open to the generic manufacturers to produce and market these drugs in their country and as a result the drug becomes cheaper.

   A generic drug is the one which can be called as the copy of the original drug after the original drug expires from the term of patent. They become available when a drug goes out of patent. Because of the increasing pressure on the budgets of both state and private health care providers, there is increasing pressure on the medical advisers/prescribers to use generic drugs whenever possible. As a result, the generic drug market supersedes the original version. Moreover the generic versions can receive approval quite quickly as these drugs need not go through the full process of clinical trials and so on. The generics manufacturers also need not require proving the equivalence of the drug to the original version because the generic drug will have the same active ingredient and a similar formulation just like the original drug.

Patent holders clearly have a lot to lose from the launch of generics and often go to great lengths to delay them. What they generally do is that they separately patent the formulation of a drug (at a later date from the patenting of the active ingredient itself) in order to, in effect, lengthen the life of the patent.

6. *Patents for Microorganisms*: According to the TRIPS provisions, all member countries should provide protection for new microorganisms. Therefore, the Patent Amendment Act 2002, which was brought into force in May 2003, provides protection for new microorganisms. The patents in biotechnology traditionally include all unicellular organisms usually having dimensions beneath the limits of vision and are self-replicating e.g. bacteria, yeasts, single-celled algae and protozoa while multicellular organisms are normally excluded; however, it includes certain self-replicating biological materials such as plasmids, replicons and viruses etc.

   Microorganism-related invention refers to inventions related to the production of new microorganism (product per se) or utilization of micro-organism for production of other substances.

   - These include traditional or conventional fermentation methods like preparation of curd, idili, dosa or vada pastes, cheese etc.
   - Bio-transformation processes for production of non-living matter like fermentation process of product such as beer, wine, vinegar.
   - Living entity of artificial origin, such as micro-organism, vaccines, transgenic animals and plants etc.
   - Biological materials such as DNA, plasmids, genes, vector, tissues, cells, replicons etc.
   - Process relating to living entities, such as isolation, purification, multiplication, etc.
   - Process relating to biological material.

Evolution of Patents in Microorganisms

Patents regarding microbes suffer from worldwide controversies as they are living entities and the word 'invention' according to Section 2(i, j) of Indian Patent Act 1970 did not clearly define patentable subject matter concerning new and useful living forms. According to the above section, 'invention' is a new useful 'manner of manufacture' or a substance produced by manufacture as a patentable subject matter only if it results in a tangible non-living matter/substance.

There have been many amendments in the laws related to microorganisms. Nowadays patent is given for naturally occurring microorganisms while it is not so in developing nations.

Before 1980, product patent was given for inventions involving microbiological processes but not for the living organisms as they were natural products. On 28 January, 1873, Louis Pasteur received a patent for the process of fermenting beer and claimed that the invention produced better and greater quantity of beer from the yeast. Pure ferment was needed to provoke or induce fermentation.

In 1980, first microbial patent was given in United States after the hearing of case *Diamond v. Chakraborty* in 1980 for novel bacterium and plasmid. Thus in United States and in many countries many microorganisms like bacteria, plant and animal viruses, filamentous fungi, protozoa and unicellular algae are patentable.

In 2001, next development took place in this regard with the signing of Budapest Treaty according to which microbes are required to be submitted in International Depository Authority (IDA) with its full description and specification. Also the signing of TRIPS agreement forced to put changes in the

Table 3.2 *Summary of Events*

Year	Event
1873	1st patent on microorganisms
1977	Budapest Treaty was signed
1980	*Diamond v. Chakraborty* case
2001	India joined Budapest Treaty
2002	Dimminaco A.G. case
2005	New Patenting Regime

criteria of patentability of living organisms. This led to second amendment in the Indian Patent Act 1970, in 2002, which specifies the following:

- Microbes are non-patentable.
- Processes pertaining to microbes are patentable.
- Section 3 was edited (the list of non patentable inventions were changed).
- The word 'plant' was deleted from Section 3(i). Thus plant treatment processes can now be patentable.
- New clause to Section 3 was added as Section 3(j), which excluded inventions on plants and animals other than microorganisms.

Further achievement regarding microbial patent was attained after the hearing of *Dimminaco A.G.* case in 2002. The company filed an application for the preparation of a live vaccine for burasitis, which was rejected by the Patent Office on the grounds of involvement of a living organism, but the patent was finally granted by the Calcutta High Court as it was clarified that there is no bar in the Act to accept a manner of manufacture patentable even if the manner of manufacture results in product containing a living organism.

In the year 2005, another amendment was done to the Indian Patent Act 1970, according to which microorganisms with genetic alteration are now patentable. Product patent for microbes and microbial inventions are now patentable. Section 5 was deleted from the Indian Patent Act 1970. Table 3.2 gives summary of the events.

Patent Laws Before and After Amendments

Patents Act 1970 before amendment included the following features regarding living entities:

- No product patent for an organism (including micro-organisms) or material per se having living entities.
- No process patents on creation of a living organism or production of other biological material/ products having living entities.
- Patents allowed on process for production of chemical products by using an organism or biological material (bioconversion).

However, the Patent Act 1970 allowed patents on the following:

- ❑ The living entity of artificial origin such as micro-organism, vaccines etc.
- ❑ The biological material such as recombinant DNA, plasmids and processes of manufacturing thereof provided they are produced by substantive human intervention.

And excluded grant of patent on the following:

- ❑ Essentially biological processes for the production of plants and animals such as method of crossing or breeding etc.
- ❑ Any biological material and method of making the same which is capable of causing serious prejudice to human, animal or plant lives or health or to the environment including the use of those would be contrary to public order and morality such as terminator gene technology.
- ❑ The processes for cloning human beings or animals, processes for modifying the germ line, genetic identity of human beings or animals, uses of human or animal embryos for any purpose are not patentable as they are against public order and morality.

Patents Act 1970 after amendment of 2005
Excludes grant of patent on

- ❑ The living entities of natural origin such as genes and micro-organism.
- ❑ Any process for manufacture or production of such living entities.
- ❑ Any living entity of artificial origin such as transgenic animals and plants, any part thereof.
- ❑ The biological materials such as organs, tissues, cells, viruses etc. and process of preparing thereof.
- ❑ Gene sequences, DNA sequences without having disclosed their functions.

7. *Plant Patents*: The plant patent protects the shape/appearance and colour of the plants and is granted to plants which are stable and reproduced by asexual reproduction, and not a potato or other edible tuber reproduced plants. Whoever invents or discovers a distinct and new variety of plant (cultivated sports, mutants, hybrids, and newly found seedlings), which can asexually reproduce, except tuber-propagated plant or a plant found in an uncultivated state, may obtain a patent thereof, subject to the conditions and requirements of plant patent.

   Specific plant patents are available only in very few countries. Patentability criteria involves the following points:

   - ❑ The plant is either invented or discovered and, if discovered, the discovery should be made in a cultivated area.
   - ❑ The plant should not be excluded by law and the part of the plant used for asexual reproduction should not a tuber food part, as with potato or Jerusalem artichoke.
   - ❑ The person who files the application should be the one who actually invented the claimed plant, i.e. discovered or developed and identified or isolated the plant, and asexually reproduced the plant.
   - ❑ The plant should be novel and not known by the people before, either in documents or in the field, more than one year prior to the date of the application.
   - ❑ The plant discovered should be different from the known, related plants by at least one distinguishing characteristic, which is more than a difference caused by growing conditions or fertility levels, etc.

Asexual reproduction is the propagation or multiplication of a plant without the use of genetic seeds, so that an exact genetic copy of the plant is being reproduced. The purpose of asexual reproduction is to establish the stability of the plant. This step of the invention must be performed with sufficient time prior to application for patent rights to allow the thorough evaluation of propagated plants or clones of the claimed plant so that the stability of the plant is assured and the specimens retain the identical distinguishing characteristics of the original plant.

Preparation of the Application

The person seeking to file a plant patent application should be thoroughly familiar with the characteristics of the plant, and must assure that the plant is stable. Invention for purposes of a plant patent is a two-step process and these two steps should be completed before the filing of the patent:

- The first step is the discovery step, which involves the identification of a novel plant. This step could be performed in any cultivated area.
- The second step consists of asexual reproduction, which tests the stability of the claimed plant to assure that the plant's unique characteristics are not due to disease, infection, or exposure to agents, which can cause a change in the plant's appearance and is transitory (without the change in the genotype).

Filing of an application before the second step of invention will result in rejection of the claim as being premature and nonstatutory. The application for filing the plant patent requires several information including Latin name of the genus and species of the plant claimed, brief description of the drawing, novelty of the claimed plant, abstract of the disclosure etc. The plant drawing is a very important part of the application and is normally photographic. The drawing includes colored photographs as it may distinguish the characteristics of the new plant. The drawings should be artistic and capable of visual representation. In preparing the disclosure of a plant patent, all parts of the plant should be keenly observed through at least one growth cycle and the observations should be recorded in detail. Because many plants (like pine trees of the same species, asparagus plants, bluegrass plants, etc.) may look very similar, but it may take the collective differences in a number of traits to distinguish a new cultivar. If the applicant fails to record the characteristics and differences at their time of availability in the growing season, then it could result in inadequate botanical description of the claimed plant. After completion of the application, it is reviewed for formalities in the USPTO Initial Processing Branch where it is assigned a serial number, assembled into a file jacket, and reviewed by application examiners for formal requirements. If the application is found complete, it is then forwarded to the examining group, where it is classified and assigned to a patent examiner and is again examined for other formalities like title, declaration, abstract, arrangement of components of the specification, completeness of botanical description, novelty and obviousness of the claimed plant. The examination typically includes the assessment of

1. *Completeness of Botanical Description:* The complete botanical description for the claimed plan includes genus and species, habit of growth, cultivar name, vigor, productivity, precocity (if exists), botanical characteristics of plant structures (i.e. buds, bark, foliage, flowers, fruit, etc.), fertility, and other characteristics which distinguish the plant such as resistance(s) to disease, drought, cold, dampness, etc., fragrance, coloration, regularity and time of bearing, quantity or quality of extracts, rooting ability, timing or duration of flowering season, etc., If the major characteristics of the plant have not been botanically described, the disclosure will be objected as incomplete (and the claim rejected) by the examiner.

2. *Novelty of the Claimed Plant*: It is important that the claimed plant should be different from the prior art, which constitutes those plants that are known to the public and are available to artisan; they may be either patented or unpatented. If the disclosure of the application does not distinguish the claimed plant over such previously known and available plants, the claim will be rejected as failing to distinguish the claimed plant over the known plant.
3. *Obviousness*: The plant will be examined based on the standard statutory and court determined tests of obviousness.

The Impact of Plant Variety Protection

UPOV system is effective in its purpose and act as an incentive for the development of new, improved varieties beneficial to farmers, growers and consumers. The report published by the UPOV in 2005 on the effects of plant variety protection in five countries, namely, Argentina, China, Kenya, Poland and the Republic of Korea, concluded the following:

- The system gave farmers, growers and breeders access to the best varieties produced by breeders throughout UPOV member territories.
- It induced economic development in the rural sector and generated economic benefits, such as varieties with improved yields lead to reductions in the price of end-products for consumers, or improved quality leading to higher value products with increased marketability.
- The system gained health benefits through varieties with improved nutritional content.
- Environmental benefits, such as varieties with improved disease resistance or stress tolerance.

Above all it gives pleasure like that of ornamental plants. These benefits may differ from country to country according to the prevailing conditions. Under the UPOV system, the method of breeding for enhancing the quality and quantity of the yield can continue to maximize the benefits of plant variety protection and plant breeding for the future.

PATENTING BIOLOGICAL PRODUCTS

Biotechnology refers to any technique that uses living organisms or part of the living organism to make a new product or modify the existing product, to improve plants and animals or to develop microorganisms for specific use. In other words, some techniques applied to living organism in order to improve them, or make products by using them for the benefit of man. Biotechnology inventions have already had a major impact on a number of industries including medical research, agricultural, animal production and health, dairy, beverages, food and waste processing (bioremediation). The potential applications of biotechnology are wide and new applications of biotechnology inventions are constantly being developed. There are arguments related to patenting of biotechnology inventions, which may be valid and are of real concern. The reasons for such a concern are the following:

- *Morality*: The genetic alteration of life is an emotional subject and is debatable and advances in this area will not be prevented merely by prohibiting patents of life forms and genetic material. However, allowing patents for such inventions may be considered as an encouragement and thus facilitates further research. For example, human cloning is non-patentable but research may proceed in this area.

- Allowing patents for these types of inventions leads to ownership and commercialization of life and reduces life forms to produce products of manufacture. It may lead to exploiting nature but further research has obtained genetically superior species of plants and animals via breeding programs. The only difference between these past practices and the use of current technology is that, biotechnology makes it easier and potentially more economical for us to select desirable traits.
- There is a widespread concern that granting patent for life forms and genetic material may encourage multinational companies to exploit the natural resources of a country without the authority and acknowledgement of, or reward to the country. However, the provision of the convention of biological diversity of 1992, 175 countries have ratified, gives signatory states the right to exploit their resources by establishing laws which prevent overseas companies from doing so.

Factors which justify patentability of biotechnology invention

- Biotechnology contributes to life-saving medical treatments and contributes towards the eradication of diseases.
- Biotechnology has the potential to provide increased and more reliable food stuffs to the world population and to provide alternative means of producing goods that will use fewer resources. Thus, it increases human welfare.
- Biotechnological advances may have positive environmental effects and may result in production processes and products that are less polluting and use less resource to clean up existing pollution and to improve waste management, to improve soil fertility and so on.

Scope of Patent in Biotechnology Industry

- Biotechnological inventions are concerned with processes occurring in living matter including plants, animals and microbes, the products so obtained and their industrial applications.
- The field of their application is broad. For example, use of fungi in bakery, wine and antibiotic industry; use of bacteria in manufacturing vaccines, plant extracts, etc.
- Classical biotechnology was concerned with naturally occurring biological processes and products and their improvements.
- This situation posed serious problems concerning patentability:
  - Patentability of living matter that reproduce itself like plants, animals and microorganisms.
  - Patentability of chemical substances produced by living organisms.
  - Patentability of microorganisms extracted from natural resources.

Problems in Biotechnology Patenting

1. Does the identification and separation of genes by conventional methods that code for well-known compounds represent a discovery or an invention? For example, insulin, a protein that has been known for some time is produced by a specific gene in the animal body. The structure of this gene was not known until recently.
2. Are claims directed to genetically engineered known compounds acceptable?

Pre-Requisites to Render a Biotechnology Invention Patentable

1. *Novelty*: The invention has to be new. Another unique thing about this qualification is that it differs between countries. Throughout the world, one of the following three main systems are adopted by different countries for accessing novelty:
   - *Local novelty:* an invention must neither be publically used nor published in the particular country in which the applicant seeks patent grant.
   - *Relative novelty:* an invention must neither be published in any country in the world nor used publically used in the particular country in which the applicant seeks the patent.
   - *Absolute novelty:* prior to filing of application, the invention must not have been published or publically used in any country.
2. *Inventive Step*: For patenting something, it must provide some advancement or step forward in technology. All elite inventions are said to lack an inventive step if it would be obvious to a person of general skills apart. The degree of thought and imagination required to render an invention patentable will differ. However, in general, it is only a small degree of imagination or a small step above what was known previousy, that will constitute an inventive step.
3. *Utility*: Another requirement for a patent is its industrial applicability, i.e. the invention must serve a practical purpose and be capable of use in some kind of industry.

Additional Requirement to Obtain a Valid Patent in Case of Biotechnology

1. *Enabling Disclosure*: The constraint for enabling disclosure is central to one of the main aims of the patent system, to promote disclosure of information to the public. The specification filed must sufficiently describe the invention along with best methods by which it may be performed in enough details to allow a person of average skill in the relative field to rework the invention without further experimentation.
2. *Deposit of Microorganisms*: It is essential to the need of filing and enabling disclosure. It is necessary as it would be impossible to accurately describe in writing all the characteristic of the microorganism. A sample can be deposited in a recognized depository like AICC, MTCC etc. Before going for the patent, the microorganism has to be deposited so that it is confirmed that it is novel or known.

Patentable Ingredients of Biotechnology

1. *RNA, DNA or Amino Acid Sequences*: Random isolated sequences generally will not be patentable if they have no utility, i.e., they have no known use at the date of filing application. For example, ESTs sequenced without any function or utility is non-patentable.
2. *DNA & RNA Vectors*: Novel vectors created in lab used for cloning or expressing gene sequences may be patentable.
3. *Cell Lines*: Artificially produced cell lines are patentable.
4. *Gene*: A gene to which genetic alterations have been made are patentable, a gene in recombinant form or newly isolated gene in pure form is patentable if its utility or function is known.
5. *Protein*: Patent protection for a protein may be granted if the protein is not previously characterized or has been isolated from a natural resource in pure form. A novel or known protein obtained through RDT may be patentable. For example, hormone expressed from recombinant vector.

6. *Microorganism*: A new strain of microorganism produced artificially transformed by recombinant vector is patentable. A microorganism newly isolated in pure form from a natural source is also patentable. A novel product produced by a microorganism is patentable. If a product produced by a microorganism is known, the process of producing the product via microorganism may be patentable.
7. *Molecular Biology Techniques*: Any novel technique(s) or processes for producing a particular molecular biology product may be patentable.
8. *Plant and Animal*: Plant varieties may be protected in most industrial countries by way of plant variety rights (also called plant patents). According to plant patents, new asexually reproduced plants can be protected with certain exceptions and ornamental designs in two different ways:
   - Plants Breeder's Right (PBR)
   - Patents

CHAPTER SUMMARY

The patent system was established to protect the invention which can be a process of making a product or a product itself. Thus these two, process and product, are the two major categories of a patent. India is member of several organizations which govern patents like World Intellectual Property Organization (WIPO), TRIPS Agreement under the World Trade Organization, Paris Convention for the Protection of Industrial Property, Patent Cooperation Treaty (PCT), and Budapest Treaty. In India, the patents are classified as a product patent, process patent and design patent. Some special types of patents are patents in textile, electrical invention, and software patent, patents in food industry, patents for microorganisms, pharmaceutical patents and plant patents. While according to WIPO, patents are classified as utility patent, design patent, plant patent.

A plant variety to get protection, it must be novel, distinct, uniform, and stable. It protects the inventor's right to exclude others from asexually reproducing, selling or using the reproduced plant. The term of plant patent granted is 20 years, however, plant are non patentable in India. Earlier only process patent was granted but later with several amendments to the patent laws, process and product patents are also granted. There are arguments related to patenting of biotechnology inventions which may be valid and is of real concern.

Patents Act 1970 before amendment:

- No product patent for living organism.
- No process patents on creation of a living organism.
- Patents allowed on Bioconversion process.

Patent Act 1970 after amendment allowed patents on the following:

- The living entity of artificial origin such as microorganism, vaccines etc.
- The biological material such as recombinant DNA, plasmids and processes of manufacturing thereof provided they are produced by substantive human intervention.

The Act of 1970 excluded pharmaceuticals and agrochemical products from the grant of patents. Thus, pharmaceutical products are not granted patents in India under the patent law. In India, patents were not granted for drugs as there was no such system for protecting them but the TRIPS agreement has placed an obligation on India to grant product patents to drugs by 2005. The plant patent protects the shape/appearance and colour of the plants and is granted to plants which are stable and reproduced by asexual reproduction, and not a potato or other edible tuber reproduced plants.

Patent are gained in biotechnology invention if it has novelty, inventive step and utility along with compulsory disclosurc and dcposit of microorganisms (Budapest Treaty). Biotechnology patents can be provided in RNA, DNA or amino acid sequences, DNA and RNA vectors, cell lines, gene, protein, microorganism, molecular biology techniques, and plant and animal.

MULTIPLE CHOICE QUESTIONS

1. Which of the following is non-patentable in India?
   (i) Artificial cell lines
   (ii) Mere sequences of genes
   (iii) Molecular biology techniques
   (iv) RNA vector
2. The term 'Petty Patent is used for
   (i) Process patent
   (ii) Product patent
   (iii) Utility patent
   (iv) Design patent
3. After 2005 amendment, the Indian Patent Act 1970 excluded
   (i) The living entities of natural origin.
   (ii) The living entities of artificial origin.
   (iii) The process of preparing any biological cells.
   (iv) All
4. The copy of the original drug after the expiry of the original drug is called
   (i) Copy drug
   (ii) Generic drug
   (iii) Pirated drug
   (iv) None
5. The aberration UPOV stands for
   (i) Union of Plant Variety
   (ii) International Union for the Protection of New Varieties of Plants
   (iii) Union for Protection of Variety
   (iv) None

REVIEW QUESTIONS

1. What is the difference between utility patent and design patent?
2. Explain the scope of patent in biotechnology industry. What problems were faced by the researchers for patenting biotechnology products?
3. Differentiate between product and process patent.
4. Are plants patentable? Explain the plant protection scenario in India.
5. According to the latest amendment in the Patent Act, which inventions related to the living entities are patentable in India?
6. What are the requirements for the patentability of biotechnology inventions?

Grant of Patent and Patenting Authorities

4

Chapter Objectives:

Patent law not only grants protection to the innovation, but also encourages the development of new innovative technology and methods for the economic growth and development of the nation. The Patent Office generally grants patent to the inventor, which makes him legal holder of the exclusive patents rights, but we should also remember that all the inventions are not patentable. There are different eligibility criteria of patentability for inventions. In this chapter we study about patentable and non-patentable inventions, patenting authorities and the powers of controller and central government. We will also study the procedure of filing the patent and the legal papers required for patenting.

INVENTION

Patent is a legal monopoly or exclusive rights given to the owner of an invention (known as patentee or assignee or inventor) by the sovereign power for a period of time. It prevents others from making, using or selling the invention in that country during the patent tenure. An invention is the outcome of an individual's creativity, which can become a boon for the society. Discovery and inventions are the two terms that should be clarified before we study the patent laws. Discovery means findings already existing in nature, such as the discovery of a new microorganism, new metal from earth's crust etc. Invention means manual or synthetic design of a material that resembles a natural material. This might be a genetically altered microorganism or entirely a new article like machines, or a new way of doing things as in a process of manufacturing.

ELIGIBILITY CRITERIA

An invention that is the outcome of an individual's thought process or creativity has to pass through certain eligibility criteria in order to get a patent. Every invention is not patentable. A patent can be granted for an invention on the following ground:

- It should be novel: should not be published earlier, no prior knowledge should exist or should have not been claimed earlier.
- It should be inventive: should not be obvious to the person skilled in art but should contain technological advancement.

- It has industrial applicability, i.e. product/process should be capable of being used in industry for commercial gain.
- It falls under patentable subject matter—it should not fall under Sections 3 and 4 of Indian Patent Act.

Thus, an 'invention' means a new product or process involving an inventive step and capable of industrial application. When we say that an invention must be novel, we mean that the described product or process should not exist anywhere in the world; otherwise such invention may not be patentable. The requirement of novelty eradicates redundancy of the existing research work done by the researchers. The invention should not be made available to the public before filing for a patent, because doing so makes the invention 'previously known' and ineligible for patent. For example, if Sahil sends a write-up to his friend to discuss his invention and his friend publishes the information in a magazine, the invention is deemed to be in public knowledge and hence lacks novelty.

Besides novelty criteria, the invention must also involve one or more inventive steps. This criterion indirectly means that the invention has to differ essentially from those that have become known previously. That is if the invention is novel, it should either involve technical advances as compared to the existing knowledge or should have some economic benefits or both. It should also be entirely different from the known solutions such that it becomes non-obvious to a person skilled in the art. For example, an architect designs a simple dining table with some very special features and applies for a patent. Although the making of the dining table is non-obvious to a layman yet, it is very simple and obvious to another architect of average skill. Hence, the invention lacked non-obviousness and will not be given a patent.

The third criterion for patentability is industrial application. As per this requirement, an invention should be capable of being manufactured by any kind of industry. By doing so, the legislators might be expressing their willingness to restrict the group of patentable inventions to be more technical and useful for the society. Industrial applicability is must in order to make the patented article reachable to an individual's home. However, this criterion differs from country to country. If the invention is useful for the society, it has to be multiplied in number, which means industrial productivity is required. Industrially reproducible articles include the methods and devices needed in commerce, building, farming, forestry, gardening, fishing, handicrafts etc.

Apart from these three essential criteria, another essential requirement is that the invention should not fall under the list of non-patentable items set by the statutory authority in the Indian Patent Act and we will discuss non-patentable items in the same chapter. Section 1 of the Indian Patent Act lists several inventions that as such are not considered industrially applicable and therefore not patentable. Thus a patentable invention is the concrete embodiment of an idea, which can be a device, a product, a process for making a product, or a new and commercial use for a previously existing product. For example, a process and product patent for a water proof jacket that allows a swimmer to swim along with sharks without causing any injury is filed. The water proof jacket emits ultrasound waves that ward off the sharks. Since the invention satisfies the patentability conditions of novelty, non-obviousness and utility, patent can be granted to the inventor. While on the other hand, if a transport vehicle with handle and seat from scooter, engine from generator, trolley from truck and horn from car, which shall serve the purpose of public transport, is designed, patent will not be granted patent as it is obvious and is a mere combinations of parts from different vehicles.

PATENTABLE INVENTIONS IN INDIA AND ABROAD

Now the question that comes to our mind is that which inventions are patentable and which are not? In a broad sense, an invention is the backbone of development of a country's economy. An invention is the outcome of an individual's brainpower, efforts and talent that proves to be beneficial to the society after its industrial applicability. Any invention is patentable in India (excluding exceptions laid down by the Indian Patent Act) if it satisfies the following criteria of

1. Novelty
2. Usefulness
3. Non-obviousness

Novelty is a fundamental requirement for all patents in all the countries, which means that the invention should not be known to the public before filing the application. For example, a lot of objections were raised to the grant of turmeric patent in United States on the grounds that it is not new and people in India have prior knowledge about the same since time immemorial. Novelty of the invention can be spoiled by prior use of the invention before filing an application for the patent, oral description and discussion of the invention in seminar or conferences not within the stipulated time of six months (in India).

The non-obviousness means that any person skilled in art in that particular subject should not be able to make out or easily guess the invention unless he applies some special mental skills.

Any invention fulfilling all the above criteria cannot be granted patent until is useful to the mankind. Therefore usefulness of an invention is also very important aspect.

We should also take care of the non-patentable inventions, which fall under Section 3 of the Indian Patent Act and the difference between discovery and invention, before filing for a patent in the Patent Office. Moreover disclosure of the invention completely (complete specification) is also essential.

The criteria of patentability of the Indian Patent Act 1970 needed modification in the field of medicine, in order to control the prices of medicine. It was also realized that inventions related to the cure of deadly diseases like cancer should not be granted patent even if they fulfil all the criteria of patentability. Finding the need of such modifications in the Patent Laws of 1970, the Act was amended in 1999, wherein only 'product patent' can be granted to the inventions in the field of medicines and compounds, but process patent was excluded. However, India after becoming a member of the WTO, incorporated the provisions of TRIPS in their domestic laws and therefore with the enactment of Patents Amendment Act 2005, the amendment process of Indian Patent Act 1970 was completed by the government. The additional provisions were as follows:

- New invention (novelty) is any invention or technology which has not been anticipated by public in any document or used in any country before the filing date of the patent application with complete specification. It should not be in public domain (Section 2, clause 1).
- Inventive step is a feature of the invention which involves technical advancement in the existing knowledge base, results in economic benefits or both and makes the invention non-obvious to a person skilled in art (Section 2, clause (ja)).
- Invention included anything new or innovative, whether a 'product' or a 'process', involving an inventive step and capable of industrial application (Section 2, clause (j)).

Section 5 of Indian Patent Act identifies several parameters for an invention to be patentable:

- It claims substances that are intended to be used as product, capable to be used as food or as medicine or drug.
- It claims substances that are prepared or produced by chemical processes (including alloys, optical glass, semi conductors and intermetallic compounds, biochemical, biotechnology and microbiological processes); patent shall be granted only with respect to the process of manufacture.

In the area of biotechnology, which is a fast growing and competent field, inventions relating to process or method of production of real, non-living substances like antibiotics, interferon, enzymes, hormones, vaccines, alcohols etc. are patentable.

The conversions using microbes (bioconversion) or chemical substances produced by using genetically engineered organisms or such existing substances can be made more economical and are patentable under the Indian Patent Act 1970 (as amended).

Software or a computer program per se, which is a set of instructions for controlling a sequence of operation of a data processing system, is not patentable because it is similar to a mathematical algorithm. But, any invention that consists of a software or computer program associated with hardware in order to perform a task (e.g. microarray image analysis, UV spectrophotometer) is considered a patentable invention.

A new solution to a problem concerning the internal operation of a computer, even if it is comprised of a program or subroutine, and involves technological features of the computer hardware or the manner in which it operates is patentable.

An invention that is the result of a combination of several elements in such a manner so as to produce a new result or to arrive at an old result with better or faster or a more economic approach is patentable.

In Other Countries

Patentable invention may vary from country to country. Patentable invention in one country may not be defined as patentable in another. In the United States, patent laws are relatively relaxed and anyone who invents anything new and useful like a new process, a machine, process of manufacture, or composition of matter, or any new and useful improvement thereof, may obtain a patent. Most other countries have a patent system similar to Malaysia, which states that an invention will be granted patent protection, based on the following criteria:

- The invention must be the first in the world.
- The invention must show inventive ingenuity.
- The invention must be useful to the mankind.

In UK and Europe, the criteria of patentability are the following:

1. Novelty
2. Inventive step
3. Industrial applicability
4. Exclusion of non-patentable inventions.

In the United States, the criteria of patentability are:

1. Novelty
2. Usefulness
3. Non-obviousness.

In the United States, as per Section 102(b), title 35, United States Code, a person shall be entitled to a patent unless the invention was in public use or on sale in this country, more than one year prior to the date of application for patent in the United States, It concludes that Section 102(b) that invalidates a patent must be based on convincing evidence. It is flexible with regard to the criterion of usefulness as it considers that the utility of an invention can be found later also.

NON-PATENTABLE INVENTIONS IN INDIA AND ABROAD

All the inventions that are novel and have some inventive step or industrial applicability are not patentable. The above criteria are more or less globally accepted and acknowledged. In contrast to the patentability, an idea, scheme or plan, any scientific principle or mathematic algorithm without any practical application or use is not patentable. Indian Patent Act provides an exhaustive list of non-patentable inventions under Sections 3 and 4. The inventions that are non-patentable include the following:

1. According to Section 3(a) of the Patent Act, any invention which is 'frivolous' or contrary to well-established natural laws are non-patentable; for example, machine that gives more than 100% performance or perpetual machine.
2. According to Section 3(b) of the Patent Act, commercial exploitation or primary use of inventions that is contrary to public order or morality are non-patentable. For example, gambling machine, device for house-breaking or anything that causes serious prejudice to health of human, animal, plant life or to the environment are non-patentable. For example, biological warfare, material or device, weapons of mass destruction, terminator gene technology, or embryonic stem cell.
3. According to Section 3(c) of the Patent Act, mere discovery of a scientific principle or formulation of an abstract theory, discovery of any living thing or discovery of non-living substance occurring in nature are non-patentable. For example, Newton's laws, superconducting phenomenon as such property of certain material to withstand mechanical shock, discovery of micro-organism, discovery of natural gas or a mineral.
4. According to Section 3(d) of the Patent Act, mere discovery of any new property, new use for a known substance or of the mere use of a known process, machine or apparatus are non-patentable unless such known process results in a new product or employs at least one new reactant. For example, new use of aspirin for heart ailments, mere new uses of neem (*Azadirachta indica*).

   For the purposes of this clause, salts, esters, ethers, polymorphs, metabolites, pure form, particle size, isomers, mixture of isomers, complexes, combinations and other derivatives of known substances shall be considered to be the same substance, unless they differ significantly in properties with regard to efficacy, For example, crystalline form of known substances. However salts, esters, ethers, polymorphs, metabolite, pure forms, particle size, isomers, complexes, combinations and derivatives of a known substance with enhanced efficacy are patentable.
5. According to Section 3(e) of the Patent Act, substance obtained by mere admixture resulting only in the aggregation of the properties of the components thereof or a process for producing such substance. For example, Combiflam [paracetamol (antipyretic) + Brufen (analgesic)], solution of sugar and colour additives in water to form a soft drink. However, a mixture resulting in synergistic properties of mixture of ingredients may be patentable like soap, detergents, lubricants, etc.
6. According to Section 3(f) of the Patent Act, mere arrangement or re-arrangement or duplication of known devices, each functioning independently of one another in a known way is non-patentable. For example, a bucket fitted with torch, an umbrella with fan, a clock and radio in a single cabinet, a flour-mill provided with sieving.
7. According to Section 3(h) of the Patent Act, method of agriculture or horticulture is non-patentable. For example, method of cultivation of algae, method of vegetative propagation of a plant or method of preparing an improved soil. However, agricultural equipments are patentable.

8. According to Section 3(i) of the Patent Act, any process for medicinal, surgical, curative, prophylactic, diagnostic, therapeutic or used for the treatment of human beings or a similar treatment of animals to render them free of disease or to increase their economic value or that of their products are non-patentable. For example, method of removal of cancer/tumour, removal of dental plaque and carries surgical processes, processes relating to therapy, method of vaccination and blood transfusion. However, surgically therapeutic or diagnostic apparatus or instruments arc patentable.
9. According to Section 3(j) of the Patent Act, plants and animals in whole or any part thereof other than micro-organisms, but including seeds, varieties and species and essentially biological process for production or propagation of plants and animals are non-patentable. For example, clones of animals and plants. However, we have a unique system of plant protection. A process for production of plants or animals if it consists entirely of natural phenomena such as crossing or selection (essentially biological process) is non-patentable.
10. According to Section 3(k) of the Patent Act, mathematical method or business method or algorithms or computer program per se are non-patentable. For example, computer program by itself or as a record on a carrier. However, new calculating machine, or a combination of hardware and software is patentable.
11. According to Section 3(l) of the Patent Act, a literary, dramatic, musical or artistic work or any other aesthetic creation including cinematographic work and television productions are non-patentable. These fall under the copyright protection.
12. According to Section 3(m) of the Patent Act, a mere scheme or rule or method of performing mental act or method of playing game is non-patentable. For example, scheme for learning a language, method for solving a crossword puzzle, method of learning a language, method of teaching/learning. However, a novel apparatus for playing game or carrying out a scheme is patentable.
13. According to Section 3(n) of the Patent Act, presentation of information is non-patentable. For example, any manner or method of expressing information whether by spoken words, visual display, symbols, diagrams, method of recording the information on carrier.
14. According to Section 3(o) of the Patent Act, topography of integrated circuits is non-patentable. For example, mask works or circuit layouts.
15. According to Section 3(p) of the Patent Act, inventions that are traditional knowledge or an aggregation or duplication of known properties of traditionally known component or components are non-patentable. For example, wound healing property of *Curcuma longa* (*haldi*), the traditional knowledge of which is already in public domain. However, any value addition using traditional knowledge leading to a new process or product, which is novel with inventive step and industrial applicability like the extraction of 'Azadirachtin' from neem plant, is patentable.
16. Inventions falling within sub-section (1) of section 20 of the Atomic Energy Act, 1962 are not patentable as a precautionary measure for national security. "No Patent shall be granted in respect of an invention relating to atomic energy". For example, inventions relating to compounds of uranium, beryllium, thorium, plutonium, radium, graphite, lithium and more as notified by the Central government from time to time. Inventions that in opinion of Central government related to production, control, use or disposal of atomic energy, prospecting mining extraction production, physical and chemical treatment, fabrication enrichment, canning or use of any prescribed radioactive substance are not patentable.

In case of medicine, the following categories are excluded from patentability while the method or process of manufacturing the following is patentable. The categories include:

(a) Medicines for internal or external use of animals or human beings.
(b) Substances that are intended to be used for or in the diagnosis, treatment, mitigation or prevention of diseases in animals or human beings.
(c) Substances that are used for the maintenance of public health or prevention or control of epidemic diseases among animals or human beings.
(d) Insecticides, germicides, fungicides, weedicides and all other substances intended to be used for the protection or preservation of plants.
(e) Chemical substances which are ordinarily used as intermediates in the preparation or manufacture of any kind of medicines or substances referred above.

In Other Countries

In United States, there are a few things which cannot be patented according to federal law and international conventions, of which the United States is signatory to. These non-patentable inventions are as follows:

- Laws of nature and the expressions of the laws of nature are non-patentable. For example, Einstein's formula 'E equals mc squared'.
- The physical phenomena like lightning, waves, and wind and the electron, proton, or other elemental particles cannot be patented. However, it is possible to receive patents for machines that produce these physical phenomena.
- An abstract idea, like voting, is non-patentable but there are patents for voting machines as they are technical expressions of the idea.
- Patents are only for technical implementations. Artistic, musical or literary works like a poem or a painting cannot be patented. Both can be subject to copyright, which is a different intellectual property right.
- The inventions offensive to public morals cannot be patented. That is, the patent cannot be used to break the law.

The USPTO often leans towards the usefulness of the invention and considers that it is in the eye of the beholder. Unlike in India, in the United States, inventions that are not much useful can also be protected as 'utility models'. Software and plants and inventions related to atomic energy are also patentable.

In United Kingdom, the following are not considered as inventions:

- Any discovery, scientific theory or mathematical method.
- A literary, dramatic, musical or artistic work or any other aesthetic creation.
- A plan or scheme or method for performing a mental act, playing a game or doing business or a program for a computer.
- The method of presentation of information.

In Europe, under the European Patent Convention, the following inventions are not considered patentable if

- The publication or exploitation of information contrary to public order or morality.
- Plant or animal varieties or biological processes are invented for the production of plants or animals.

In China, patents are not granted to

- Scientific theory, discovery.
- Rules and methods for mental activities or game.
- Methods for the diagnosis or treatment of diseases.
- Animal or plant varieties.
- Substances obtained by means of nuclear transformation.

In Germany, the following inventions are not patentable:

- Discoveries, scientific theories and mathematical methods.
- Aesthetic creation, plans, rules and methods of intellectual activities or games, specifically computer software but if the software is combined with the technical invention, it is patentable.

Therefore, we can conclude that the patent system is more or less similar in all the countries and India follows an exhaustive list of non-patentable inventions.

Patentability in Microorganism-Related Inventions

Micro-organisms include all unicellular organisms having dimensions beneath the limits of vision and are self-replicating, e.g. bacteria, yeasts, single-celled algae and protozoa. They fall under the criteria of patentability along with certain self-replicating biological materials such as plasmids, replicons and viruses etc. Multicellular organisms are normally excluded from it. In case of microbes, the 'invention' refers to

- The production (not discovery) of new micro-organism (product per se)
- Utilization of micro-organism for production of other substances.
- Bio-transformation processes for production of non-living matter like fermentation process product such as beer, wine, vinegar

Biotechnological inventions on micro-organism refers to inventions relating to the living entity of artificial origin, such as genetically altered micro-organism, vaccines, transgenic animals and plants etc..., Biological materials such as DNA, plasmids, genes, vector, tissues, cells, replicons etc..., process relating to living entities, such as their isolation, purification, multiplication etc...

Several amendments were made in the Patent Act regarding inventions involving living entities. For example, according to the Patents Act, 1970 (before amendment), the following laws were followed for the living entities:

- No product patent was granted given for an organism (including micro-organisms) or material per se having living entities.
- No process patents was given on creation of a living organism or production of other biological material/products having living entities.
- Patents were allowed on process for production of chemical products by using an organism or biological material (bioconversion).

Whereas after the amendment of the Indian Patents Act, 1970 there were a few changes related to the living entities. They allowed patent on the following:

- The living entity of artificial origin such as micro-organism (genetically altered), vaccines etc.
- The biological material such as recombinant DNA, plasmids and processes of manufacturing thereof provided they are produced by substantive human intervention.

But, it excluded grant of patent on

- Essentially biological processes for the production of plants and animals such as method of crossing or breeding etc.
- Any biological material and method of making the same which is capable of causing serious prejudice to human, animal or plant lives or health or to the environment including the use of those would be contrary to public order and morality such as terminator gene technology.
- The processes for cloning human beings or animals, processes for modifying the germ line, genetic identity of human beings or animals.
- Uses of human or animal embryos for any purpose are not patentable as they are against public order and morality.

Finally, the Patent Act 1970 after 2005 amendments also excludes grant of patents on

- The living entities of natural origin such as genes and micro-organism.
- Any process for manufacture or production of such living entities.
- Any living entity of artificial origin such as transgenic animals and plants, any part thereof.
- The biological materials such as organs, tissues, cells, viruses etc. and process of preparing thereof.
- Gene sequences, DNA sequences without having disclosed their functions.

However, the law allowed patent on the genetic modification of these living entities but with human interference. Many amendments occurred in this area specifically because of various following issues on allowing patents on microorganism, which will be discussed in detail later in further chapters.

(a) Morality issue
(b) Ethical issue
(c) Access to biotech inventions—public health issue
(d) Environment issue
(e) Bio-piracy issue.

Now, as we know which inventions are patentable and which are not, What is the next step after knowing the inventions as 'patentable'? Of course, the inventor would like to file the patent for the invention. So, where to file the application? And the answer is 'Patent Office'. The applicant can apply to the Patent Office falling in the applicant's territory.

PATENT OFFICE

An application for the patent is filed in the Patent office. The Patent Office is governed by the Office of the Controller General of Patents, Designs & Trade Marks (CGPDTM). This is a subordinate office of the Indian government and administers the Indian law of patents, designs and trade marks. The administration of patent-related matters in India is looked after by the Patents and Trademark Office, which comes under the Department of Industrial Policy and Promotion (DIPP) as shown in Figure 4.1, which has segregated their offices based on different intellectual properties like office for registering design, trademark, IP management etc...

These offices for different IPs are located at different places. There are four patent registry offices in India, five trademark registry offices, a GI registry office and an office for NIIMS and patent information. The location city of these offices are given below.

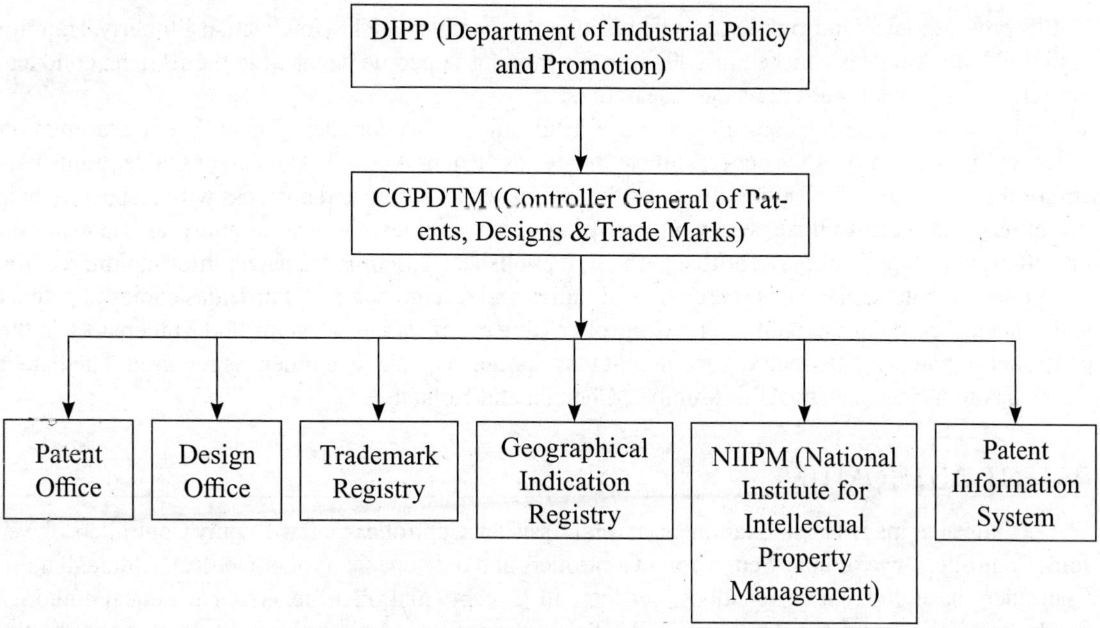

Figure 4.1 *Hierarchy of Indian Patent Offices*

Patent Registry Office

1. Kolkata (Head Office)
2. Delhi (Branch Office)
3. Mumbai (Branch Office)
4. Chennai (Branch Office)

Trademark Registry Office

1. Mumbai
2. Kolkata
3. Delhi
4. Chennai
5. Ahmedabad

Geographical Indication Registry Office

Chennai

Design Office

Kolkata

NIIM, PIS Office

Nagpur (established in 1980 by the government of India as a national centre of excellence for training, management, research education in the field of IPR). It provides service for the patent search.

PIS provides latest information to scientists and researchers. IPTI (Intellectual Property Training Institute), which was established in 2002 imparts training to people engaged in the IP field, conducts awareness programs for attorney and researchers.

Patent Office (three regional offices and a head office) also conducts Patent Agent examination twice a year and approves the successful candidates as 'Patent Agents'. The Patent Office grants patent for the protection of invention. It serves the interest of inventors and business with respect to their inventions. The Patent Office works on zonal basis. It examines application and grants patents on inventions when applicants are entitled to them; it publishes, disseminates patent information, records assignment of patent, maintains search files of Indian and foreign patents. It provides copies of patents and official records to the public. The Controller General of Patent, Designs and Trademarks is the controller of patents. The Central government may appoint as many examiners as required. The Patent Office has four branches in Delhi, Mumbai, Chennai and Kolkata.

PATENT AUTHORITIES

The IP Office has many Patent Examiners, several Assistant Controllers, a few Deputy Controllers, fewer Joint Controllers, two or three Senior Joint Controllers and only one Controller General. Although these Controllers have different designations, yet they all (except Controller General) have equal authority to administer the Patent Act. The appointed officers are required to discharge their functions under the direction of the Controller. There can be many patent examiners and the number of officers reduces with increase in position in the hierarchy. The hierarchy of patent authorities in the office is the following:

- Controller General (Patent, Design and Trademark)
- Senior Joint Controller (supports the Controller General)
- Joint Controller (reports to Senior Joint Controller)
- Deputy Controller (monitored by Joint Controller)
- Assistant Controller (monitored by Deputy Controller)
- Controller
- Patent Examiner/Senior Examiner (examines the patent application).

The Controller has general and specific powers and is entitled to withdraw any matter pending before an officer. If anyone files an opposition against the patent, the matter is resolved by the Controller. An opponent can file a representation in the appropriate office within 3 months from the date of publication of the application or before the grant of patent. It should include a statement and evidence in support of representation. The Controller along with the evidence submitted and the arguments at the time of hearing will consider the representation. The Controller may reject the representation by the opponent and grant the patent to the applicant or accept the representation by the opponent and refuse the grant of patent within 1 month from the completion of the proceedings. Patent Examiner searches for prior art, objections or oppositions under any ground specified in the Patent Act and reports to the Controller who has the power to accept or reject the Examiner's report. This report sent to the Controller is not open for public.

The General and Specific Powers of the Controller and the Central Government

The general powers of the Controller are as follows:

1. The controller has the authority to exercise the powers equivalent to that of civil court (Section 77), which includes awarding costs, issuing commissions for the examination of witness of

documents, receiving evidences on affidavits, summoning and enforcing the attendance of any person, reviewing his/her own decisions on application made within the prescribed time and manner.

2. The controller can correct any clerical error in any patent or in any specification or other documents or in application for a patent or any clerical error in any matter entered in the register (Section 78) but the correction made must be based upon a request in writing made by any person interested and accompanied by the prescribed fee. The correction can also be made without a request but then the Controller has to give the notice of the proposal to the applicant or patentee and the nature of the proposed correction has to be advertised in the prescribed manner before incorporating the correction.
3. The Controller has the power to call for evidence to be given by affidavit. Oral evidences can also be taken by his permission and any party may be cross-examined on the contents of his/her affidavit (Section 79).
4. The Controller has powers to cautiously hear any party and give any such party an opportunity to be heard and give decisions accordingly (Section 80).
5. The Controller has the power to extend the time for doing any act related to grant of patent (Section 81).
6. The Controller is entitled to award cost depending upon the circumstances of each case (Rule 122(2)).
7. The Controller has the power to review the records in case of any mistake or error or when new and important matters of evidences come into existence. {Section 77(1)(f))

The specific powers of the Controller are as follows:

1. The controller has the power to refuse or require amended application in certain cases. If the application or any other document put ahead is not in compliance with the requirement of the Patent Act, the Controller can either require for its amendment or refuse it.
2. The Controller has the power to give directions to the co-owners of the patent in case to multiple proprietor of the patent. He can direct in accordance with the application as to the sale or lease of the patent or any interest therein, the grant of patent, or the exercise of any right.
3. The Controller has the power to make orders related to the date of application. He may direct the applicant on getting the request from him and before the acceptance of the complete specification that the application shall be post-dated to the date not later than 6 months from the date on which it was actually made and proceed accordingly.
4. The Controller has the power to reject or accept the complete specification if it appears to him as a case of anticipation unless the applicant satisfies the Controller that the priority date of the claim of his complete specification is not later than the date on which the relevant document was published.
5. The Controller has the power for potential infringement, if it appears to the Controller that an invention in respect of which an application for a patent has been made cannot be performed without substantial risk of infringement of a claim of any other patent, the Controller may direct a reference to that other patent to be inserted in the applicant's complete specification by way of a notice to the public.
6. The Controller has the power to make orders regarding substitution of applicants. The Controller can direct that the application shall proceed in the name of the claimant or claimants and the applicant or the other joint applicant or applicants, accordingly, as the case may require.

7. The Controller has the power to adjourn applications for compulsory licenses. If he gets the application for revocation of non-working patents or compulsory license and finds that the time since the sealing of the patent and the said application is minimal and is not sufficient for the invention to be worked on a commercial scale, he can further adjourn the case hearing. However, the period of adjournment cannot exceed 1 year.

The Controller has all the powers starting from the date of application of patent to the grant or till the expiry of the patent. But in September 2003, The Indian Government constituted the Intellectual Property Appellate Board (IPAB) to hear and make judgements on appeals made against the decision of Registrar under Indian Trademark Act, 1999 and Indian Geographical Indication of Goods Act, 1999. In 2007 however, it could also adjudicate upon appeals for patents against an order, decision or direction of the Controller, which could lead to any interlocutory order. Sections 116 and 117 deal with the provisions related to the appeal. The appellate board IPAB has its headquarters at Chennai and has sittings at Delhi, Kolkata, Ahmadabad, Mumbai and Chennai.

According to the provision of IPAB (Procedure) Rules 2003, every appeal should be made in the prescribed format with indicated fee within 3 months of the decision of the Controller/Central government.

Powers of the Central Government

The Patent Act 1970 has granted certain powers to the Central government regarding the 'inventions' patented. The government has the power to prohibit some category of people from using the invention and also has the right to import or manufacture by or on behalf of the government any machine or apparatus or article for which the patent is granted or the process by which these products are made and the process patent is granted. Any process for which the patent is granted can be used by the government or used on behalf of the government for its own use. Any drug or medicine can be used by the government for its own use or for distribution in any dispensary, hospital or other medical institution which the government specifies. The Central government has the power to use the invention for the government. It can acquire the invention from the applicant or patentee for a public purpose and the patentee in turn are compensated by the Central government. If it appears to the Central government that it would be contrary to the public interest to use the invention, then the patentee is informed about the use of the invention. The government has the right to give the compulsory license but also includes the right to sell the invention on non-commercial basis.

Application for the Grant of Patents

Patents are not valid worldwide; they vary from country to country. Its protection is a territorial right and therefore, Indian patent is effective only within the Indian territory. However, filing an application in India enables the applicant to file a corresponding application for same invention in other countries, within or before expiry of 12 months from the filing date in India. Therefore, separate patents should be obtained in each country if the applicant requires protection of his invention in those countries also. For example, a person has created a coffee machine and has taken a patent in country 'A'. Another person with the same design and process can take a patent in country 'B'. But, if the first person wants to hold monopoly right of his machine in country 'B' also he has to file a patent in country 'B' as well.

A patent application has to be filed at the appropriate Patent Office in the prescribed format along with the prescribed fee. An application can either be a provisional application, a complete application or international application.

- A 'Provisional Application' is the provisional application generally filed to get an early application date (priority date). It is generally filed at a stage where some more experimentation is still required to make the invention perfect. It requires less specification of the invention. It cannot be filed in India if the applicant has already filed the application for the same in a foreign country (convention country) and if the application is a PCT application.
- A 'Complete Application' is the final application which has to be filed within 12 months (extendable to 15 months) of filing the provisional specification. It includes detailed explanation of the invention.
- An 'International Application' is the application which helps in applying the patent in a number of countries simultaneously. These are also known as PCT (Patent Co-operation Treaty) application.

Patent Nominee

Patents give statutory rights to the inventor for his/her innovation, hard work in favour of the institute, city or country as a whole and in turns he/she enjoys fame, monitory benefits and motivation to do further research in the specific field of study. It is an accepted norm across the world that the person entitled for the grant of patents is generally

– an inventor,
– an inventor's assignee, or
– legal representative or successor in title of the inventor.

An 'inventor' is anyone who invents or produces something new or innovative by experimentation or investigation or should have contributed intellectually for the invention. But anyone assisting in the lab or routine work to create an invention doesn't deserve to be an inventor. For an inventor it is important to have the written records of the experiments conducted in the lab.

An 'assignee' is anyone to whom a title, claim, property, interest or right has been transferred. It can be the organization or institute where the inventor has worked or used the resources. According to the Indian Patent Act, 1970 Assignee is 'assignee of the assignee' and the legal representative of a deceased assignee and references to assignee of any person including reference to an assignee of a legal representative or an assignee of that person.

A 'legal representative' is the one who represents the inventor in the Patent Office. He has all the papers and documents necessary for the application of patent. He can be a patent agent or lawyer. It denotes a person who under law represents the estate of a deceased person (If a person who is the inventor is suffering from any deadly decease).

A patent application can be filed either by true or first inventor or by his assignee, either alone or jointly with any other person. Legal representative of any deceased person can also make an application for patent. If the application is filed by the assignee, proof of assignment has to be submitted along with the application.

- If a researcher in a pharmaceutical company invents a medicine, his/her company will automatically own the patent right to that medicine as the researcher has used all the resources of the company. The company may be required to pay the inventor certain amount as compensation or royalty. In Germany, if the company decides not to apply for the patent, the employee has the right to apply for the patent himself/herself.
- In a situation where the inventor is an employee of a company, the company owns the rights to apply for the patent. The exception is United States, where only individual person who is the

inventor and an employee of the company may apply for a patent. The employee can assign his/her rights to the company. The filing is done on behalf of the employee but the rights immediately go to the company.

- In India, according to Section 6 of Indian Patent Act, an inventor can individually apply for the patent rather than the company applying for it. To be eligible for the patent, the person has to be true inventor of the particular invention. But in case of inventor's death, before the filing of patent or before getting grant of patent, the person who is entitled for the patent are his/her legal representatives. An assignee of the true inventor is also entitled for the grant of patent. The true owner or the successor in title is entitled for the grant of patent rights.

From 20 July 2007 the Indian Patent Office has put in place an online filing system for patent application. More information for filing online application is available on the website of Patent Office (i.e. www.ipindia.nic.in). This facility is also available for filing trademarks application.

Procedure for the Grant of Patent

In general, the patent rights are granted by National Patent Offices. So, in each country, patent protection for an invention is to be obtained individually. Each country has to follow the procedural formalities, which generally comprises three steps:

1. The person or company seeking patent protection must file an application for patent at the relevant Patent Office.
2. The Patent Office performs a novelty search, which involves checking all the literature available for finding documents that describes the invention partially or completely. Only those documents that were published before the date of filing the application are considered in this research.
3. An examiner decides whether patent can be given or not on the basis of the report generated by the novelty search. If after that there is still an invention left, and the invention falls under the criteria of patentability, the applicant is granted a patent.

In India, the major steps for granting patents involve

1. Filing of an application for patent with complete specification.
2. Examination of application by Patent office.
3. Advertisement of acceptance of application with complete specification.
4. Opposition to grant of patent if any. The opposition can be made at several steps but before and after the grant, also known as pre-grant and post-grant opposition respectively.
5. Hearing the parties in case of any opposition.
6. Grant and sealing of the patent.

The procedure for patent grant is explained in Figure 4.2 to show precisely every stage till the grant of patent. In India, the procedure for granting patent involves several lengthy steps discussed below. The procedure starts with the filing of patent application.

1. Filing Patent Application

Patent applications in India are of six following types:

- Ordinary application
- Convention application

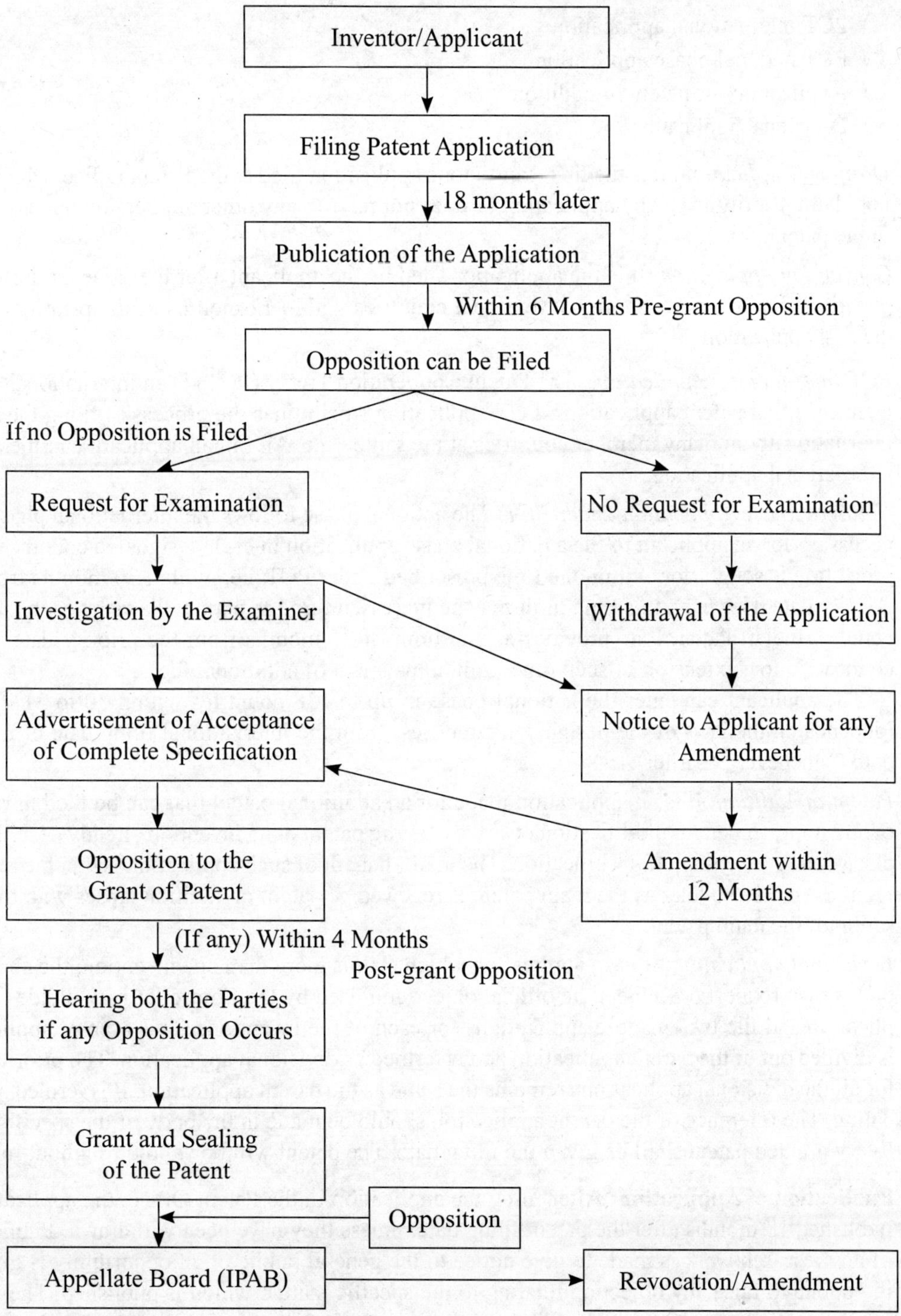

Figure 4.2 *Procedure for Granting a Patent*

- PCT international application
- PCT national phase application
- Application for patent of addition
- Divisional application.

Ordinary Application: It is the first stand-alone application filed at the Patent Office, which does not claim priority from any application or does not refer to any other application under process in the patent.

Convention Application: It is the application filed by the applicant after the same or similar application, filed in one or more conventional countries within 12 months of the priority date of the first application.

PCT International Application: The Patent Cooperation Treaty (PCT) is an international agreement for filing patent applications. PCT application streamlines the process of filing the patent internationally in many member countries at the same time. An Indian applicant can file a PCT international application.

National Phase Application under PCT: The national phase follows the international phase. It is necessary for an applicant to file a national phase application in each designated country, where protection is sought for, within the time prescribed under PCT, i.e., within 30 months from the priority date. However, this time limit may be increased through national laws by each member country. Indian Patent Law provides a time limit of 31 months from the priority date. Some countries allow extension of such time limit on payment of additional fee.

The applicant can enter the national phase in up to 138 countries within 30 to 31 months (depends on the laws of the designated countries) from the international filing date or priority date (whichever is earlier).

Patent of Addition: It is an application made for an additional patent that can be filed in respect of any improvement or modification over the existing patent or an invention already described or disclosed in the complete specification. The major benefit of such application is that the renewal fee is exempted so long as the main patent is renewed. A patent of addition lapses with the cessation of the main patent.

Divisional Application: It is an application which claims more than one invention; the applicant on his own request or to meet the official objection raised by the Controller may divide the application and file two or more applications for each of the inventions. This type of application is divided out of the parent application and is termed as divisional application. The priority date for all the divisional applications remains the same as the parent application. It is termed as ante dating. The reference of the parent application should be made in the body of the specification. Every granted patent shall be given the filing date. The patent will be valid throughout India.

2. **Publication of Application:** After filing the application in the Patent Office, the application is published 18 months after the patent filing date, unless they have been withdrawn. Publication of any research work is made to give notice to the general public or an opportunity is given to the public to raise any objection relating to the specific matter, which is published. The patent application is not open for the public until the period of 18 months expires. During this period, the invention is blocked for some time. It is extremely important to publish an application of patent since the inventor claims to have invented a particular method, product or process, which

is novel, non-obvious and industrially useful. It is essential because it is this invention for which the inventor is going to get the patent, enjoy its benefits, and get the right to stop others from infringement. If after the publication of this work it is found that the invention was not novel or genuine, further stages for the grant of patent will stop and patent will not be granted. Thus, this step of publication is compulsory and precondition for the grant of patent. This period of filing opposition is 6 months and any objection for the publication has to be filed within this time period. If no opposition is filed by that time, next step is taken by the inventor for the grant of patent.

3. **Opposition to the Grant of Patent:** According to Section 25 of Patent Act 1970, anyone who finds that the existing work has already been done, or is wrongly acquired, or it is published earlier and is in knowledge of the people, or there is lack of inventive steps, can file opposition. Opposition can also be made if the invention lies in the list of non-patentability or if the information is inadequate. The main objective of this step is to give an opportunity to any person to give a notice of objection. If the applicant successfully passes this step, it can be concluded that no pre-existing data or publication of this work is present; as a result the application may move for further steps like examination.

4. **Examination of Application:** After publication of the application, if no objection is filed, the process of examination of the application proceeds. In case if the Controller finds that the patent application falls under the category of defence, he might skip the step of publishing the application.

   At this stage, all the applications accompanied by complete specification are examined substantively. The inventor has to make a request to the Patent Office for examination of the application and this requisition has to be made within 48 months from the date filing the application. This examination is carried out truly on the request of the inventor/applicant in the prescribed manner. If he/she fails or forgets to file the application for examination, the application will not proceed and would be treated as withdrawal. This provision was made compulsory in the Patent Amendment Act, 2002. The examination of the application is done in order to see

   - whether the specifications given in the application are perfect according to the provision of law;
   - whether the results obtained by the investigation conducted are in accordance with the methods and results given in the specifications;
   - whether there is any ground for lawful objection to the grant of patent.

   This examination report has to be submitted within 18 months from the date of its reference. If the examiner finds that certain changes are to be made in the application, the Controller is under the obligation to send a notification to the applicant to make the relevant changes. If the applicant fails to respond for the amendments within 12 months, the Controller can discard or reject the application. On the contrary, if the applicant makes the necessary amendments and files the application with these changes, it is accepted by the examiner and a copy of acceptance is sent to the applicant.

5. **Opposition to the Grant of Patent:** The opposition filed after the publication of the application is known as pre-grant opposition while the opposition filed after the advertisement of acceptance of complete specification is called post-grant opposition. This can be done within 4

months of acceptance of application. The patent application can be opposed by the opponent party on the following grounds:

- If the patent is anticipated
- If the patent is wrongly acquired
- If the patent has prior publication
- If the patent falls under non-patentable invention
- If the applicant has given inadequate description of the invention
- If the applicant fails to disclose information about the invention.

After receiving the notice of opposition, the patent office grants an opportunity to both the parties to present their argument and if the opponent is found to be correct the application for grant for patent ceases. There are several landmark cases wherein patents were rejected due to oppositions by India. For example, the neem patent challenge, the turmeric patent challenge, and the Hessian patent challenge.

6. **Grant of Patent:** After the acceptance of the complete specification and disposal of the opposition, a patent is granted. It is then sealed and entered into the register. The request for sealing of the patent is to be made by the applicant within 6 months of acceptance of complete specification. This can only be extended in case if the applicant dies or if the applicants are more than one and any one of them dies. Also, if any application related to the proceeding is pending before the Controller or High Court. The patent is granted for a period of 20 years (according to TRIPS agreement Section 53, amended in 2002) by the patent office in a specific form laid down in Rule 57 of Patent Rules. The patent can be renewed or kept alive by paying a renewal fee according to Section 53(2). Patent grant is given countrywise and is effective throughout India. Patent gives the patentee certain rights like holding, using and selling the patent.

Patent Specification

Specification means description of the invention. Every patent application must have specification. Specifications may be provisional or complete. By provisional specification we mean ‘the nature of the invention’ and by complete specification we mean ‘description of the invention’ including drawings, claims and abstract. Thus, it specifies the nature as well as the procedure of formation of the invention in simple and unambiguous language. The type of information required for provisional and complete specification is given in the Table 4.1.

The contents of the specifications are described in Sections 9, 10 and 11 of the Indian Patent Act. The contents of specification include the following:

- Title of the invention.
- Full description of the invention and its method of application or usability.
- Drawing model (if any) to accompany the description of the invention.
- Claiming a part or whole of the invention which defines the scope of the invention for which protection is claimed.
- Abstract of the invention is necessary for providing the technical information on the invention. This abstract can be amended by the Controller for better clarity of the subject or invention.

The procedure for grant of patent varies from country to country but it is more or less similar everywhere. The procedure for grant is to a very small extent similar to that followed in India.

Table 4.1 *Information Required for Provisional and Complete Specification*

S. No.	Complete Specification	Provisional Specification
1	Title	Title required
2	Abstract	Abstract (not required)
3	Written description	Written description required
4	Drawings, where ever necessary	Drawings, if necessary
5	Sample or model, if required by the examiner	Sample or model, if required by the examiner
6	Enablement and best mode	Enablement and best mode (not required)
7	Claims	Claims (not required)
8	Deposit (microorganisms)	Deposit (microorganisms) (not required)

Documents Required for Filing the Patent

Some important documents should be arranged while filing the patent, which may vary from time to time and as directed by the Controller, but following are some of the basic requirements:

- Application form in duplicate.
- Provisional or complete specification in duplicate. If the provisional specification is filed, it must be followed by the complete specification within 12 months.
- Drawing in duplicate (if required to explain the invention).
- Abstract of the invention in duplicate.
- Information and undertaking listing the number, filing date and current status of each foreign patent application in duplicate.
- Priority document (if priority date is claimed) in convention application.
- Declaration of inventorship where provisional specification is followed by complete specification or in case of convention/PCT national phase application.
- Power of attorney (if filed through Patent Agent).
- Fees (to be paid in cash/by cheque/by demand draft).

CHAPTER SUMMARY

A country generally grants patents to an inventor for his or her invention (not discovery), which eliminates others from copying, using or selling his or her invention in that country. An invention according to the Section 2(1) (j) means a new product or process involving an inventive step and capable of industrial applicability. A patent is granted for an invention based on certain criteria, which is novelty, inventiveness, industrial applicability, non-patentable subject matter. The patent can be granted to an inventor, or an inventor's assignee, or legal representative or successor in title of the inventor. Patents are not provided for some inventions given below even if they fulfil all the criteria of patentability.

Frivolous inventions, inventions contrary to well-established natural laws; inventions falling within Section 20(1) of the Atomic Energy Act, 1962; commercial exploitation or primary use of inventions that is contrary to public order or morality; mere discovery of a scientific principle or formulation of an abstract theory; mere discovery of any new property or new use for a known substance; mere arrangement or re-arrangement or duplication of known devices, each functioning independently of one another in a known way; substance obtained by mere admixture resulting only in the aggregation of the properties of the components thereof; method of agriculture or horticulture, process for medicinal, surgical, curative, prophylactic, diagnostic, therapeutic or other treatment; mathematical method or business method or algorithms or computer programme per se; a literary, dramatic, musical or artistic work; presentation of information, mere schéme or rule or method of performing mental act or method of playing game; topography of integrated circuits; inventions that are traditional knowledge or an aggregation or duplication of known properties of traditionally known component or components.

An application for the patent is filed in the Patent Office, which is governed by the Office of the Controller General of Patents, Designs and Trade Marks (CGPDTM). An applicant can apply in the Patent Registry Office, located at Kolkata (Head Office), Delhi, Mumbai or Chennai (as Branch Offices) or any of these offices and the major steps for granting patents in India involves filing of an application for patent with complete specification, examination of application by Patent Office, advertisement of acceptance of application with complete specification, opposition to grant of patent if any (the opposition can be made at several steps but before the grant), hearing the parties in case of any opposition and finally grant and sealing of the patent.

The Controller of patents is the Controller General of Patents, Designs and Trademark and is the supreme power in the hierarchy of the officers (patenting authorities) and enjoys general and specific powers.

MULTIPLE CHOICE QUESTIONS

1. The date of priority is
   (i) The date on which the patent application with complete specification is filed at the patent office.
   (ii) The date on which the patent application with provisional specification is filed at the patent office.
   (iii) Both
   (iv) None
2. The patent application is closed for a period of
   (i) 18 months
   (ii) 24 months
   (iii) 48 months
   (iv) 6 months
3. Who is the head of the Patent and Trademark office?
   (i) The Examiner
   (ii) The Controller
   (iii) The Controller General
   (iv) The Joint Secretary
4. Section 3 of The Patent Act explains
   (i) Patentable invention
   (ii) Non-patentable invention
   (iii) An invention
   (iv) None
5. A patent can be given to
   (i) an inventor only
   (ii) an assignee
   (iii) a patent agent or legal representative
   (iv) any one of the above

REVIEW QUESTIONS

1. How can you define invention in case of living entities like microbes?
2. How is a patent obtained/filed?
3. What is patent specification? Which are the various types of patent application?
4. What are the powers of the government related to compulsory license?
5. What are non-patentable inventions?
6. What is the eligibility criterion for filing the patent application?

Patent Owner: Rights and Duties

5

Chapter Objectives:

It is true that the patent owner or the inventor enjoys the exclusive monopoly rights for his/her invention. A patentee has all the rights to make use of his/her invention for making money or for commercial purposes but still the rights are not absolute. In this chapter, we will study all the legal rights and duties of the patent holder along with its limitations and also how these rights can be transferred and how can the lapsed patents be restored? The chapter also makes us aware about infringement of different intellectual properties, types of infringement and the remedies against such infringement.

OWNERSHIP OF PATENT

Patent right is an intangible right and in general, the right to own a patent goes to the inventor but this does not happen always as the owner of the patent may be the inventor, the inventor's assignee, the legal advisor or the inventor's employer (as discussed in Chapter 4). The person who contributes to the conception of a novel idea to practicality is the inventor. The person who contributes financing, marketing or other auxiliary assistance (in lab or field) is not considered as an inventor. However, the patents can also be owned by people other than the inventor. The people who can own the patent are as follows:

- An *inventor* is anyone who invents or produces something new or innovative by experimentation or investigation or has contributed intellectually for the invention. But anyone assisting in the lab or engaging in routine work to create the invention are not considered as inventors. For an inventor, it is important to have the written records of the experiments conducted in the lab.
- An *assignee* is anyone to whom a title, claim, property, interest or right has been transferred. It can be the organization or institute where the inventor has worked or used the resources. According to the Indian Patent Act 1970, an assignee is "assignee of the assignee and the legal representative of a deceased assignee and references to assignee of any person including reference to an assignee of a legal representative or an assignee of that person."
- A *legal representative* is the one who represents the inventor. He has all the papers and documents necessary for the application of patent. It denotes a person who under law represents the estate of a deceased person (if the inventor is suffering from any deadly decease). He can be the patent agent or lawyer.
- *A person or a company* can also hold the patent. In case of inventions made by a company's employee, the right of exploitation and ownership is credited to the employer (as the employer provides the platform and financial support to the employee), though the right of acknowledgement as author

of the invention remains with the inventor, who is also entitled to a fair compensation. Under the contract of employment, the inventors may be required to assign inventions to their employers. In most European countries, ownership of an invention may pass by itself from the inventor to their employer by rule of law if the invention was made by the inventor in the course of the inventor's normal or specifically assigned employment duties.

- Patent can be granted to two or more persons and they are called *joint inventors*. A joint owner of the patent can enjoy all the rights of the patent for his/her own profit but this right is subject to the condition that they do not infringe with the patent rights of the other owners. In some countries, each proprietor or inventor may freely license or assign their rights in the patent to another person while in other countries the law prohibits such actions without the permission of the other proprietor(s).

The owner of the patent is entitled to granting licenses to others as well as assigning his/her patent rights to others. Patent rights is a privilege given to the inventor by the government for his/her dedication and innovation and allows the inventor to enjoy those exclusive rights. But it is important to identify the inventors. For example, US patent laws require the identification of all individual inventors. Failure to name an inventor, or naming a non-inventor as an inventor, can invalidate any patent granted. Inventors can obtain patents and sell them to others as it is their right and the person who now owns the patent enjoys the same rights as the inventor. The patent also is also used to prevent others from exploiting the claimed inventions.

RIGHTS OF PATENT HOLDER AND CO-OWNERS

The rights of the patent holder fall under Section 48 of the Indian Patent Act 1970. The exclusive rights are as follows:

1. *Right Before Stealing*: The patentee has the exclusive right to hold, make, use, sell or distribute the patented product in India or use the method or process of product formation for economic gains or commercial purposes. These rights are exercisable by the inventor (or the one whose name is given for the granting of patent) during the patent period of 20 years.
2. *Right to Assign and License*: Section 70 of the Indian Patent Act 1970 explains the right to assign the patent to others or grant license to other person. It deals with the right of the patentee to grant patent to others or assign patent to others or deal with the patent for any consideration. A co-owner also has the right to assign patent to others or grant license to any third party.
3. *Right to Surrender the Patent*: Section 63 of the Indian Patent Act 1970 deals with the right of the patentee to surrender the patent. The patent right is an exclusive right and remains with the patentee throughout the term of the patent but it does not mean that the patentee has an obligation to carry the monopoly till the patent expires. The patentee has the liberty to surrender the patent during its term, after giving a notification to the controller.
4. *Right to Exploit the Patent*: Section 24 of the Indian Patent Act 1970 specifies that after the publication of the advertisement regarding the acceptance of complete specification of the patent application and before the date of sealing of the patent, the patentee has all the privileges and rights of the patentee. The owner of the patent in accordance with Section 19 shall have the exclusive right to exploit the invention, to grant permission for the exploitation of the invention and to assign the patent to another person.
5. *Right for Exclusive Marketing*: The applicant enjoys the monopoly right to sell, distribute, market and deal with his inventive product in the country. The purpose of EMRs is to ensure that the

innovator can market free copies of his product. Medicines and drugs, excepting intermediates, were not patentable as products till 2005. Only the process of manufacture (process patent) was patentable. But after 1 January 2005, Section 24 of the Act stipulated that India has to receive applications for patents containing claims for drugs and agro chemical products with the consideration of granting EMR if an application is made (claimed in a Black Box application). Upon getting the EMR, the applicant has the exclusive right to sell or distribute the invented product for a period of five years from the date of grant or till the date of grant or rejection of the application for patent, whichever is earlier.

6. *Right to Sue for Infringement*: A patent is an intangible property for a patentee and it becomes his legal right to protect the patent or invention from infringement. He/she are entitled to file a suit in case of an infringement.
7. *Rights of Co-owners*: Co-ownership or joint ownership is given when two or more persons contribute to the same invention. The contributions may be made in such a manner that they cannot be separated from one another. It is not necessary that the contributors contribute the same amount of work at the same place, or contribute to the same subject matter of every claim of the patent. The rights and obligations that in general are enjoyed by the single inventor are now shared by the multiple inventors until they have signed upon a different agreement. If a dispute arises among the co-owners regarding sale, lease or licensing of the patent, they can approach the Controller of Patents who shall decide upon the matter.

Section 50 of the Act lays down the rights of the patent co-owners, which are as follows:

- The co-owners have equal undivided share in the patent. But if they sign any contract regarding the share, the share will be according to the agreement signed by the patentees.
- The co-owners have no right to grant a license or assign his rights in a patent to a third party without the consent of the other co-owners.
- A co-owner is entitled to exploit the patent for his own benefit without accounting to the other co-owners. This again is based on the existence of any contract. Each one is free to use the invention independently. Any co-owner can license the patented invention to others and need not share any royalty with the other co-owners.
- If a patented article is sold by one or more persons registered as proprietor. The rights are vested in them in such a way as if they were vested in a single person.

Co-ownership and partnership are two different relations. Partnership is equal share ownership by the two inventors (50–50) or accordingly while co-ownership means 100% for all the people who own. Partnership is the result of an agreement while the ownership is the result of work done. Co-owner has the right to transfer his rights to any third person without the consent of the other owner while partner doesn't have such rights. The co-owner is free to exploit his invention in any form he wants but it is not the case with the partner. After the death of one owner, the intellectual property is transferred to personal representative (according to the application filed) and not to the other co-owner unlike in a partnership.

DUTIES OF PATENT HOLDER AND CO-OWNERS

Rights are granted either as per the laws or arise out of contract and give us freedom but duties are our responsibilities towards those rights. They restrict us to be within a boundary of ethics. Similarly, patents grant exclusive rights to the patentee to hold the monopoly and it becomes the duty of the patentee to make sure that the rights granted are not abused.

- The patentee/co-owner should assure that the invention is not used unjustly.
- The patentee/co-owner should assure that no act that is prejudicial to the public is performed.
- The patentee/co-owner should assure that the patent is used in India in such a manner that reasonable requirement of the public is taken care of.
- The patentee/co-owner should assure that the product is made available to the Indian people at an affordable and reasonable price.
- The patentee/co-owner and the licensee should inform the Controller in writing about the extent to which the patented invention is commercially used in India.

TRANSFER OF PATENT RIGHTS

A patent is a transferable property and the patentee has the right to transfer, sell or mortgage the patent according to his will or requirement. This is done in writing and is known as 'assigning the patent'. The one who is assigned the patent is called the 'assignee'. Once the patent is transferred, the assignee becomes the patent holder and enjoys all the rights of the original patent holder. There can be various reasons of patent transfer like deceased patentee, financial transaction, a merger, a takeover or a demerger or the result of an operation of law such as an inheritance process, or in a bankruptcy. It is also transferred because a person who is good at coming up with ideas is not always good at marketing. The different ways of patent transfer are as follows:

- Assignment
- License
- Operation of law.

1. **Assignment**: An assignment is the transfer of all the rights by the patentee to the other person. In case of patent, it involves the sale and transfer of ownership of a patent by the assignor to the assignee; in case of trade mark, it involves the transfer of ownership of a trademark application or trademark registration from the assignor or owner to the other. The assignor is the on record owner of a patent application or patent, trademark application or trademark registration. An assigner transfers or assigns ownership to an assignee. Sometimes it becomes mandatory to assign the patent because of the contract that the employee has signed with the employer.

   An assignment is irrevocable and permanent. It is essential that the assignment is in writing and registered. An assignment may be of the entire right or title. There are three types of assignments: legal assignment, equitable assignment and mortgages.

   Legal Assignment: When the patent is assigned through an agreement and is registered by assignee's name, it is known as legal assignment. It is the right of the legal assignee to get his/ her name entered in the patent register in the Controller's office as the proprietor of the patent, after which the legal assignee is free to exercise all the rights conferred by the patentee.

   Equitable Assignment: When a certain amount of share of the patent is given to another person, it is called an equitable assignment. The name 'equity' implies equality of right or claim to an asset in intellectual property. It is a document other than the agreement, by which the patentee agrees with another person to hand over to him/her a specific share of the patent, which will have immediate effect. A person with such right is not entitled to register his/her name on the patent register maintained by the Controller. This type of assignment can be converted into legal assignment by getting a written agreement and can be registered later.

Mortgage: When patent rights are wholly or partly transferred to obtain money, it is called a mortgaged assignment. A mortgage of the intellectual property passes the ownership rights to the mortgagee until the mortgage has been paid back and a retransfer from the mortgagee (lender) back to the mortgagor (the borrower) is made. On repayment of the money, the mortgagee is entitled to retransfer the patent in the original owner's name. The mortgagee is not entitled to register his name in the patent register maintained by the Controller.

2. **License:** A license is an authority given to a person to do some act in the absence of which his or her action will be considered as illegal or non-functional. A patentee may permit others to make, use, or exercise the invention by giving a license, which otherwise would not be allowed. The license is a contract signed between the two parties in writing and the terms agreed upon by them (including the payment of royalties) is specified in the application filed with the Controller. In simple words, it is just the permission to use the invention. It can be given to one or more persons depending on the patentee. Licences are of the following types.

- Voluntary license
- Statutory license (e.g. compulsory license, licenses of right)
- Exclusive license
- Expressed and implied license.

Voluntary License: It is simply the power given to the other person to make, use and sell the patented article as agreed upon in the terms of license in writing. In this type of licensing, Central government and the Controller have no roles to play. The terms and conditions of the license are mutually settled between the two, the patentee and the license seeker. It can be cancelled if the license seeker fails to follow the conditions laid down.

Statutory License: It is an authoritative practice followed by the government to empower the third party to use the patented article without the consent of the patent holder in public interest or as allowed by policy. The patentee here is helpless and is forced to give the license of his invention to the third party or to the government. This is done for public interest if the invention is very much useful to the public. The government considers that the interest of the public is supreme than the personal interest. Usually the patentee receives some royalties set by law or arbitrarily.

Compulsory license is an example of this type of license. Under certain circumstances, the Indian Patent Law provides adequate powers to the Controller of Patents to issue compulsory licenses to deal with certain situations like when reasonable requirements of public are not satisfied, a very high royalty is quoted by the patentee, when the invention is not worked in the territory of India (Section 84), in case of extreme or urgent situation like war or epidemic (Section 92(1),(3)), and under Section 92A, compulsory licence can also be granted for exporting the pharmaceutical product to any country incapable of manufacturing pharmaceutical products for the benefit of the people there, when working of a patent requires another related patent or on notification by the Central government, the Controller can grant a license to an interested person.

The Central or state government can use the invention or its process for its own purpose either with or without royalty. Under Section 84, anyone can make an application to the

Controller for granting compulsory license after three years from the grant of that patent. The United States does not recognize compulsory licenses, but there are other nations having compulsory licenses. It is also known as 'equitable remuneration'.

Exclusive License: It is the right given to any one person excluding all others, even the patentee, from the use of invention. Any one or more rights of the patented invention can be conferred from the bundle of rights owned by the patentee. The rights may be divided and assigned, restrained entirely or in part. For example, this applies to software license, as the software law supports software transactions and protects intellectual property included within the software; 'copyright' confers a number of rights on the copyright owner like the right to reproduce a copyrighted work and to make changes in it. These rights can be divided among two or more licensees. So, a copyright owner might give one person the exclusive right to print copies of the work, and another person the exclusive right to make and publish translations of the work. Or the rights might be limited geographically, so that one person has the right to print works in one territory, and another person has the same rights in another territory. Each of these persons will be an exclusive licensee for the purposes of the Copyright Act. Thus the exclusive license is granted by the patentee to another person excluding himself or herself.

The individual who is granted with the license is the only one allowed to produce, distribute or make use of that intellectual property. But a question will appear in your mind as to why such licenses are given, which excludes the patentee from using or selling his invention? There are many reasons. Firstly, such a license may be granted to an author of an original work who has copyrights for that work. The writer of a book may be granted the exclusive rights to distribute and sell the book, a painter of a picture or composer of a song may be given the exclusive rights and license to the distribution of their art. The most important thing is money that a patentee can get in lieu of the license.

Expressed License: It is the one in which permission is given in expression of terms. The terms and conditions of the license are very clearly and expressly declared in this type of license.

Implied License: It is the one in which permission to use the invention is not given or expressed clearly in writing. For example, when a web page is viewed by a person and downloaded through the Internet, he can use a copy of the web page. It is also clear that the web page is protected against unauthorized copying by copyright law. But it would not make a sense if the author sues the user who viewed his page as the author always wants the others to view his web page. Therefore if the document is downloadable, it can be inferred that the author has automatically given end users an implied license to download and view the web page. The extent of this implied license is unclear. This form of licensing is different from expressed license and not in a written format while it is an understandable and indirect form of licensing.

3. **Operation of Law:** Patent is a form of abstract property that can be transferred by the patentee like any other physical or movable property. It can also be transferred by way of operation of law in case of death of the patentee, bankruptcy or dissolution of a company (if the patentee is a company). Any person who by way of operation of law is entitled to the patent has to apply to the Controller for the registration of his title.

   Assignment Versus License: It is good to understand the difference between assignment and license as we have studied both. An assignment is the transfer of all the proprietary rights by the patentee or assigner to the assignee while license is the right to work the invention but the proprietary rights remains with the patentee. An assignee can reassign his rights to the third person while the licensee cannot change the title or cannot reassign his rights to the third person. An assignee is assigned with all the rights that an owner can enjoy while it is not the case with license. An assignment has the right to sue the infringer while the licensee is not empowered with the right to sue anyone for the infringement in his name.

LIMITATIONS OF PATENT RIGHTS

A patentee has all the rights to make use of his/her invention and use the way he/she likes, exploit it to make money also commercially but still the rights are not absolute. Every country has some exceptions to the exclusive rights of the patentee, which can be taken by the third party without the will of the patentee. The third party can enjoy the benefit of the invention at any time during the lifetime of the patent (20 years) with or without any compensation. The following are the exceptions:

- Government use of the patent
- Compulsory license
- Defence use of the invention
- Revocation of patents.

Government use of Patents: Section 99 of the Indian Patent Act illustrates the fact that government has the power to make use of the invention for the benefit of the public or country as a whole or to sell the invention non-commercially. This can be done by any authoritative person of the government or directly by the governing bodies. The government can use the invention for its own use or import the patented matter. It also has the right to prohibit anyone from using the invention if the government finds that the invention is being misused either by the patentee or any other person. If the public has intense interest in the invention and as the government is of the opinion that public interest is higher than the interest of the individual person, the government has the right to use the invention for public. The government notifies the patentee and the others, whose name is indicated in the patent register regarding the invention, and with its publication in the official gazette, the patent is transferred to the government and it enjoys all the rights enjoyed by the patentee.

Compulsory License: Compulsory license is the step taken by the government in situations like patent abuse, emergency or unaffordable cost of the patent. The Controller has the right to issue the compulsory license 3 years after the grant of the patent and it is he who sets the terms for its grant. Section 89 of the Act implies all the objectives behind granting the compulsory license and the circumstances that lead to the grant differ from one situation to another and therefore it has to be flexible. Such license can be issued in case of extreme emergencies like wars or epidemics, for example (as discussed earlier).

The other reasons can be as follows:

- If the requirement of public with respect to the invention is not satisfied or the invention is not worked on the commercial scale as expected.
- If the patented invention is not available to the public at an affordable price.
- If the patented invention is not worked within the Indian territory.

The Controller by the recommendation of the Central government can make the order for the 'license of right' if the Controller is convinced of any of the above facts.

Defence use of the Invention: The Controller when receiving an application regarding the opposition of a patent on the grounds that the invention is relevant for the defence purpose, he gives the notice to the government for prohibition or restriction of publication of the invention. The government after confirmation of the matter directs the continuation of prohibition or restricts the invention.

Revocation of Patent: Patents are given to the inventor for his novel invention, which has some industrial applicability and could be commercialized for human welfare. It has to be worked in India on commercial scale with full capacity and should not be confined to the research/ experimental laboratory because the public interest is considered supreme to personal, but if such conditions are not fulfilled, the patent can be withdrawn or revoked considering that the patent is non-functional (under Section 64).

Patent can be revoked by

- Appellate board
- Central government
- High Court
- Controller
- Commissioner.

There can be several reasons for the revocation of patents, few of which are given below:

Non-Payment of Renewal Fee: The patentee after getting the patent has to give a maintenance fee to maintain the patent till the date of possession, If the patent holder misses the renewal/maintenance fee of the patent within the prescribed time given by Patent Office, the patent becomes inactive or lapses.

An opposition can be filed for the patent to the Controller by submitting the application form (14) with a fee of Rs. 6000 within 2 months from the date of publication of the invention. If no opposition was filed, the Controller easily restores the patent upon payment of unpaid renewal fee with some additional late fee as prescribed. If the Controller sends a copy of the notice of opposition to the applicant and listens to both the parties and if they remain unsatisfied with the decision of the Controller, any of the two can file appeal in the appellate board for the decision.

Public Order or Morality: If the Central government finds that the patent or the method of its execution may create nuisance or chaos in the public or in any form harmful to the public, it can take the decision to revoke the patent after a hearing with the patentee (Under Section 66).

Atomic Energy Act: If after getting the patent, at any point of time, the Controller realizes that the patent falls under the purview of Atomic Energy Act, 1962, the Central government may direct the Controller to revoke the patent (under Section 65). The Controller in turn issues notice to the patentee and the assignees to have a hearing, which may result in revocation of the patent.

Compulsory License: Patent can be revoked upon the issue of compulsory license (under Section 134).

Examiner's Report: Upon the receipt of adverse report by the examiner after examining the application (under Section 101).

Counterclaim by Infringer: A person who was accused of infringing the patent can also counterclaim the patentee and file petition in the court for revocation of the patent on some valid grounds (under Section 128).

Surrendering of Patent: Patent may be revoked if the patentee surrenders the patent (under Section 137).

Ineligibility to Apply for Patent: The revocation can also be done if the patent is granted to a person who is not entitled to apply for it (under Section 138):

- If the patent is wrongfully obtained by the patentee.
- If the subject of claim does not fall under the title 'invention'.
- If the invention is not novel and is publicly known in India or elsewhere.
- If the complete specification in the application does not clearly define the procedure of invention or the invention itself.
- If the invention is obvious and involves no inventive steps.
- If the patent is based on false suggestions or representation.
- If the patentee knowingly imparts false information in the application regarding the patent material.
- If the source of origin of biological material is not disclosed or falsely disclosed by the applicant.
- Patent can be revoked completely or partially by the court at any time after the grant on the basis of petition filed by minister or any other person.

Patent of Addition: Under Section 82 of the Act, if a patentee files an application for 'patent of addition', he/she will get the patent only when the former patent is revoked.

RESTORATION OF PATENTS

The patent right lapses due to several reasons as discussed earlier. The patentee has the right to file the application for restoration and get the patent restored. Patents can be restored till the last day of 19th month (which cannot be extended further) after the date of lapse of the patent. If the patent has ceased due to non-payment of renewal fee then a grace period of 6 months is given with late fees for the restoration of the patent. For restoration of the revoked patents, some basic documents are required.

1. An application by the patentee or his legal representative for restoring the lapsed patent where the patentee has to specify the reason of lapse of patent (under Section 60 of Indian Patent Act 1970)
2. Form 15 with the prescribed fee (approximately Rs. 6000 or as specified)
3. Evidence to support that the cause of lapse of the patent was unintentional.

As far as 'patent of addition' is concerned, no extra fee is required to restore it but if the controller is convinced that the cause of the lapse or delay in renewal of patent was unintentional, the application will be published in the official gazette, else it will be rejected.

After the restoration of the patent by the patentee, the rights enjoyed by him/her might be restricted or constrained by the Controller in order to protect the rights of those people who might have begun to avail themselves of, or have taken steps by contract to avail themselves of the patented invention between the date when it ceased to have an effect and the date of the advertisement of the application for restoration of the lapsed patent.

INFRINGEMENT OF PATENT RIGHTS AND OFFENCES

Infringement is defined as breaking of a rule or agreement. It denotes encroachment upon others' belongings, intrusion or interfering with some legal rights. For example, invading the boundary of a landowner's real estate is called 'trespass', unlawful use of an area of a real-estate property is called 'encroachment'. Similarly, an encroachment upon a patentee's claims is called 'infringement'. Both are civil wrongs but unlike a trespass, patent infringement is lawfully wrong and is governed by law. An intellectual property infringement is the infringement or violation of an intellectual property right, which belongs to the intellectual property holder. There are several types of intellectual property rights, such as copyrights, patents, design and trademarks. Therefore, an intellectual property infringement may be a 'copyright infringement', 'patent infringement' or 'trademark infringement'.

Patent infringement consists of the unauthorized making, using, offering for sale or selling any patented invention within the territory of a country, or importing into the country any patented invention during the term of the patent, which varies from one type of intellectual property to another and is 20 years in case of patents. The basic purpose behind granting the patent is to confer exclusive rights to the patentee so that he/she might exercise certain powers/rights like the following:

- Excluding others from making, using and selling the invention without his or her consent.
- Preventing other parties from making, using and selling the invention for profit gains.

It is not always that the infringement is a complete infringement of the intellectual property. It can also be a partial infringement. Each component of the claim is important and defines the scope of the patented invention. Sometimes a few components from of the patents are infringed known as partial infringement. So it's important to protect the entire components to save the property from partial infringement. In India, Sections 104 to 114 of Indian Patent Act 1970 provides guidelines to the patent infringement.

Determining Infringement: Sometimes it becomes difficult to identify the essential and non-essential elements of the invention, though it is done according to the set guidelines. It is an important to differentiate between the two because it determines whether an act amounts to infringement or not. To determine whether an infringement has actually taken place, it is important to know the extent of the monopoly right conferred on the patentee, and whether such infringement amounts to making, using, selling of the product or using of the process. The direct way of determining infringement is to keep a market watch on all the products released in a particular technology domain and keep an eye on the competitor's product. It is important so that the competitors could not intervene in the company's revenue, market share and goodwill. The products in the market should be keenly examined. This work can also be done by taking the help of a Patent Agent. A company should also keep track of published patent applications of its potential competitors, which can be done by doing a patent watch in the technology area. Patent infringement can be determined in two steps:

- The claims are analysed by studying all the relevant patent documents to see if the product or process 'reads on' one or more patents described by the claims of one or more patents.
- The product or process is examined and compared to see whether it is substantially described by the claims or not.

The extent of protection of an invention is defined by 'claim'; it informs the general public that this specified part is restricted or protected. The test that determines the infringement varies from country to country, but in general it requires that the infringing party's product falls within one or more of the claims of a patent. The process employed involves 'reading' a claim of interest. If all of the claim's elements are found in the technology, the claim is said to 'read on' the technology and if a single element from the claim is missing from the technology, the claim does not literally read on the technology and the technology does not infringe on the patent with respect to that claim.

Types of Infringements

Patents give their owners the right to exclude others from practicing the claimed invention. Unauthorized practice is called 'infringement', which is of following types:

Direct or Literal Infringement: It is the most common form of infringement that occurs when a product substantially close to a patented product/ invention is marketed, sold, or used commercially without taking the inventor's permission. It involves making, using, selling, offering the invention for sale and importing the invention. Anyone who makes, uses, or sells the patented invention becomes a direct infringer.

Indirect Infringement: It occurs when a person knowingly or unknowingly helps the other person in infringement. If a person actively encourages others to make, use, or sell the invention, such an inducer is an indirect infringer. If the middleman knowingly helps the infringement of a product, then it is known as 'contributory infringement'. It includes inducing infringement, contributing to infringement.

Contributory Infringement: Contributory infringement can be committed by knowingly selling or supplying an item for which the only use is in connection with a patented invention. A person can have the benefit of good faith or ignorance in case of indirect or contributory infringement but there is no such defence for direct infringement. In response to allegations of infringement put by the inventor or patentee, an accused infringing party generally asserts one or more of the following points:

- That the inventor/patentee was not practicing the patented invention.
- That he was not performing any infringing act in the territory covered by the patent.
- That the patent has already expired.
- That he has obtained a license of the patent.
- That the patent or any particular claim(s) alleged to be infringed is found to be invalid, because the invention in question does not meet patentability criteria or includes a formal defect, rendering the patent invalid.
- That the patent holder is infringing patent rights belonging to the accused infringing party, and the party may resolve the dispute in settlement or cross-licensing.

ACTIONS AGAINST INFRINGEMENT: REMEDIES/RELIEF

The patentee is provided with the exclusive rights in written documents, which are equivalent to one's physical property and so it is very important to protect one's property. Every patentee has the right to protect his/her right, which cannot be infringed by anyone. In anticipation of such a possibility, the patent law portrays remedies available in the situations where infringement of the right has taken place. Indian courts receive two types of cases:

- Patent infringement cases
- Patent administrative cases.

Patent infringement case involves patentee or patent assignees that pursue damages caused by the infringer. These cases include patent infringement cases, disputes related to ownership of patents, disputes related to patent rights, rights for application, patent contract disputes, disputes on assignment of patent rights, patent licensing and disputes related to revocation of patents.

According to the Indian Patent Act 1970, infringement cases should not be instituted in any court lower than the district court in India. But if the defendant files a counter-claim against revocation of the patent, then the suit, along with the counter-claim, will be transferred to the High Court for final decision. The following is the hierarchy of the court in case of patent infringement disputes.

District Court
(Under Section 104)
↓
High Court
↓
Supreme Court

Patent administration cases involve Intellectual Property Office (as a defendant) and the applicant (patent seeker). The case includes disputes on grant of a patent, patent invalidation or upholding and disputes on compulsory licensing. The appeal for such cases is made by the applicant to the Appellate Board under Section 117A of Patent Act 1970. The following is the hierarchy of court in case of patent administrative disputes:

Controller
↓
Appellate Board
↓
High Court
↓
Supreme Court

Infringement of patents is the violation of the statutory rights and for their violation, civil remedies are available. Not only the inventor/patentee but also the exclusive licensee (if the license is registered), a compulsory licensee (if the patentee refuses to institute the suit), the assignee, the co-owner of the patent can have the right to sue the infringer. Basically the remedies are of three kinds.

- *Civil remedies*, which includes injunction damages or account of profit, delivery of infringing copy and damages for conversion.
- *Criminal remedies*, which includes imprisonment of the accused or imposition of fine or both.
- *Administrative remedies*, which includes an order by a statutory power to ban the import of infringing article into India when the infringement is by way of such importation. According to Section 106 of the Indian Patent Act 1970, the following remedies are available for infringement:
    - Injunctive relief or injunction (order made by the judge)
    - Damages (including treble damages for wilful infringement)
    - Accounts of profit
    - Order for delivery or destruction
    - Certificate of validity

Injunction

It is a form of unbiased/equitable remedy in the form of court order. It is a civil court order which puts legal restriction on others to protect the patent right of the patentee so that no infringements occurs. Here, the infringement party can be asked to do or can be asked to refrain from doing certain acts. Injunction can be either be *temporary* or *permanent* (based on time period) or *prohibitory* or *mandatory* (based on decree or government authority), provided under order Section 39, rule 1–2 of Code of Civil Procedure, 1908.

Temporary or preliminary or provisional or interim injunction is the remedy granted to restrict the activity of a defendant temporarily until the court's decision. Permanent injunction is granted only after the trial when the court finally concludes that the defendants' product infringed on the plaintiff's patent. Prohibitary injunction forbids the defendant to do some acts. It is governed by provisions of Section 38 of the Indian Patents Act. Mandatory injunction requires the defendant to do some particular act according to Section 39. Violation of an injunction is considered as contempt of court.

Damages

It is a kind of relief or remedy given to the patentee in terms of monetary compensation for damages by infringement like economic harm due to loss of profit that the patentee could have earned had the infringement not taken place. The judicial authorities have the authority to order the infringer to pay the patent holder such amount of damages, adequate to compensate for the injury the patent holder has suffered because of an infringement. The damage is calculated on the basis of exploitation of the invention by the patentee, if the patentee manufactures the invention or the patented product then the damage could be calculated by estimating the profit that the patentee could have made had the infringement not taken place. In other case, if the invention was exploited through the grant of license, the amount of damages that could be claimed would be the amount of royalty that could have been earned by the patentee if the patent was licensed to the infringer.

Accounts of Profit

Damages are recovered and the profits are claimed. The gain that the infringer attains is the profit and the loss that the patent holder suffers is damage. It is important to determine the extent to which the invention was appropriated so that the profits made by the infringer can be assessed. A patentee has the right to hold the amount of profit out of his invention or out of his lost profit by the infringer, which he has gained by reason of infringement.

Order for Delivery or Destruction

According to the Patent Amendment Act 2002, the court has the power to seize, forfeit or destruct the infringing goods without payment of compensation.

Certificate of Validity

When a suit is filed for the revocation of the patent claiming the validity of the patent, and if it is found by the court that the patent is valid, the court grants a certificate of validity. These kinds of proceedings are normally heard by the High Court. A suit for revocation is revoked if

- the invention, claimed in any claim of complete specification, was claimed earlier in a valid claim of any other patent granted in India, i.e. it has already been claimed in prior specifications of some other patent;
- the patent was granted on the application of a person who was not entitled under the provision of the Patent Act to apply for the patent.

However, if the patentee is granted with the certificate of validity by the court then he is entitled to

- obtain a final order or judgement in his/her favour;
- obtain an order for payment of his/her full costs, charges and expenses incurred relating to such claim.

Limitations on IPR Remedies

The patents should be checked for infringement regularly because a statute of limitation for initiating a civil action is within 3 years after the claim accrued while a criminal proceeding must be commenced within 5 years after the cause of action arose. Thus, the period of limitation for filing the suit is 3 years from the date of infringement.

Defender's Defence

When a suit for infringement is filed, the defendants may put forward clarifications or innocence in the matter that can defend them. The various escape routes that is generally followed by the defenders or infringers are the following:

- Invalidity of the patent: the infringer might put a question on the validity of the patent or invention.
- The patent device was already disclosed.
- The patent has expired.
- The patented invention was not been practiced.
- The patent holder was engaged in fraud or other misconduct during the patent application process.
- The accused device did not infringe any of the claims in the patent.
- Valid license to use the patent.
- The person concerned is not entitled to file the suit for infringement.
- The implied license is there to use the invention.
- Unawareness about the existence of the patent.

Infringement of Copyright

A copyright is infringed if a person knowingly or unknowingly copies or takes the work of an author or creator without his permission, or without an authoritative letter like license or agreement for monitory gains. But on the other hand, if the work of the author or creator is used or copied for non-commercial use, for academic purpose, for review or criticism or for other private use, it is not considered as an infringement. Generally a symbol is used in order to make people aware of the copyrighted material. Software on internet is available to check for the infringement of the copyright.

The plaintiff is entitled to all civil remedies (for which the District Court has the exclusive jurisdiction) available against infringement like

- Injunction
- Damages
- Accounts of profit.

Criminal remedies include punishment for infringing the copyright, which under Section 63 of the Indian Copyright Act, 1957, are as follows:

- Imprisonment for 6 months but which may extend to 3 years
- Fine or penalty, which is not less than Rs. 50,000 but which may extend to Rs. 2 lakhs.

The punishment in case of a second and subsequent conviction shall not be less than 1 year but which may extend to 3 years with fine, which shall not be less than Rs. 1 lakh but which may extend to Rs. 2 lakhs. Therefore it is advisable to take the prior written permission from the author in order to avoid infringement claims before using the copyrighted work.

Infringement of Trademark Rights

Rights in trademarks are generally acquired through the use of the trademark or by using the trademark in a geographic area. The damage in this case occur in two different ways:

- If it is consumers find that there are similar type of trademarks being used on a number of different goods and services, the original mark loses its distinctiveness.
- If the original mark is used in such a way that the consumer knows, because of the context or the usage, that there is no connection between the owners of the respective marks. However, use of the mark by the other party brings the trademark owner's mark into disrepute or shows the trademark in a bad light. For example, a cold company uses a slogan 'enjoy Pepsi' on its posters and advertisements and suddenly a cigarette company also starts using the slogan 'enjoy cigarette' on its posters, though there is no connection between the two, the latter company is supposed to have brought disrepute for the former company.

An infringer can be the one who directly uses or threatens to use the registered trademark, any agent of infringer or an owner of a company. The plaintiff is entitled to remedies under Indian trademark law such as

- Infringement action: in case of registered trademark.
- Passing off action: in case of unregistered trademark.

Remedies/Reliefs

There are remedies available for infringement. Passing off occurs when one trader attempts to pass off his goods by misrepresenting them so as to make the consumers believe that his goods are the same as those of another trader. For example, use of a mark 'Nieke' on caps with a similar getup to pass it off as 'Nike'. The type of relief to which a plaintiff is entitled is as follows:

- An injunction restraining further use of the infringing mark.
- Damages or an account of profits.
- An order for delivery-up of infringing labels and marks for destruction or erasure.

An injunction is a judicial process or order restraining a person from continuing with wrongful act. Injunction may be the following types:

- *Anton Piller Order*, *Ex Parte Order*: Order passed on the application of the plaintiff without giving the defendants a notice of the application. This is done in case of strong prima facie evidence or if failing to pass such order causes irreparable damage to the plaintiff.

- *Mareva Injunction*: Court's power to freeze defendant's assets.
- *Interlocutory Injunction*: Order to restrict the defendants from continuance of the acts which amount to infringement. It can be interim injunction granted for a limited period *ex parte* without notice in cases of urgency.
- *Perpetual Injunction*: Order to completely and forever restricting the defendants from continuance of the acts, which amount to infringement. Such order comes when the suit is finally decided.

Infringement of Design

The design patent holders have the right to sell the design, import the design for sale or publish or expose for sale. The term of such protection is 10 years, which is extendable to 5 more years. A person who copies the design for commercial purposes is the infringer of that design. But for filing a suit against the infringer, the design should be registered.

Infringement

It is considered as infringement if the infringer uses the identical or similar design on his products and exercises exclusive rights given to the owner or uses the design without authorization from the owner during the term of the protection within territory of the owner of design. Innocent infringement occurs when a person unknowingly uses the design non- commercially and no damage occurs to the owner.

Remedies

The remedies available for infringement are as follows:

- Damages
- Injunction
- Statutory damages: not more than 25,000/- per contravention and not more than 50,000/- per design.

PATENT AGENT

The Patent Agent is the one who works on behalf of the applicant, drafts the patent application and guides the applicant about the peculiarities of procedures in filing the patent, takes the application through various stages needed for the grant of patent. Patent agents should be registered in the Patent Office under the Section 2(1)(m) of the Patent Act, without which he/she is not eligible to practice. To qualify for registration as a patent agent, the candidate should fulfil the following criteria:

- He should be an Indian citizen.
- He should be more than 21 years of age.
- He should hold a graduate degree in science, engineering and technology from any Indian university or equivalent qualification.
- He should have a degree of L.L.B in addition to the above qualification.
- He should have qualified the exam for Patent Agent.
- Functioned as an examiner or discharged the functions of a Controller for a total period of not less than 10 years
- Paid the prescribed fee.

Whereas a person is not eligible for registration as a patent agent for the following reasons:

- He is considered of unsound mind by the court.
- He has been considered by the court for an offence.
- He has been found guilty of misconduct/negligence of his duties if he is a Chartered Accountant.
- He has been found guilty of professional misconduct, if he is a lawyer.

If a person fulfils the above criteria for the Patent Agent, an application is made by the person entitled to apply for patent agent, which is verified by the Controller and if the Controller is satisfied with the eligibility conditions laid down by the Act for the applicant, he enters the person's name in the patent register and he/she becomes entitled to certain rights. The patent agent has the following rights:

- Practice before the controller
- Verify all applications and other communications that are addressed to the Controller in writing.
- Prepare all documents related to patenting.

But, the Controller has the power to cancel the name of the patent agent from the patent register at any point of time if the Patent Agent is convicted of any offence and sentenced to imprisonment or if found guilty of misconduct in his/her professional capacity, which according to the Controller makes him unfit to hold the post of Patent Agent. The other reason for cancellation can be the death of Patent Agent or Patent Agent's willingness to withdraw his name, if the Patent Agent's name is not restored in the patent register or any reason that causes the Controller to cancel the deal with the Patent Agent.

CHAPTER SUMMARY

Patent is a statutory right and a property that belongs to the patent owner or the one who files a patent for his innovation. The patent can be owned by the inventor, an assignee, a legal representative or a company. There are several specific rights which these owner and co-owner possess are

- Right before stealing
- Right to assign and license
- Right to surrender the patent
- Right to exploit the patent
- Right for exclusive marketing
- Right to sue for infringement
- Rights of the co-owner.

These rights can also be transferred or assigned to other person by the ways of assignment (legal, equitable, mortgage), license (voluntary, statutory, exclusive, expressed and implicit), and operation of law. However, these rights are not absolute. They are prone to limitations like government use of the patent, compulsory license, defence use of the invention and revocation of patents. Whenever rules or rights are made, laws are also made to protect them from illegal use or infringement so there are provisions made by the law to punish the infringer for his/her illegal actions. The infringement can be the following:

- Direct or literal infringement
- Indirect infringement
- Contributory infringement

The actions taken in response to these infringements are known as 'remedies', which include injunctive relief or injunction (order made by the judge), damages (including treble damages for wilful infringement), accounts of profit, order for delivery or destruction and certificate of validity. The infringer has the right to defend himself in different ways, for example either pointing out the invalidity of the patent or marking the ineligibility of the patentee.

MULTIPLE CHOICE QUESTIONS

1. Certificate of validity is given by
   (i) Controller
   (ii) High Court
   (iii) Patentee
   (iv) Either Controller or High Court
2. To apply for the patent agent, the age limit is
   (i) 18 years
   (ii) 21 years
   (iii) 35 years
   (iv) After retirement
3. What remedies are available for the infringement?
   (i) Injunction
   (ii) Damage
   (iii) Order for delivery or destruction
   (iv) All
4. What are the limitations of patent rights?
   (i) Making, using, selling the invention
   (ii) Compulsory license
   (iii) Damages
   (iv) Certificate of validity
5. The co-owner of the patent has right to
   (i) Right to assign and license
   (ii) Right to surrender the patent
   (iii) Right to exploit the patent
   (iv) All

REVIEW QUESTIONS

1. What is the difference between rights and duties?
2. Can patent rights be transferred? If yes, then to whom can these rights be transferred?
3. Define infringement. How can patent be infringed?
4. Which part of the patent document is responsible for the protection of an invention? Explain.
5. Who is a Patent Agent? What is the role and eligibility of a Patent Agent?
6. What are various types of licences? Differentiate between license and assignment.

Protection of Plant Varieties and Farmers' Rights Act, 2001

6

Chapter Objectives

An efficient plant variety protection system is necessary to speed up agriculture development and to motivate investment and research in this area. In this chapter we study the criteria for protecting plant and the method of protecting plant and its products. The chapter primarily focuses on plant variety protection and Farmer's Right Act, the infringement and remedies related to it.

METHODS OF PROTECTION OF PLANT AND PLANT PRODUCTS

The Plant Patent Act was enacted by U.S. Congress in 1930. It was primarily introduced to benefit the horticulture industry by encouraging plant breeding and increasing plant genetic diversity. Specific plant patents are available only in very few countries. An efficient plant variety protection system is necessary to speed up agriculture development and to motivate investment for research and development of new varieties of plant. An efficient system is also required to protect plant varieties, farmer's rights, and plant breeder's rights and also to develop new plant varieties. There are five basic methods to protect the plant and plant products that are used in the United States, Europe and Australia where the systems are of longer standing and widely used. Plant protection is also discussed briefly in Chapter 3. In this chapter, we will discuss more about plant varieties and farmer's right. The five basic methods of protecting plants and its products are as follows:

- *Patents on Plant*: Utility patent, plant patent (limitation on the type of plant that is patentable)
- Plant breeder's right
- Trade secrets
- Genetic mechanism (hybrids, restriction technologies)
- Contracts not involving an exclusionary right conferred by a national government (Material Transfer Agreements [MTA], Technology Use Agreements [TUA]).

Patent on Plants

The countries such as United States, Australia and the continent of Europe provide plant protection if the application meets all the necessary requirements and standards for patentability. According to WTO agreement, those countries which do not provide such protection must provide an alternative way to protect plants and its products.

Utility patent distinguishes between patents and other specific intellectual property claims in several ways. Utility patent of United States is similar to that of standard patent awarded in Australia and Europe. Utility and standard patents protect rights in transgenic plants, new varieties of plants (United States only), plant groups, individual plants and their descendants, plant traits, plant parts, plant components (particular genes or chromosomes), plant products (e.g. fruits, oils), plant material used in industrial processes (cell lines used in cultivation methods), reproductive material (e.g. seeds or cuttings), plant culture cells, plant breeding methods, vectors and processes involved in the production of transgenic plants. Utility patent grants the owner the right to exclude others from making, using, selling (or offering for sale), importing the patented invention for 20 years from the first date of filing the application.

Plant patent (specific plant patents) is available in a very few countries. It is provided for new plant varieties, mutants, hybrids, cultivated spores if they reproduce asexually except tuber-propagated plants and the plants found in an uncultivated state. The other modes of asexual reproduction in plants are grafting, bulbs, apomictic seeds, rhizomes and tissue culture.

The requirement for getting utility and standard patent include novelty, non-obviousness or an inventive step, usefulness, enablement, claim clarity and written description. In contrast to utility patent, plant patents only protect a single plant or genome and the protection conferred is quite limited. Plant patents are granted on the entire plant, and only one claim per plant patent is permitted. It does not protect plant characteristics, mutants of the patented plant and the techniques of its cultivation. The utility patent and plant patent can both be obtained to protect the same plant.

Plant Breeder's Right

It is required for protection under TRIPS and International Union for the Protection of Plant Varieties, (UPOV). There are some signatory countries that follow a different mechanism for awarding intellectual property rights to plants. Some examples are Plant Variety Certificates (United States), Plant Breeder's Right (Australia), Community Plant Variety Rights (European Union) or a TRIPS-conforming *sui generis* System (India). The term 'plant breeder's right' is synonymous with plant variety right, discussed later in the chapter.

Trade Secrets

Plants can also be protected by keeping them as trade secret. It requires efforts and care to keep the new plant variety secret or confidential and out of public domain. This process of protection has been used in the United States for decades to protect parental lines of hybrid corn. Gene sequences of inbred plant varietal lines can also be protected by this law but sufficient efforts are required to preserve the secrecy of gene sequences.

Genetic Mechanism

This can be done by making genetic hybrids or by using restriction technologies like the following:

- *Hybrids*: Specialized plant breeding can also act as an alternative to intellectual property protection. The breeder selects plant with specific, useful traits and then crosses these plants with plants of different varieties that also have some attractive traits or characters. The resulting progeny is called hybrids. Hybrid selection therefore becomes a way for the plant breeder to protect their varieties from exploitation as they are safe in the knowledge that the farmer or customer can only access the trait reliably for one generation.

Seeds resulting from hybrids show an extremely poor ability to reproduce the trait of interest in their next progeny. Farmers or the customers must obtain more seeds from the breeder if they wish to continue to use the same hybrid plants.

This method of protection is inexpensive and does not require legal protection but on the other hand, the breeder has no enforceable remedy available to him, except that under trade secret law or by contractual agreement.

- *Genetic Use Restriction Technologies*: Genetic Use Restriction Technologies (GURTs) allows control over gene expression of an organism and also allows restrictions on the use of the organism or trait. There are two main types of GURTs: variety-level GURT (v-GURT) and trait-level GURT (t-GURT).

  In case of v-GURT, the seeds of the affected plant variety are made sterile while t-GURT results in the expression of a selected trait. t-GURT introduces a mechanism for trait expression into the variety, according to which the expression of a trait can be turned on, or off, by treating with specific chemical inducers. The gene of interest can thus be expressed in a crop at particular stages or generations.

Contracts

The laws of contracts as opposed to that of intellectual property laws are not governed by the international agreements. The examples of the agreements are Material Transfer Agreements (MTA) and Technology Use Agreements (TUA).

- *Material Transfer Agreements (MTA)*: These are legal agreements between a provider and a recipient party used when research material is being transferred between institutions. It contains a written description of the material that is transferred and includes any limits on the material that the provider wishes. For example, restricting or limiting the non-commercial use of the transferred material or restricting the material to a specific field of research. If the material is used for the research that results in a publication, then it becomes necessary to acknowledge the source of the material.

  The materials most often transferred to the institutes include plant varieties, transgenic plants, cell lines, germplasm, vectors, chemicals, equipment or software. The agreement is often used to protect the ownership rights of the provider and also protect the material from unauthorized use.
- *Bag Labels*: Bag label contracts are another form of legal protection that can be applied to plants, especially seeds. These explicit contracts are described on a bag label, sewn into the seal of a bag. On breaking the seal or opening the bag, it is considered that the purchaser agrees to comply with the contract. These contracts are similar to what is commonly known as 'shrink wrap licenses' in software.
- *Technology Use Agreements (TUA)*: A technology use agreement is signed commonly between technology suppliers and farmers who use the technology and control the right to plant a given seed on a specific area of land for a certain period of time. This form of property right enforcement is generally used in the United States and other countries. In some cases, the producers reserve the right to inspect the field of the contracting farmer and to take samples to ensure the compliance of the farmer with the TUA. A violation of a TUA gives rise to a claim for damages if a breach of contract occurs.

Under the TRIPs provisions of WTO Agreement, it has become mandatory for the member countries to provide protection for the new plant varieties. TRIPS provisions have given the member countries two options for the protection of new plant varieties:

(i) Protection under the patent law itself
(ii) Protection by a separate system (called *sui generis* system)

India has opted for the second category namely *sui generis system*. Accordingly Indian Parliament has passed the "Protection of Plant Varieties and Farmers Rights Act 2001" to give recognition to Article 27(3)(b) of the TRIPS agreement and the act was signed on 30th October 2001 and was accepted and appreciated throughout India. The Rules for this legislation is being framed and it is expected that this legislation will be brought into force soon.

A *sui generis* System (India)

Many developing countries have an agricultural economy and such an economy is dependent upon farmer-produced seed varieties that are both maintained and further adapted to their local growing conditions by small-scale farmers. Developing countries with such an economy want to acknowledge the rights of farmers for their contribution to crop conservation and development and the sharing of their knowledge on adaptive traits. They also want to encourage farmer-to-farmer exchange of new crop/plant varieties that are adapted to the local growing conditions. As a result, some developing countries have chosen a *sui generis* system of plant protection that is not compliant with UPOV. The system allows farmers to improve and adapt the seed in order to make it more successful in the local conditions. Under the Indian Protection of Plant Varieties and Farmers' Rights Act 2001, plants are divided into four main classes: new varieties, extant varieties, essentially derived varieties and farmers' varieties.

New Varieties

New variety is novel, distinct from all the existing varieties in at least one characteristic. It might have improved yields, higher resistance to pests or diseases and/or better quality yield. Such new improved varieties with the uses of modern technology of plants results in tremendous increase in agriculture production of a country.

Extant Varieties

Extant variety is available in India and is notified under Section 5 of Seeds Act, 1966, a variety about which there is common knowledge in public domain.

Essentially Derived Varieties

Essentially derived variety is essentially derived from an initial variety or from a variety which itself is predominantly derived from such initial variety while retaining the expressions of the essential characteristics that result from the genotype or combination of genotypes of such initial variety. It is clearly distinguishable from the initial variety and conforms (except for the differences which result from the act of derivation) to such initial variety in the expression of the essential characteristics that result from the genotype or combination of genotypes of such initial variety.

Farmers' Varieties

Farmer's variety means a variety that has been traditionally cultivated and evolved by the farmers in their field, or is a wild relative or land race of a variety about which the farmers possess common knowledge.

ESSENTIALITIES OF PLANT PROTECTION

The requirements for protection of plants are novelty, distinctness, uniformity and stability. A new variety shall be registered under this Act if it conforms to the following criteria:

- **Novelty:** A new variety is considered as novel if the propagating and harvested material of such variety has not been sold in the market or disposed of by the breeder for exploitation of such variety, before the date of filing the application for registering the protection of the variety. In India, the distance between these two events should be less than a year in order to consider the variety as novel.
- **Distinctiveness:** A new variety is considered as distinct if it is clearly distinguishable by at least one essential characteristic from any other variety whose existence is in common knowledge in any country at the time of filing of the application.
- **Uniformity:** A new variety is considered uniform if subject to the variation that may be expected from the particular features of its propagation if it is sufficiently uniform in its essential characteristics.
- **Stability:** A new variety is considered stable if its essential characteristics remain unchanged after repeated propagation or, in case of every cycle of propagation, the variety remains unchanged at end of each such cycle.

The TRIPs agreement states that the countries can protect plant varieties through a patent system. The Plant Protection Act provides a framework for intellectual property for protection of plant varieties. Such rights are known as Plant Variety Rights Or Plant Breeder's Right. The period of protection of the plant like trees and vines is 18 years, which is renewable after 9 years and for other crops it is 15 years, which is renewable after 6 years. In case of extant varieties, the term of protection is 15 years from the date of the notification.

PLANT VARIETY PROTECTION AND FARMER'S RIGHT ACT

Plant Variety

According to the taxonomic classification, a plant variety results from the lowest sub-division of the species. It lies lowest in the hierarchy of the plant kingdom (Kingdom → Division → Class → Order → Family → Genus → Species → Variety). Plants may be very different within the same species based on characteristics that could be recognized from any other variety. The UPOV Convention (Article (VI)) defines plant variety as

'A plant grouping within a single botanical taxon of the lowest known rank, which grouping, irrespective of whether the conditions for the grant of a breeder's right are fully met, can be

- defined by the expression of the characteristics resulting from a given genotype or combination of genotypes,
- distinguished from any other plant grouping by the expression of at least one of the said characteristics and
- considered as a unit with regard to its suitability for being propagated unchanged.'

Therefore, a plant variety is eligible for protection if it has distinct recognizable characteristics from any other variety and remains unchanged throughout the generation in the process of propagation; otherwise it is not considered as a variety within the UPOV system.

The system of breeding started by the end of eighteenth century when the innovative farmers realized that considerable further progress can only be possible by systematic selection. However the rediscovery of Mendel's law of heredity in the twentieth century contributed to the establishment of plant breeding on a scientific basis. Plant breeding resulted in creation of genetic variation in a plant species, which could be then selected based on the characters so desired that could be inherited in a stable form. For example, varieties of rose plant can be vegetatively reproduced by propagating a bud or a stem cutting from a plant of the variety.

Need for Protection

The objective of the breeders is to produce a variety that is an improvement over the existing variety, in terms of high yield and quality, resistance to pests, diseases and stress or survival in unfavourable environmental conditions like drought. In order to meet the requirement of the increasing population and minimizing the burden on the natural environment, the modern technology of plant production has to be combined with high-performance varieties in order to get great achievements in agricultural productivity. But this is a difficult challenge as many useful characteristics are not controlled by any one or two genes. Moreover, it takes a lot of investment in terms of time and money. Large-scale breeding work requires significant annual investment on land, equipments like greenhouses, growth chambers, laboratories and skilled scientific manpower. It also involves market risks as changes in market requirement may eliminate the possibility of return on investments.

In order to reward the breeders for their labour and investments on new varieties, it is important to provide an effective system of plant variety protection, with the aim of encouraging the development of varieties of plants, to provide sustainable progress in agriculture, horticulture and forestry for the benefit of the society. Improved varieties are a necessary and a cost-effective means of improving productivity, quality and marketability for farmers. In addition, plant breeding has wider economic and environmental benefits. In the absence of Plant Breeder's Right, there would be nothing to prevent others from multiplying the breeder's variety or selling it without the consent or recognition of the breeder.

Thus, the need for plant variety protected emerged in order to minimize the pressure on the natural environment, in order to get high throughput yield and less wastage.

Objectives of Protection

1. To set up an effective system to protect plant varieties, the farmer's right and breeder's right.
2. To promote the development of new plant varieties.
3. To recognize the rights of the farmers and to protect the contribution of the farmers in contributing towards improving and making plant genetic resources accessible for the development of new plant varieties.
4. To encourage investment in research and development in this area.

United States is one among the nations that grants plant patents. Plant patents are granted subject to satisfaction of the following conditions:

1. The plant must either be invented or discovered. If discovered, it should have been made in a cultivated area.
2. It has not been sold or released in United States more than a year prior to the dare of the application.

3. It should not be the one which is excluded by law (e.g. potato).
4. It has not been put into public domain.
5. If the new plant is shown to differ from already existing and known related plants by at least one distinguishable characteristic.

The World Agricultural Forum carried out a research and the results revealed that India was far behind in terms of filing patents with respect to herbal, medicinal and agricultural wealth. Out of 416 herbal patents filed during the period 1996–2001, United States had 134 and Canada had 66 patents. But India had only 18 patents. Out of that ginger, tea and aloevera received the highest number of patent applications. Patenting of herbal formulations and products are discussed more due to mainly two reasons:

1. Physicians firmly believe that herbal formulations are less toxic and have minimum side effects than allopathic medicines.
2. They cost less than allopathic medicines.

Under the provisions of Indian Patent Act 1970, the process of extraction of medicinal herbs in any form is patentable, if any novelty resides in the process. Germany has taken a number of patents regarding the process of extraction of different components in the last two decades. The process of preparation of any bioactive component in pure form or any mixture thereof is patentable with reduced term of monopoly under Section 3H of Indian Patent Act 1970. The process for cultivation of medicinal herbs is not patentable and so is any process to increase its economic value.

The Indian Parliament approved the Protection of Plant Variety and Farmer's Right Act in November 2001. The Act provides protection to the rights of farmers. The rights of the breeders are protected to grant them monopoly for using and selling the seeds and planting the material for new plant varieties. Under Article 39(iv), the farmer is entitled to save, use, sow, resow, exchange and share or sell his farm produce including seed of a protected variety. The breeder has control of the commercial marketplace without threatening the farmers' ability to practise his livelihood.

The Indian Act also contains provisions for 'benefit sharing' whereby the local communities are acknowledged as contributors of land races and farmer varieties in the breeding of 'new' plant varieties. It is these extra provisions granting rights to both breeders and farmers, which make the Indian system a *sui generis* method of protection. China and Thailand are other examples of countries that do not implement a UPOV style protection system.

Benefit Sharing

It is defined as sharing of benefits gained by the breeder from a variety developed from indigenously derived plant genetic resources [Section 26(1)]. The authority after receiving the copy of certificate of registration publishes the contents and calls for any claims for benefit sharing to the registered variety in prescribed manner. On receiving the claim for benefit sharing, a copy is sent to the breeder of the variety and he will be given an opportunity to submit his opposition to the claim. The authority may invite claims of benefit sharing of any variety registered under the Act, and shall determine the quantum of such award after ascertaining the extent and nature of the benefit claim, after providing an opportunity to be heard, to both the plant breeder and the claimer. After the case hearing, decision is made by the authority.

The breeder must deposit the amount of benefit sharing that has been fixed by the Authority in the National Gene Fund. Every breeder has to deposit such quantity of seeds or propagating materials including the parental line seeds of registered variety in the National Gene Bank as specified in the regulations. A breeder can give the authority of selling, producing or marketing the registered variety under limitations and conditions provided in the regulation and the licensee has to make an application to the registrar along with the prescribed fee for the same.

All the varieties are not registered. The researchers are given the right to use any protected variety for the purpose of research and experiment. If the researcher uses the registered variety repeatedly then the authorization letter from the breeder is required. The right of the farmer to save, use, exchange, share or sell his farm product of a variety is protected under the Act, but if the farmer sells the reproduction under the commercial marketing arrangement then he is not entitled to the right under the Act.

Registration of Plant Variety

The Central government established a registry, for the purposes of this Act, which is known as the Plant Varieties Registry. A register called the 'National Register of Plant Varieties' is maintained at the head office of the Registry, wherein all the names of the registered plant varieties are entered with the names and addresses of their respective breeders, the right of such breeders in respect of the registered varieties, the particulars of the denomination of each registered variety, its seed or other propagating material along with specification of salient features thereof and such other matters as may also be prescribed.

Registration of a plant variety gives protection only in India and confers upon the rights holder, its successor, agent or licensee the exclusive right to produce, sell, market, distribute, import or export the variety. All the varieties are not registered. The varieties that have to be prevented from commercial exploitation in order to maintain public order or morality or the health of human, animal or plant or to avoid serious impact on the environment are not allowed to be registered. Therefore any genus or species can be excluded from the scope of protection by the Central government in favour of public interest.

The application for protection under the Act can be made by any of the following persons:

- Any person claiming to be the breeder of the variety.
- Any successor of the breeder of the variety.
- Any person being the assignee or the breeder of the variety in respect of the right to make such application.
- Any farmer or group of farmers or community of farmers claiming to be the breeder of the variety.
- Any person authorized to apply on behalf of farmers.
- Any university or publicly funded agricultural institution claiming to be breeder of the variety.

Procedure of Registration

The process of registration followed in India includes the following basic steps.

- *Completion of the Application Form:* Completion of the form and filing of the application is done by the eligible person. It has to be accompanied by an affidavit sworn by the applicant that such variety does not contain any gene or gene sequence involving terminator technology. The application should contain a statement containing brief description of the variety bringing out its characteristics of novelty, distinctiveness, uniformity and stability. The application should also contain a complete passport data of the parental lines from which the variety has been derived along with the geographical location in India from where the genetic material has been taken and if any contribution is made in breeding by any farmer, village community, institution, or organization in breeding, evolving, or developing the variety, their data is also required. It should also contain a declaration that the genetic material or parental material acquired for breeding, evolving, or developing the variety has been lawfully acquired.

- *Review by the Registrar*: After the application with all the formalities is completed, it is checked by the registrar and if he finds it unsatisfactory, he can either direct the applicant to amend the application or alternatively reject the application.
- *Publication*: After the Registrar accepts the application either absolutely or subject to any conditions, it will be advertised in the prescribed manner along with its photographs or drawings. Within 3 months of the publication of this application, any person may give notice of his opposing the application to the Registrar in the prescribed format.
- *Opposition*: Any person can oppose the application if the person opposing the application is entitled to the breeder's right as against the applicant; if the variety is not able to get registered under the protection of Plant Varieties and Farmers' Rights Act, 2001 Act; if the registration of this variety will not be in public interest or if the variety may have adverse effect on the environment. However, if no opposition is made (or if made, the opposition was rejected) the Registrar will issue a certificate of registration to the applicant.

Authority

The Central government appoints an authority under the provision of Section 3 of the Act by publishing it in the Official Gazette. Such an authority is known as 'Protection of Plant Varieties and Farmer's Rights Authority' and comprises of a chairperson with 15 members. The Chairperson, to be appointed by the Central government, shall be a person of outstanding calibre and eminence with long practical experience to the satisfaction of that government, especially in the field of plant varietal research or agricultural development while the members of the Authority, to be appointed by the Central government, shall be with the following hierarchy:

- The Agriculture Commissioner, Government of India, Department of Agriculture & Cooperation, New Delhi, ex-officio
- The Deputy Director General in charge of Crop Sciences, Indian Council of Agricultural Research, New Delhi, ex-officio
- The Joint Secretary incharge of Seeds, Government of India, Department of Agriculture & Cooperation, New Delhi, ex-officio
- The Horticulture Commissioner, Government of India, Department of Agriculture & Cooperation, New Delhi, ex-officio
- The Director, National Bureau of Plant Genetic Resources, New Delhi, ex-officio
- One member not below the rank of Joint Secretary to the Government of India to represent the Department of Biotechnology, Government of India, ex-officio
- The Government of India to represent the Ministry of Environment & Forests, Government of India, ex-officio
- One member not below the rank of Joint Secretary to the Government of India to represent the Ministry of Law, Justice and Company Affairs, Government of India, ex-officio

- One representative from national or state level farmers' organization to be nominated by the Central government
- One representative from a tribal organization to be nominated by the Central government
- One representative from the seed industry to be nominated by the Central government
- One representative from an Agricultural University to be nominated by the Central government
- One representative from national or state level women's organization associated with agricultural activities to be nominated by the Central government
- Two representatives of state governments on rotation basis to be nominated by the Central government.

The Registrar General is the ex-officio member secretary of the Authority. The Chairperson of the Authority presides the meetings of the Authority. A National Register is placed at the head office of the Registry for entering the names of all the registered plant varieties along with the names and addresses of the respective breeders. All orders and decisions of the authority shall be authenticated by the signature of the Chairperson or any other member authorized by the Authority on his behalf. The chairperson is the chief executive of the Authority and has powers as stated under the Section7 of the Act and has to perform the duties prescribed.

Functions of Authority (Section 8)

It shall be the duty of the Authority to promote and encourage the development of new varieties of plants and to protect the rights of the farmers and breeders. There are certain functions that has to take care by the authority such as the following:

- It should ensure that seeds of the varieties registered under this Act are available to the farmers and providing for compulsory licensing of such varieties if the breeder of such varieties or any other person entitled to produce such variety under this Act does not arrange for production and sale of the seed in the manner as may be prescribed.
- The registration of extant varieties subject to such terms and conditions and in the manner prescribed.
- Developing characterization and documentation of the varieties registered under this Act.
- Documentation, indexing and cataloguing of farmers' varieties.
- Compulsory cataloguing facilities for all varieties of plants, seeds and germplasm for compilation and germination.
- It should also ensure the maintenance of the Register.

Compulsory License

Any person, after expiry of 3 years from the date of registration, can apply to the Protection of Plant Varieties and Farmers' Rights Authority for a compulsory license for undertaking production, distribution and sale of the seed or other propagating material on the grounds that the reasonable requirements of the public for seeds or other propagating material of the variety have not been satisfied or that the seed or other propagating material of the variety is not available to the public at a reasonable price similar to other patents. The applicant has to write an application and after hearing both the parties, the Protection of Plant Varieties and Farmers' Rights Authority in consultation with the Central government may pass an order for the registered proprietor to grant the license on such terms and conditions as the protection of Plant Varieties and Farmers' Rights Authority deems fit. Furthermore the Protection of Plant Varieties and Farmers' Rights Authority will determine the duration of the compulsory license on a case-to-case basis but in no case the duration of the license can exceed the total remaining period of the protection.

Infringement and Remedies

Infringement is defined as taking the rights of the other person. The Protection of Plant Varieties and Farmers' Rights Act 2001 clarifies that the right is infringed by a person in case of the following:

- A person who is not being the registered proprietor of the variety under the Act sells, exports, imports or produces such variety without the permission of the registered proprietor.
- A person uses, sells, exports, imports or produces any other variety, giving this variety, the denomination identical or similar to that of the registered variety in order to cause confusion in the mind of the general public in identifying the variety that has been registered.

If a person who is not the original breeder of a variety or the licensee of the variety sells, exports, imports or produces the variety, then it amounts to infringement of the right of the breeder. A suit of infringement has to be brought to a District Court and not to any other court inferior to it. In the suit, the rights holder may seek an injunction and either damages or a share of the profits. The order for injunction could include interlocutory order for discovery of documents, preserving of infringing variety or documents or other evidence that are related to the subject matter of the suit, and attachment of such property of the infringer that the court deems necessary to recover damages, costs or other pecuniary remedies, which may be finally awarded to the rights holder.

The relief which a court may grant in any suit for infringement related to this area is referred to in Section 65. It includes an injunction, damages or a share of the profits at the option of the plaintiff. The order of injunction under sub-section (1) may include an *ex parte* injunction or any interlocutory order for any of the following matters:

- Discovery of documents.
- Preserving of infringing variety or documents or other evidence that are related to the subject matter of the suit.
- Attachment of such property of the defendant which the court deems necessary to recover damages, costs or other pecuniary remedies which may be finally awarded to the plaintiff.

Farmers' Rights

A farmer who has developed or bred a new variety of plant shall be eligible to register his variety under the protection of Plant Varieties and Farmers' Rights Act, 2001 similar to the breeder of a variety. Farmers, who are involved in the conservation of genetic resources of land races, wild relatives of economic plants and their improvement through selection and preservation, shall be eligible to register his variety for recognition and reward from the Gene Fund. The condition that applies is that the material so selected and preserved has been used to donate genes of varieties registered under the Act. Moreover, a farmer shall also be entitled to save, use, sow, re-sow, exchange and share or sell his farm produce including seed of a variety protected under the Act in the same manner as he was entitled before the coming into force of the Act provided that the farmer shall not be entitled to sell branded seed of a variety protected under the Act.

The breeder shall be required to deposit the seed or propagating material including parental line seeds of a registered variety to the Authority. An applicant has to submit a fixed amount of seed sample (breeder seed) with prescribed germination percentage, physical purity and phyto-sanitary standards. The applicant shall also submit along with the seed/propagating the seed quality test report.

UPOV CONVENTION (PLANT VARIETIES) 1961

The International Union for the Protection of New Varieties of Plants (UPOV), established by the International Convention for the Protection of New Varieties of Plants, is an independent intergovernmental organization having legal personality, with headquarters in Geneva. The acronym UPOV is derived from the French name of the organization, *Union internationale pour la protection des obtentions végétales*. The Convention was signed in Paris in 1961 and entered into force in 1968. It was revised in Geneva in 1972, 1978 and 1991.

The Act of 1991 entered into force on 24 April 1998. The 1991 Act contains detailed provisions concerning plant varieties and the Authority's rights. The council of UPOV consists of the representatives of the member of the union. The UPOV members and the UPOV Secretariat maintain contact with the government and also provide legal, administrative and technical assistance for growing number of member states. The Secretariat is directed by Secretary General who is assisted by a Vice Secretary-General.

Functions of UPOV

As of 2011, the union has 70 member countries. Some of the developing countries have been adopting the alternative *sui generis* options of the UPOV Convention for the protection of plant varieties. As a result the number of contracting states gradually increased from the strength of 46 in the year 2000, 52 in 2002, 68 in 2009 and the strength of 70 in 2011.

According to it, the following is the eligibility criteria for protection of plant variety:

- Distinctness (from existing commonly known varieties)
- Uniformity (in its relevant characteristics)
- Stability (throughout the generation)
- Novel (not commercialised earlier)

The mission of UPOV is to provide and promote an effective system of plant variety protection, with the aim of encouraging the development of new varieties of plants, for the benefit of society. After the conclusion of an agreement between the World Intellectual Property Organization (WIPO) and UPOV, the Director General of WIPO is the Secretary-General of UPOV and WIPO provides administrative services to UPOV.

The WTO's Agreement on Trade-Related Aspects of Intellectual Property Rights (TRIPs) requires member states to provide protection for plant varieties either by patents or by an effective *sui generis* (stand alone) system, or a combination of the two. Most countries meet this requirement through UPOV Convention-compliant legislation. India adopted a plant breeders' rights law, which has been rejected by the UPOV Council as not meeting the requirements of the treaty.

The following functions are performed by the UPOV:

- It promotes international harmonization and cooperation among the member countries.
- It brings legislation on plant varieties to the member countries.

- It ensures that the basic concepts of the plant varieties must be included in the local laws.
- It gives a platform to share views and experiences.

India as a member of TRIPs agreement also agreed to join the Plant Breeder's Right but the move to join UPOV was strongly opposed due to following reasons:

- India is an agrarian economy where seeds are essentially produced by farmers and farmers' co-operative and not by private corporations; UPOV provides only breeder's right but ignores the farmer's right. It will restrict the rights of the farmers to save seeds and to replant them, which is a practice followed by 75 percent of the Indian farming community.
- UPOV is applicable to industrial economies and not to agricultural economies.
- UPOV laws are applicable to those nations that provide high subsidies to agriculture.
- The cost of UPOV system is very expensive and the Breeder's Right Certificate costs in lakhs, which small companies, farmer's cooperatives and farmer breeders are unable to bear.
- UPOV model has the potential to aggravate the erosion of biodiversity, which can prove extremely dangerous, especially in poor countries. Farmers cannot afford chemicals and genetic engineering, which is essential to compensate crop vulnerability.
- Contrary to the developed nations, research is conducted in India by public institutions like various agricultural organizations. The control of plant varieties resting with big seed companies or the privatization of genetic resources can have a negative effect on research.
- India's joining UPOV could have 'a domino effect' on nine other Asian developing countries that are currently consulting UPOV on their national legislations.

There can be other alternative for the developing countries like a *sui generis system* of legislation, which takes a balanced approach between giving rights to farmers, formal plant breeders and traditional communities on their genetic resources.

The law provides exclusive rights to the plant breeders with some exceptions, for a period of 20 years from the date of grant or, in the case of trees and vines, for not less than 25 years.

CHAPTER SUMMARY

To speed up agriculture development and to motivate investments in research and development of new varieties of plant, an efficient plant variety protection system is necessary. An efficient system is also required to protect Plant Varieties, Farmer's Rights, and Plant Breeder's Right and also to develop new plant varieties. The five basic methods of protecting plants and its products are by providing patents on plant, plant breeder's right, trade secrets, genetic mechanism and contracts not involving an exclusionary right conferred by a national government. Under TRIPs provisions, it is mandatory to the member countries to provide plant protection and has given the member countries two options for the protection of new plant varieties:

1. Protection under the patent law itself
2. Protection by a separate system (called *sui generis* system)

India has opted for the second category namely *sui generis* system, where the criteria of patentability involve novelty, distinctiveness, uniformity and stability. The plant variety seeks protection in order to conserve biodiversity and encourage the development of plant varieties production. The other objectives of such protection are the following:

- To improve over the existing variety.
- To get high yield and high-quality products.
- To obtain pest resistance varieties.
- To obtain disease and stress resistance varieties.
- To obtain varieties that can survive unfavourable environmental conditions.
- To minimize burden on the natural environment.

In order to meet these objectives, the International Union for the Protection of New Varieties of Plants (UPOV) was established by the International Convention for the Protection of New Varieties of Plants, which is an independent intergovernmental organization having legal personality. In case of infringement, remedies like injunction, damage and accounts of profit are also available.

MULTIPLE CHOICE QUESTIONS

1. Which of the following method of plant variety protection is used in India?
   (i) Trade secret
   (ii) Plant patent
   (iii) Sui generis
   (iv) Genetic mechanism
2. The plant variety about which there is common knowledge in public domain is
   (i) New variety
   (ii) Extant variety
   (iii) Farmer's variety
   (iv) Essentially derived variety
3. The criteria of patentability in plants does not include
   (i) Novelty
   (ii) Distinctiveness
   (iii) Industrial applicability
   (iv) Uniformity
4. Injunction and damages are the types of
   (i) Infringements
   (ii) Remedies
   (iii) Acts
   (iv) None
5. The authority for the protection of plant variety and farmer's right act is appointed by
   (i) The Central government
   (ii) The Agriculture Commissioner
   (iii) High Court
   (iv) None

REVIEW QUESTIONS

1. Explain the concept of 'benefit sharing'.
2. Briefly describe the procedure for registering a plant variety.
3. What are the various methods of protecting plant and its products?
4. What are the criteria of protecting plants? Explain in brief the objectives of the Plant Variety Protection and Farmer's Right Act.
5. What is the difference between Farmer's Right and Breeder's Right?
6. Write a short note on the international union for the protection of new varieties of plants. Is India one of its members?

Patent Law: Present Scenario 7

Chapter Objectives:

Intellectual property is an important weapon required for cutting down monetary crises in the field of research and development. The recognition and identification of intellectual property (IP) assets has gained equal or higher importance than any other form of property. IP assets are increasing day by day in every branch of engineering and technology. With the growth of patents in various fields, management of patents are also required to get the optimum benefit or profits. Here we have tried to give a brief picture of the present scenario in patenting life forms, gene and bioinformatics patenting and the methods to manage intellectual property rights (IPR).

PATENT AND ECONOMY

The economy of a country is directly proportional to its growth in industries, marketing and business, research and innovation and on its natural assets like agriculture, research and development. Nowadays, business is globalizing and erasing the geographical boundaries. Companies are developing products with a view to market it globally. Therefore, creativity and innovation is essential in every field in order to get the products absorbed in the global market. Continuous growth and survival in the market requires imagination, which leads to innovation, which in turn leads to wealth. Therefore, the importance of the international conventions and treaties in patents are increasing gradually in different countries. International convention benefits business between countries resulting in mutual benefit, and researchers in commercializing their invention and creation. Today, globalization has propelled the inventors also to network their invention across the globe, recognizing the invention of others, respecting new inventions and also keeping a track of those who use other's invention illegally. For economic growth, creativity and innovation is required in every field whether transport system, road construction, entertainment devices like television, radios, satellite connections, high definition TVs, communication system like phone, fax, Internet and other emerging construction technologies. Earlier the important elements of business processes were land, building, machinery and capital but now new assets like creativity, imagination and knowledge are becoming important. People are focussing on these new assets that are intangible. These intangible assets are now showing the way to achieve tangible assets.

Intellectual property is an important power tool for the strength and development of the country. Industrialization has brought greater changes in the economy of the country. Earlier the intention behind an invention was to disseminate the knowledge to the people for their welfare and nothing was expected in return. As a result the inventors were left with nothing but satisfaction and prestige but in today's world, the inventors along with prestige and satisfaction are also enriched financially for their efforts, and knowledge and time devoted to the invention for the welfare of the society. The institutes are engaged in research and development, and the business houses are also concentrating on research and development. As a result, the number of research personnel working in research and development department is also increasing. The business houses consider intangible assets as hidden values, which are hidden in innovation, new ideas, and imagination that has the potential to lead them to success.

Patent being an important element of the intellectual property forms an important part of business houses and play an indisputable role in generating income for the company and for the country. Thus, it is important to protect the patent globally. The prototype for the today's international patent protection system was created in Paris in 1883, which provided two fundamental patent rights:

- The inventor will enjoy the patent rights in all the member countries also. For example, if a person has been granted patent in China, then his patent is valid in China but he can acquire patent for the novelty of his invention globally.
- Each applicant is treated the same regardless of nationality, which means equality in national treatment.

Global protection for patent is based on multinational treaties that have led to a fair degree of uniformity, reciprocity and predictability between various nations. Patents fetch economic benefits, which trigger the research activities and result in further inventions and research innovations, which could be further utilized for large-scale industrial use or commercialization. It may act as a catalyst for the improvement and development of technology. Increasing patent numbers result in new products, help develop new marketing strategies, new markets, new joint ventures, inflow of new investment and finally generation of new profits. For example, if a new drug is formulated, this new product has to be launched in the market after proper planning. Doctors should be convinced and satisfied about the new drug, and new markets have to be searched and investments done on all these promotional activities. But once it is accepted by the society, it generates money and profits.

Thus, patents act as a vital catalyst for the generation of profit to the business houses, research organizations, institutes and for the economic development of the nation. Today, the value of a company does not depend on physical assets alone but also includes the staff capabilities, the quality of research work done and the number of patents possessed. Along with the possession of patent, it is also important that the society or any individual of society should not misuse this tangible asset. Unauthorized usage of the invention without paying royalty to the inventor or lifting any secret information from the patent office leads to offence, which results in penalty and punishment.

The risks related to intellectual property in a company or organization is theft, piracy and its unauthorized use. In research organizations also the intellectual property assets are at risk of theft due to competition for fame and stability. Thus patent management is required. Patent management does not only deal with preparing plans and strategies but also deals with situations of infringement activities. Immediate action has to be taken against infringers so as to track the usage of patents across the globe. Thus, it is imperative to manage patent along with organization inventory such as human resources, cash and other activities on a regular basis. Every organization appoints a manager or legal officer specially to look into such issues of patent management. Nowadays, the insurance companies are coming up with new insurance products for the IP assets like a product design, business process, customer information and research data.

PATENT MANAGEMENT

Patent management system is used to obtain and manage the patent. Patent management is an important aspect of intellectual property. It includes various management functions such as the following:

- To formulate the objectives of the organisation for obtaining patent
- To design a system of protection of patents
- Allotment of budget to improve the existing patent
- Formulating the strategies for commercializing the patents
- Forecasting the market and consumer behaviour
- Creating the research environment
- Making applications to patent authorities for granting patents
- Documentation of patents
- Keeping track of authorized and unauthorized users for infringement
- Ownership verification
- Keeping an account of income generation of individual patent
- Valuation of patent
- Fixing the royalties
- Maintenance of records.

The management of patent is bidirectional from the patentee and from the organization. Once the patent is obtained by the inventor, the process does not end there; the patentee will also have to invest time, money and energy in managing the patent during the term of 20 years.

The inventor has to pay considerable attention in enforcing the patent, checking the infringement and making changes in the patent. Patent is taken in order to exploit the invention at the maximum so careful consideration is required in licensing or selling the patent with a view to maximize profits.

- Money is required to pay maintaining fees, restoration and in case of objection procedures.
- If the patent holder finds that infringement of his invention has occurred, he can file a case against the infringer for infringement, or nullification if he finds that the patent does not fulfil the requirement set by the Patent Act.
- Patentee can file application for amendment in the patent. Amendment is registered by means of a deed and entered in the patent register with retroactive effect.

There are different types of deeds that have specific formal requirements and specific costs associated with each like licences, right of pledge, seizure, surrender, assignment of patent, change of name, nullification, and claim of patent. Technological advancement, knowledge of subject and benefit of patents, leads to increase in the number of patents application; as a result the complexities associated with managing patents are also increasing.

Ownership of patents is the main issue for patent management. An inventor is always the owner of the patent. Regular periodic checking is done to ensure that the inventor is the owner on file for his patent; it should not have been erroneously transferred to someone else. The invention can also be leaked or copied from the institute (when the patent holder is the institution or its employees) as there is a lot of time gap between the date of application and the date of grant of patent.

PATENT GROWTH

The growth of any research organization or company depends on the number of patents achieved so every organization or institute or company now has its research and development laboratory. There are continuous innovations and new products are launched in the market with new technologies: for example, health care services, pharmaceutical products, biotechnology, technology usage in washing powder, brushes, tooth pastes and several day-to-day articles. Sustainable development requires continuous improvement upon the existing products, which leads to economic growth of not only the organization but also the country. Patents motivate the employees for the continuous development. Good marketing strategies, good brand name, better products, research and development and provision of patent protection can lead any organization to success.

The trend of patent filing in our country has tremendously increased. *Economic Times* of 7 January 2009 reported that 'a total of 35,218 patent applications were filed, 6040 from domestic and 29,178 from foreign applicants in the last fiscal'. In India, 184 patents are held by the Council of Scientific and Industrial Research, 56 by Ranbaxy, and 19 by Dr. Reddy's Laboratories. Globally, IBM holds the highest number of patents, i.e., 3248 followed by Matsushita Electric Industrial company with 1934 patents, which is followed by Canon with 1805 patents. India holds very less number of patents in software industry.

The Indian pharmaceutical sector has come a long way, from being almost no where during 1970 to a prominent provider of health care products, meeting almost 95% of country's pharmaceutical needs. Currently, the Indian pharmaceutical industry is valued at approximately $8 billion. Indian pharmaceutical industry has over 20,000 units, of which, around 260 constitute the organized sector, while others exist in the small-scale sector. The focus of the Indian pharmacy companies is also shifting from process improvisation to drug discovery using bioinformatics tools and setting R&D laboratories. Indian companies are setting up their own R&D setups and are also collaborating with the research laboratories like CDRI, IICT etc. We should not forget the upcoming and booming application of bioinformatics in drug discovery and development, which is expected to reduce the time for drug discovery by 30% and the annual cost of developing a new drug by 33%. Now pharmaceutical companies are expected to invest more on attaining or developing affective bioinformatics software for drug designing.

Though innovations and strengthening of the patent system is important for industrial growth, it is equally important to take necessary steps to safeguard the sanctity of our patent system and prevent filing and grant of frivolous non-patentable subject matters, which is being addressed.

PATENTING IN LIFE FORMS

Living organisms were not patentable until the first patent application of Bursitis vaccine, which was filed in the Patent Office. The office rejected the application on the grounds that the invention is a living organism. But Calcutta High Court ruled out the rejection and directed re-examination of the application. This decision was a landmark in biotechnology patents. New opportunities were opened in India for patenting micro-organism-related invention and doors were opened for research on animals, human beings, plants and a race for getting the patents in biotechnology started. Biotechnology, microbiology and pharmaceutical industries were the focus.

A number of patent applications were filed for the grant of patent on DNA and its constituents. Thousand of patents have been granted on human genes and more are in the pipeline. There are a number of controversies regarding DNA sequencing, for they are natural and not an invention involved in it.

Whereas vitamins and antibiotics are also natural products but when they are purified, they have tremendous commercial value. However, certain areas like animal and human cloning is not granted patent due to ethical reasons. Canada being a major industrial country in biotechnology also prohibits patents in life forms, which is a financial loss to the biotechnology companies. The biotechnology companies are pressurizing the government to revise the decision of Canadian Supreme Court by bringing amendments to the Patent Act.

The dispute for granting patent in the field of biotechnology started from oil-eating genetically engineered micro-organism back in 1970, which was later resolved by the Supreme Court with the view that the microbes are soulless, mindless, lowly forms of life and anything under the sun made by man could be patentable, if it meets all the criteria. It started in 1985, when the patent was awarded to Chakraborty and Kellogg for 'Bacteria capable of disseminating the environmentally persistent chemical compounds'. The patent for first genetically modified plant went to Kenneth Hibbard, Paul Anderson and Mellanie Barker for 'Tryptophan overproduction mutants of cereal crops' in 1986. The first patented animal was made by Philip Leder and Timothy Stewart as 'Transgenic non-human mammals' in 1988, called the 'Harvard Mouse' or 'Oncomouse', a mouse that was genetically altered to make it more susceptible to developing breast cancer. United States became the first country in the world to issue a patent for an animal that was labelled later as 'the product of the year' by a popular magazine. Patents are also awarded to human cells, expressed sequence tags, single nucleotide polymorphisms and isolation of stem cells.

Laws in this area are still being framed in developing countries and it may take some more time to define the laws relating to living organisms. In India, the need to grant patent has to be re-examined. It is considered that there are many grey areas in defining the scope of patentable microorganisms, non-biological and microbiological process multilaterally. Patenting life forms in India is different from that of the developed countries. The patent laws in United States are flexible in this matter. On 16 April 1994, India signed GATT along with 116 nations and further the rules of TRIPs agreement imposed the compulsion that the patent protection should be available for all the fields of technology including agriculture, health care and energy. TRIPs also stressed on patentability of biological materials such as plants and animals. According to it,

- The process of production of plants and animals are non-patentable.
- Microorganisms per se, non-biological and microbiological processes are patentable.

In India, however, the microbes that already exist in nature are non-patentable but genetically modified version of the same microbe that result in high output or has commercial value are patentable. The patent system in India was established in 1970 and went through several amendments till 5 May 2006. According to the draft, Patent Manual of India 2008, there is a difference between discovery and invention. Discovery is adding something to the human knowledge. In case of living entities, invention should also fulfil the criteria of novelty, non-obviousness and industrial applicability. The mandatory requirement of the patent law is that it should provide the detailed information of the patentable invention, referred as 'sufficiency of disclosure' but the living organisms are difficult to describe in words. Therefore, a depository of living entities is made, known as International Depository Authority (IDA), which is involved in the deposition of microbes for the grant of patent. Budapest Treaty, which is an international treaty signed by India, recommends the IDA for countries; IMTECH Chandigarh in India is one of such IDA.

In India, patents related to microorganisms and other biological materials are subjected to 'product patent' unlike other developed countries. The term of such patents was 5 years from the date of grant, but now from 20 May 2003, India started granting patents related to microorganisms and the term was extended to 7 years from the date of filing the application for patent. Presently, the grant of patent for microbiological invention is for a period of 20 years from the date of filing.

Amendments to the Indian Patent Act added that chemical processes including biochemical, biotechnological and microbiological process are patentable; microorganisms that are lyophilized as an end product are patentable. A process using microbe to produce a substance and the substance itself can both be patentable; the process of biosynthesis of new microorganisms is patentable. The number of applications for the grant of patent in the field of pharmaceuticals, biotechnology are increasing day by day as a large number of microbes are applicable in food industry, medicines etc.

Many fears arisc out of possible adverse unforeseen consequences of patenting microorganisms and genetically engineered organisms. So to prevent any biohazard to the human or animal population and ecosystem, biosafety measures are undertaken so that sustainable growth occurs. The other side of the story is that life patents also threaten to obstruct the scientific and technological research, in that the patents award monopoly rights on organisms or their components, transform the product of evolution, which is natural into a private property, patent monopolies lead to higher cost of medicines and treatment, which is unaffordable for most of the patients.

Moreover, patenting life forms brings religious and ethical issues with them, which are discussed in the following chapters in appropriate detail.

BIODIVERSITY AND IPR

Biodiversity is the treasure in a developing country like India. India is classified among the 12 mega-diversity centres of the world. In agro-biodiversity, India has 167 crop species and 320 species of wild crop relatives and several species of domesticated animals. India is considered to be the centre of origin of 50,000 varieties of rice, 1000 varieties of mango, 100 varieties of pepper and several other varieties of pigeon-pea, turmeric, ginger, sugarcane, gooseberries etc. and ranks seventh in terms of contribution to the world's agriculture. India has a rich and varied heritage of biodiversity.

The developed countries have excellent laboratory set-up for experimental research but are not gifted with biodiversity. Therefore, the flow of biodiversity moves from developing to developed countries. Whereas the flow of patents is in opposite direction as a result the unprotected flow of genetic information from the developing countries to the capital-rich developed countries occurs mainly through patents and Plant Breeders' Rights (PBR), which results in loss of biodiversity. In the last few years there has been significant developments related to intellectual property rights (IPRs) and biodiversity.

Two major international agreements, both legally binding, deal with this issue: the Convention on Biological Diversity (CBD) and the Agreement on Trade-Related Aspects of Intellectual Property Rights (TRIPs) of the World Trade Organization (WTO). In addition, the World Intellectual Property Organization (WIPO) and other international institutions are increasingly becoming active on the subject.

India is a member of the Biological Diversity Convention. India signed the convention on 5 June 1992, which came into effect on 29 December, 1993. The convention conserves biodiversity. The Central government has established the National Biodiversity Authority for regulating, transferring and using biodiversity resources at the national level. The Biodiversity Act, 2002 has applicability throughout India.

Functions of National Biodiversity Authority (NBA)

- The authority grants approval to applications for patents relating to biological research in foreign countries.
- The authority imposes terms and conditions for paying royalty, secure equitable sharing of benefits that arise out of the use of accessed biological resource and their by-products.

- The authority gives advice to the Central Government on matters related to conservation and sustainable use of biodiversity. It also advices the State government to choose the areas that can be notified as heritage sites.
- The authority grants permission to the interested people to acquire biological resource in India, permits them to acquire knowledge related to the biological research and transfer of results related to the biological resource.

The Effect of IPR on Biodiversity

During this century, it is believed by most of the authorities that an alarming proportion of the genetic variability of our major food plants has become extinct. Thus, the conservation and development of the remaining crop diversity is a matter vital global concern. For increasing the sale, farmers often sow different and more commercially viable seeds and sometimes various government schemes force them to adopt specific seeds or new plant varieties. Thus commercial agriculture tends to increase genetic uniformity and this, in turn leads to genetic erosion. IP system encourages commercial agriculture, which accelerates genetic erosion. Biotechnology research also focuses on commercial agriculture and leads to demand for IP protection as more and more people focus on genetically altered or hybrid varieties that have potentially negative consequences for genetic diversity (loss of genetic diversity).

Plant Variety Protection (PVP) certificate has lower thresholds than the standards required for patents, so it is easier to avail of them. Although, there are requirements for novelty and distinctness for a PVP certificate, yet there is no equivalent of non-obviousness (inventive step) or industrial application or utility. Thus, PVP laws allow breeders to protect the varieties with very similar characteristics, which mean that the system is governed by commercialization only without any genuine improvements in agronomic traits. Similarly, the requirements for uniformity (and stability) in UPOV-type systems exclude the local varieties developed by farmers that are more heterogeneous and less stable genetically. These characteristics make them more adaptable and suited to the agro-ecological environments in which the majority of poor farmers live.

Furthermore, a genetically engineered organism may produce unanticipated harmful effect on other species in its new environment that may cause further biodiversity erosion and ecological degradation. Improved seeds require more fertilizer and pesticide consumption, which makes tremendous contribution towards biodiversity loss, and have direct impact on floral, faunal and microbial population.

Biodiversity is basically required for our sustainability to maintain soil fertility; it optimizes soil management in rain fed belts, ensures food security, range of foods ensure nutritional balance, provides a range of fodder to the cattle, keeping them healthy and productive.

BIOINFORMATICS PATENTING

In addition to the rights protecting gene-related invention, drug screening methods and recombinant DNA experiments involving manipulated microbes, other rights such as database rights, confidential information and copyright are also available for biotechnology and bioinformatics, which need more focus.

Bioinformatics is the marriage of biotechnology and information technology resulting in the solution for biological problems like protein structure and function prediction, primer designing, molecular modelling, drug designing and several types of analysis like microarrays and image analysis, sequence analysis, phylogenetic analysis etc. It involves the collection of huge amount of biological data or information from various fields like molecular biology, biotechnology, microbiology, medicine or clinical biology, agriculture biology etc.

Bioinformatics is an advanced field requiring the expertise of biotechnology, chemistry, physics, mathematics, statistics, computer science and software programming to solve complex biological problems. Bioinformatics data management has patentability requirement as the product of bioinformatics involves

- collection of protein and nucleotide sequences;
- molecular structures like three-dimensional structures of isolated proteins;
- structure of genes, with or without drug binding sites;
- analytical computer software, tools, algorithms (sequence analysis tools like BLAST, FASTA, CLUSTAL W);
- gene expression data;
- networks of interacting molecules in a biological system or cell;
- software/hardware tools for visualization, pattern recognition, gene prediction, docking, molecular modelling, etc;
- computer-implemented protocols or software for data collection, storage, processing and analysis;
- biological integrated circuits;
- mapping techniques, sequence analysis and comparison techniques; and
- designed primers.

Obtaining intellectual property protection for bioinformatics and bioinformatics-related technology is essentially an important process in order to promote the progress in this area and motivate the researchers involved in the field of bioinformatics. Patents not only exclude others from using the protected technology, but also provide monitory gains and monopoly rights to the patent holder for making, using and selling the technology. Research in this area involves lesser risks of biohazards and so should be encouraged.

Types of intellectual property protection in bioinformatics involve the following.

Patents: The biotechnology companies and entrepreneurs involved in such inventions can obtain legal monopoly rights to protect their technology from being manufactured and sold by competitors; thus patents act an important incentive for technology development, protection and innovation because innovation requires motivation, which can be gained by monetary satisfaction. Out of the various types of patents, utility patent is very much associated with bioinformatics inventions, and can be obtained for a new, useful and non-obvious process, machine, manufacture or composition of matter or new and required improvement on any of the above process or product.

Trade Secret: Trade secrets can be used in the field of bioinformatics for securing the secrets like software code, manuals, databases, factual laboratory data, formulas, processes and algorithms.

Copyrights: Copyrights can be used to protect bioinformatics-related material such as software, code, books, scientific articles, web pages, manuals, computer algorithms, graphic networks, multimedia works, manuals, etc.

Trademarks: Trademarks in bioinformatics are used to protect the trade names, product names, domain names, service marks or slogans for bioinformatics companies.

During 2000 and 2001, bioinformatics patents were given for computer-based methods of determining the actions of drug candidates on cellar targets, methods for modelling molecular interactions for rational drug design, use of 3D protein structures in rational drug design and bioinformatics database structures. As the volume of data is growing exponentially, the scientific community is seeking patent protection in this field in order to remunerate their investments. It is high time for India that companies and academicians should realize the present challenges and opportunities set up in the field of biotechnology and bioinformatics through the IPR regime.

GENE PATENTING

Gene patenting is included in biotechnology patents but is discussed here as it is highly controversial and of great importance in the present patenting scenario. The story of gene patenting started with the case of *Diamond vs Chakrabarty* on 16 June 1980 in the United States for the genetically altered oil-eating bacteria (*Pseudomonas* sp.), which was rejected earlier until the decision of US Supreme Court that held that genetic alteration of a bacterium DNA makes the natural product artificial and so is patentable. After this decision and the Human Genome Project, the US Patent and Trademark Office is flooded with applications for inventions that include DNA sequence.

DNA (deoxyribonucleic acid) consists of a chain made from four types of nucleotide subunits, a phosphate group, and one of the four bases: adenine (A), cytosine (C), guanine (G), and thymine (T). The different combinations of these four bases give rise to different sequences that have the capability of carrying the code of a certain characteristic, which can be hereditarily transferred to the next generation and this is called a gene. It is a part or a stretch of very long DNA. A gene patent is patent granted for isolated gene/DNA sequences, its chemical combination/sequence of bases arranged in a particular fashion, the process of obtaining the gene or using the gene for any particular purpose, or a combination of such claims.

Gene patent may claim for

- isolated natural gene sequences;
- use of these isolated gene sequences for specific purpose; and
- genetic alteration of these natural sequences by adding a promoter or other changes to make it more useful.

However, patents on genes have only been granted on isolated gene sequences with known functions. The gene sequence can be utilized in four different ways.

- *Diagnostic Testing*: A DNA sequence can be used as a probe that binds to DNA from an infectious agent and carries a detectable fluorescent molecule, which helps in testing.
- *A Vaccine*: Apart from live attenuated bacterium, a vaccine might also consist of a DNA sequence unique to a disease-causing virus or bacterium.
- *Gene Therapy*: In gene therapy, a normal gene replaces a malfunctioning gene. Thus, a normal version of gene is required as a treatment measure.
- *Genetic Counselling*: It provides information about an individual's likelihood to develop a specific condition or disease.

The subject of gene patenting is wrapped around with controversies and arguments within the scientific community. The debate on gene patenting started in 2010 with some events like the *Myriad and Monsanto* case in March 2010 where US district court invalidated the claims of Myriad on isolated BRCA1, BRCA2 DNA sequences associated with breast and ovarian cancer. While the patent on the gene BRCA2 was issued by the British Patent Office on 27 November 1997 to the Institute of Cancer Research (ICR) in London and Duke University, which covers the protein-encoding portion

Table 7.1 *Some of the Controversies in Gene Patents*

S. No.	Favouring Gene Patent	Against Gene Patent
1	Patents on gene lead to the development of life-saving medicines	DNA sequences/gene are blueprints of life and play a special role in carrying the important information to construct a human.
2	Gene patenting will force the disclosure of secret information, e.g. Genentech patent on human insulin gene enabled pharmaceutical company Eli Lilly to develop insulin for diabetics, 'Humulin'	Gene is very closely related with species identity, so no parts of it should be controlled by corporate interest
3	Isolation of a gene makes it 'artificial' as no isolated gene sequence occurs in nature. Thus it should be patentable as not natural.	In case of humans, DNA is unique and therefore possess intrinsic value of sacred kind
4	A patented gene differs from its intracellular counterpart in that it is no longer a part of a chromosome and patents claims only the protein coding part of a gene, not the entire gene	DNA bears the image of God and is a product of nature, not human ingenuity
5	DNA sequence exists with a known function or use, but genetic alteration makes it different from their form inside a cell and so should be patentable	Plants, animals and microorganisms comprise life on earth and a part of nature. These species, or their molecules or parts, should not be converted to corporate property through patent monopolies.

of the gene, and the claims include development of pharmaceuticals, diagnostic tests, and a method to produce the protein, cloning of Dolly sheep in May 2010 ignited the debate over the ethics of gene patenting.

Table 7.1 highlights some points of controversies regarding gene patenting.

But there occurred a compromise on such patents as in the words of Hanson: 'One possibility that is acceptable to those religious leaders who oppose gene patenting is "Process Patent", whereby the processes involved in the manipulation of particular gene to serve a certain function are patented rather than the genes themselves'. Between 1981 and 1995, 1175 patents were granted worldwide related to human DNA sequences. Major problems regarding gene patenting is that it is a large biological information molecule whose sequences vary considerably limitlessly. A gene coding a protein can have millions of possible alternative sequences, and claiming any one will not give automatic claims on others and it will not be possible to avoid infringement. We know well that even a single base change in DNA can cause unbelievable effects on the individual, but this is not the case always; concerns are only when the changes are made in the coding part of the DNA.

The Indian scenario faces recent controversies regarding biotechnology patents. The developed countries are trying to usurp ownership of basmati rice, neem and turmeric and it is necessary for India to take advantage of IPR. Indian biotechnology scientists have been successfully working in the field of synthetic organic chemistry and biosciences like biochemistry, microbiology and molecular biology for the same. India can play a role in the further investigation into their chemistry, and in synthesis and processing of these molecules. The Indian Patent Office's guidelines for the unity of invention clarifies that when a genetically modified gene sequence/amino acid sequence is novel and involves an inventive step and has industrial applicability, it is eligible for claims like

- gene sequence/amino acid sequence,
- a method for expressing gene/amino acid sequence,
- an antibody against that that protein/protein sequence and
- a kit made from the antibody sequence.

Thus, it is clear that genetic modification of a gene is necessary and so the kit made from such a sequence is patentable. Further clarification can be found in the draft manual of 2005 in annexure I, which provides examination guidelines for patent application relating to inventions in the field of chemicals, pharmaceuticals and biotechnology. It is mentioned in the annexure I, in the list of patentable and non-patentable invention, that the following are patentable:

- Biological material such as recombinant DNA, plasmids
- Process of manufacturing thereof

But the gene sequence and DNA sequence with unidentified function are non-patentable. Thus, Section 3(c) and the draft manual of 2008 and 2005 illustrates that the isolated naturally occurring DNA would be considered as discovery and is not patentable in India. The Controller General of Patents Designs and Trademarks in India is the authority who grants patents. The country has a Patents Act (1970) and Patents Rules (2003) and their amendments which apply to patents but there is an immense need for legislation and concrete guidelines for biotechnology-related inventions; else we will face delays and blockages to be encountered regarding patenting in this field.

The majority (approximately 80 per cent) of DNA patent holders are universities and non-profit organizations that have never enforced a patent. The motto of academic researchers to apply for patents is to protect their research as well as to gain recognition on their scientific discovery. If the patent is not applied for a discovery, it could result in inhibited access to their research. The competing lab can make a similar discovery and gain a patent and exercise their rights as patent holders. But there are certain issues like the issue of gene patenting, which are at risk as their patentability affects patients, industry, researchers and others.

The Human Genome Project was completed in 2001 and the US Patent Office has granted patents to nearly 60,000 DNA-based patents covering genetic variations and related gene sequencing technologies. Approximately 2600 patents have been awarded for for isolated DNA.

NEW PATENT REGIME

Intellectual property faces challenges in today's world with fast changing technologies, especially in the electronic industry. For example, VCRs has been replaced by VCDs, VCDs are replaced by DVDs and finally these are replaced by Blu Ray. Floppies have been replaced by pen drives, cables have been replaced by the optical fibres, cassette player has been replaced by MP3 player, iPods have been replaced by Walkman and so on. Due to fast changing technology the patented products lose their importance within a short period of time and the time and money spent on acquiring them will be wasted.

Therefore, continuous research and innovation is required in order to survive in the global market. To meet the demands of the fast changing world, new modifications are made to the products and because microbiology and biotechnology has many upcoming promises for the future, the relationship between biotechnology, bioinformatics, microbiology and pharmaceutical industry is also becoming cohesive to meet these expectations. The technological developments in these upcoming and progressive fields are responsible for a number of challenges to the IP assets.

CHAPTER SUMMARY

Globalization of business is responsible for the growth and development of most of the countries and is essential for survival in today's business. Continuous growth and surviving in the market requires imagination, which leads to innovation, which in turn leads to wealth. Therefore, the importance of the international conventions and treaties in patents are increasing gradually in different countries. India has also become member of many international conventions. Fast-changing technology requires speedy inventions and so most of the companies are engaged in research and development involving a large number of people in research. Now research is not limited to the research institutes facilitated by the government, but has entered business organizations also. Most of the private companies have R&D units so as to improve over the existing products for long-term survival in the market.

The inventors or the institutes are benefitted monetarily to replenish the time and money spent on the research. Indian pharmaceutical sector has exponentially progressed in drug discovery using bioinformatics tools. Patenting in biotechnology, living organisms and bioinformatics is very promising and has wider scope. The dispute for granting patents in the field of biotechnology started from oil-eating genetically engineered microorganism back in 1970, which was later resolved by the Supreme Court favouring microbial patents. The laws in developing countries are still being framed and it may take some more time for them to define the laws relating to living organisms. According to India, the need to grant patent has to be re-examined.

In India, the microbes that already exist in nature are non-patentable but genetically modified version of the same microbe, which results in high output or has commercial value, are patentable. Amendments to the Indian Patent Act added that chemical processes including biochemical, biotechnological and microbiological process are patentable; microorganisms that are lyophilized as an end product are patentable. However, patenting microorganisms opens the door for several biosafety, religious and bioethical issues, which will be discussed later in the following chapters. In the new patenting regime, bioinformatics brings up new challenges and opportunities for the researchers in the field of genomics, proteomics, drug designing and other related areas. Gene patenting is a controversial issue in countries including India. The Indian Patent Office's guidelines states that if a genetically modified gene sequence/amino acid sequence is novel, involves an inventive step and has industrial applicability, it is eligible for the claims like gene sequence/amino acid sequence, a method for expressing gene/amino acid sequence, an antibody against that that protein/protein sequence and a kit made from the antibody sequence. A genetically engineered organism may produce unanticipated harmful effect on other species in its new environment that may cause biodiversity erosion and ecological degradation. Unprotected flow of genetic information from the developing countries to the capital-rich developed countries occur mainly through patents and Plant Breeders' Rights (PBR), which results in loss of biodiversity. Thus, in order to protect the biodiversity loss due to the knowledge of IPR or any other reason, India has become a member of the Biological Diversity Convention, which was signed on 5 June 1992 and became effective on 29 December 1993, which is applicable throughout India. The convention seeks to conserve biodiversity. The Central government has established the National Biodiversity Authority for regulating, transferring and using biodiversity resources at the national level. Patenting in this field is required to be firm since personalized medicines can be brought to homes by commercial organizations, which is possible only through patents.

MULTIPLE CHOICE QUESTIONS

1. India signed the convention on biodiversity on
   (i) 29 December 1993
   (ii) 5 June 1992
   (iii) 28 April 1977
   (iv) 1 January 1995
2. Patent management involves
   (i) Record maintenance
   (ii) Infringement check
   (iii) Ownership verification
   (iv) All
3. Bioinformatics data management involves data like
   (i) Gene expression data images
   (ii) Sequences of DNA and RNA
   (iii) Structure of Protein
   (iv) All
4. Bioinformatics software can be protected by
   (i) Copyright
   (ii) Trade Secret
   (iii) Trademark
   (iv) Utility patent
5. Lyophilized microbes as an end product of a biological process is
   (i) Patentable
   (ii) Non-patentable
   (iii) Patentable only outside India
   (iv) None

REVIEW QUESTIONS

1. What place does India occupy in the new patenting scenario?
2. How has Indian pharmaceutical industry progressed after the TRIPs agreement?
3. What role do IPR play in bioinformatics industry?
4. How are patents managed?
5. What is the effect of rapid technological advancements on IPRs?
6. What controversies are associated with gene patenting? Explain the relationship between IPR and biodiversity.

Introduction to Biosafety

8

Chapter Objectives:

The aim of biosafety is to reduce or eliminate accidental exposure to infectious agents and to prevent release of infectious agents to the environment. Infectious agents include bacteria, fungi, viruses, parasites and other cell cultures that can pose a risk to environment, animal and human health. This chapter deals with the various risk levels and its extent of pathogenicity. It explains how to manage risk and details emergency procedures. It introduces the backbone of biosafety in the form of Cartagena Protocol on Biosafety, which is a precautionary approach towards biosafe environment. There is also an introduction of various organizations to take proper measure, to regulate, manage or control risk associated with the use and release of genetically modified organisms (GMO).

OVERVIEW OF BIOSAFETY

Biosafety, in the broader term, is the prevention of large-scale loss of biological integrity focusing both on ecology and human health. The more an environment and its original processes are altered due to acts of man, the less biological integrity it holds. However, if the change in the processes takes place naturally without any human intervention, the integrity of the environment is maintained.

Over the past three decades, our ability to transform life forms has revolutionized modern biotechnology. Scientists can isolate DNA from various species, alter them with precise accuracy and transform them from one organism to other. For example, a gene from cold water fish can be transformed into tomato genome to make frost resistant tomato plants or a bacterial gene can be used to make a plant-insect resistant The resultant product in such transformations is called living modified organisms (LMOs) or genetically modified organisms (GMOs). The initial success of the commercialization of the first transgenic crop has led to increased scientific focus on genetic transformations and dozens of crops and animals have been modified—some for higher yield and/or improved nutrition and many others for better medical treatments and new industrial products.

However, this scientific pursuit of creating LMOs or GMOs has left many questions unanswered. These questions revolve around the interaction of the modified product with the ecosystem—its evolution and interaction with other species, gene transfer from GM plants to wild types through wind pollination or insect-resistant plants tending to repel even the beneficial insects that help in pollination. Even as the scientific community is working hard to solve these questions, we do not have all the answers yet, partly because the pace of research in genetic transformation has been much faster in the last decade and partly because observations around such issues need more time to be monitored since it could take a few generation of the product to show an effect. Whichever be the case, there is a potential risk of bio-agents used in transformations getting released to the environment and also an unknown risk of the effect of the GM product on its ecosystem. Biosafety then is the application of knowledge, techniques and equipment to prevent personal, laboratory and environmental exposure to any such biohazard while maximizing the benefits of biotechnology.

RISK ASSESSMENT

Risk is a measure of the probability of release of an altered organism or bioagent into the environment times the hazard posed by that biological material or agent. A hazard is any adverse effect that can be identified and measured. Risk assessment involves determination of potential and anticipated adverse effects of the recombinant DNA research. Generally, risk assessment consists of hazard identification, hazard analysis, consequence analysis, risk determination and risk evaluation. Risk assessment is made on the basis of risk groups and biosafety levels.

Risk Groups and Biosafety Levels

On the basis of their relative risk, bioagents are classified under four risk groups. Risk indicators include pathogenicity of the bioagent, mode of transmission, availability of vaccines for prevention and availability of medicines for treatment if the infection occurs.

Bioagents are classified under risk groups such as the level of risk with 'Risk Group 1' is lower than the level of risk with organisms classified under 'Risk Group 2' and so on. The four risk groups are as follows:

- Risk Group 1 (RG1) – Bioagents classified under this risk group are not found to cause any disease in healthy adult humans or animal, e.g. *E coli, Bacillus subtallis*
- Risk Group 2 (RG2) – Bioagents classified under this risk group are known to cause disease, which is rarely serious with limited potential for transmission and for which preventative or therapeutics is often available, e.g. *Hepatitis B, Salmonella*, etc.
- Risk Group 3 (RG3) – This risk group contains organisms that are associated with serious or lethal human disease for which vaccination/medication may be available, e.g. *Flavivirus, Rhabdovirus*.
- Risk Group 4 (RG4) – This group has organisms that are associated with lethal human disease for which vaccination/medication is not readily available, e.g. *Arena viruses*.

The four biosafety levels deal which the four risk groups defined above.

- Biosafety Level 1(BSL1) – This level deals with Risk Group 1 (RG1).All experimental work at this level can be done on an open top bench. This level does not require any special containment and/or equipment to work.
- Biosafety Level 2 (BSL2) – At this level, there is restricted access to laboratory and biological safety cabinets must be available. Gloves, lab coats and autoclaves are a must when working at BSL2.
- Biosafety Level 3 (BSL3) – Since this level deals with a much higher risk group, the laboratory must be isolated and ideally be in a separate building, with double door entry and directional inward airflow. Medical surveillance and additional training is required when working at BSL3.
- Biosafety Level 4 (BSL4) – When dealing with biological hazards at this level, the use of a Hazmat suit and a self-contained oxygen supply is mandatory. The entrance and exit of a level four laboratory should have multiple showers, a vacuum room, an ultraviolet light room and other safety precautions designed to destroy all traces of the bioagent.

The Process of Risk Assessment

Comprehensive risk assessment is needed to analyse and decide the level of containment appropriate for the experimentation based on the risk group. Generally in this risk assessment exercise, features like the organism used for experimentation and virulence, pathogenicity, infectious growth, environmental stability, route of infection, availability of vaccines etc. are taken into account. Any strain which shows higher pathogenicity is be handled at a higher containment level. The assessment also includes the type of manipulation that is planned for the higher risk group. The process of risk assessment consists of following steps:

- *Hazard Identification*: Identification of any genotypic and phenotypic features of GMO that may have adverse effect on environment, human or animal health.
- *Hazard Analysis*: Evaluation of likelihood of these adverse effects being realized, taking into account all the risk levels and the kind of exposure it might have when exposed or released in the environment.
- *Exposure Assessment*: This is to assess the level of risk consequences it can have on human and animal health and at the same time its implications on the environment.
- *Risk evaluation*: Whether or not the risks evaluated are acceptable or manageable. It includes identification of the strategies to manage the risks.

Risk Assessment for Planned Introduction of GMO

Risk assessment for planned introduction of GMOs is done to identify and evaluate the potential adverse effect of introduction of GMO in the environment including biological diversities and human health. The following factors are taken into account while assessing the risks.

- Biological characteristics of the recipient or the parental organism including taxonomic status, centre of origin, genetic diversity and habitat where they are likely to persist or proliferate.
- Characteristics of the vector including its origin, source and its host range.
- Genetic characteristics of DNA insert; modification and manipulation introduced or planned.
- Detection and identification methods including their specificity, sensitivity and reliability.
- Complete environmental information of the location, climatic and ecological characteristics including relevant information of the biological diversity of the environment in which planned introduction is proposed.

Risk Assessment for the Release of Transgenic Crops

In case of a release of transgenic crops, the following factors are taken into account:

- The characteristics of the promoter—whether they are organ-specific or constitutive.
- Nature of the marker gene used.
- Location and proximity of related crops in relation to isolation – distance needed for the prevention of pollination.
- The chances of inter pollination with wild relatives and the chances of survival of the transgene; for example, if a critical transgene for insect or herbicide resistance is transferred to the weed, it may become more persistent.
- Possible disturbance to the ecosystem by the introduction of the novel gene.
- Effect of the transgenic plant on the flora and fauna of their phyllosphere (area near leaf) and rhizosphere (area near root).

Risk Assessment of Food and Additives Obtained from GMOs

In assessment of risk of food obtained from transgenic crops, the following points are considered:

- Characterization of the food crop that has been modified
- Potential of any introduced DNA to encode for harmful biomolecules like allergens
- Safety of proteins encoded by transgene
- Conformance of any known plant toxicant and important nutrients within acceptability level in the new variety
- Mandatory compliance of labelling for GM food.

To assess the inherent risk in biotechnology and to take proper measures to ensure biosafety, there are different regulatory bodies all over the world that are responsible for the approval of guidelines and processes, right conduct of participating organizations and to ensure that GMOs are not posing any harm to the environment, animal and human health. These regulatory bodies are discussed in the next section in detail. Within the convention of biological diversity, which raises the concerns of the impact of biotechnology application on biodiversity and describes the need of precaution in safe handling of GMOs, the Cartagena Protocol promotes biosafety by establishing practical rules and procedures for the safe handling, transfer and the use of GMOs.

CARTAGENA PROTOCOL ON BIOSAFETY

In 1995, the Convention established an open-ended ad hoc working group on biosafety to develop a draft protocol on biosafety. After a lot of negotiations within the parties, the final draft was adopted on 29 January 2000 as an international legal binding agreement that addresses potential risks posed by GMOs. Known as the Cartagena Protocol on Biosafety, the protocol for the first time set out an intricate and comprehensive regulatory system for ensuring the safe transfer, use and handling of GMOs and its trans-boundary movement to prevent any adverse effect on biodiversity or any probable risk to humans.

The Cartagena Protocol on Biosafety is the first effort to regulate the movement of genetically engineered organisms. This international agreement was established in conjunction with United Nations Convention on Biological Diversity (CBD).

The Cartagena Protocol promotes and ensures biosafety by establishing rules, procedures and good practices for the safe transfer, use and handling of GMO, with the specific attention on regulating movements of these organisms between countries. It features two sets of procedures: one in which the GMOs are intentionally introduced to the environment like transgenic and the others that are to be used directly as food or feed. Both the procedures are designed in a way to ensure that for trans-boundary movements, the recipient country is provided with all the information it needs to make an informed decision on whether to accept the GMO or not. Governments exchange this information through an organization called Biosafety Clearing House and make their decisions on scientifically sound risk assessment and on the precautionary approach. Finally when a country decides to allow the import of GMO, it is mandatory for the exporter to provide all the important related documentation. Governments also establish the methods for managing any risks identified during risk assessments and they must continue to monitor and control any risk that may emerge in the future both in traded and domestically produced GMOs.

Silent Features of the Protocol

- The protocol seeks to protect biological diversity from the potential risks arising from GMO and LMO.
- All the regulatory bodies or parties working under this protocol must be allowed to ban a GMO if they are not convinced that the GMO is safe for the environment and human health.
- The protocol must prohibit any release of GMO in the major centres of diversities.
- The protocol also mandates that the parties should have a domestic regulatory framework on biosafety to serve as a basis for the national implementation of the protocol.
- The main aim of the protocol is the establishment of Advance Informed Agreement (AIA) procedure for the trans-boundary movement of GMOs. This requires the exporter to notify the importer with all the information needed to accept or refuse the import and/or even impose certain conditions on the import according to the basis of the risk assessment.

For sustainable effectiveness over the long term, the protocol also contains a number of important provisions like capacity building, public awareness and participation, financial mechanism, etc.

CAPACITY BUILDING

In common terms, capacity building is an ongoing process through which individuals, groups, organizations and societies enhance their ability for development challenges. Under the Cartagena Protocol, capacity building requires that all member countries cooperate in the development and strengthening of human resources and institutional capacities in biosafety for the effective implementation of the protocol. For each member country, it translates to having skilled personnel and a regulatory framework to assess the risks and make informed decisions to manage or avoid the adverse effects of any GMO on the environment. The protocol also encourages governments to assist each other with scientific and technical training to promote more awareness for building capacity for better and effective working of a bio-safe environment.

Components of Capacity Building

The protocol envisages for capacity building in the following areas:

- Risk assessment, risk management, detection and monitoring of LMOs
- Institution building including labs and equipment for testing LMOs
- Scientific, technical and institutional collaboration
- Human resource development including training in scientific skills
- Facilities and methods for inspection of LMOs
- Awareness, education and participation
- Information sharing and data management.

Advance Informed Agreement (AIA) for Intentional Use of GMO

The Advance Informed Agreement (AIA) procedure applies to the first intentional trans-boundary movement of GMOs for intentional introduction into the environment of the importer. It includes four components: notification by the exporter, acknowledgment of notification by the importer, the decision procedure and opportunity for review of decisions. The purpose of this agreement is to make sure that the importing country has both the opportunity and the capacity to assess risks that may be associated with the GMO before agreeing to its import. The importing country must indicate the reasons on which its decisions are based (unless consent is unconditional). An importer may, at any time, in light of new scientific information, review and change a decision. An exporter may also request the importer to review its decisions.

A Simplified System for Agricultural Commodities for Direct use of GMOs as Food or Feed

There is a large category of GMOs that is intended to be used as food or feed directly or for processing, like GM corns, soybean or other genetically modified agricultural products. For this category of GMOs, the Cartagena Protocol proposes a simpler procedure compared to the AIA used for intentional use.

Under this procedure, a party must inform other parties through the Biosafety Clearing-House, within 15 days, of its decision regarding domestic use of LMOs that may be subject to trans-boundary movement. This helps the international trading system retain total transparency.

The Biosafety Clearing-House (BCH)

The Biosafety Clearing-House has been setup by the Cartagena Protocol to facilitate the exchange of scientific, technical, environmental and legal information on GMOs and LMOs. Using the information available with the clearing-house, member countries can implement the protocol more effectively. The Clearing House is a repository of national laws, regulations and all the guidelines set up for implementing the protocol. It contains summaries of all the risk assessments and environmental review, as well as detailed technical information.

Documentation of the Export

There is a strong focus on export documentation as a part of the Cartagena Protocol. For GMOs that are intended for direct introduction to the environment, the documentation on the shipment should clearly state that it contains the particular GMO, its unique traits, requirements for its safe handling, its storage needs and names and address of the importer and the exporter. Alternately when the shipment is for agricultural commodities involving direct use as food or feed or for processing, the shipment must clearly indicate that it contains living modified organisms (LMOs) and that they are not intended for the introduction in to the environment.

An Approach to Public Awareness and Participation

It is very important that each individual understands the need for biosafety and needs and processes related to LMOs. The protocol therefore calls for cooperation on promoting public awareness and education for the safe transfer, handling and use of GMOs. The protocol requires parties to consult the public in the decision-making process, to make public the final decision taken and to inform public about the means of access to the biosafety clearing-house.

Different Organizations and Database Information on Biosafety

The International Plant Protection Convention (IPPC)

This agreement protects plants by assessing and managing risks of plant pest that are associated with the GMO. All the GMOs that pose a threat to plant as pest comes under this treaty. The IPPC allows government to take the initiative to prevent or circumvent the spread of such pest.

The Codex Alimentarius Commission

The Codex Alimentarius Commission deals with consumer health and food safety. The commission has established an intergovernmental task force on food derived from genetic engineering. It is also responsible for developing standards and guidelines for genetically modified food and lays emphasis on labelling GMOs so that the consumer can make an informed choice. It has declared international guidelines for biosafety, which have to be followed strictly in all the organizations dealing with GMOs.

Convention on Biological Diversity (CBD)

It was established in 1992 with a focus on conserving biological diversity. It raises the concerns of potential impact of biotechnology application on biodiversity and emphasizes and elaborates the needs and precautions to be taken in safe handling of biotechnology products. Its regulation and guidelines has been the base for the international biosafety regulatory systems through the Cartagena Protocol on Biosafety.

World Trade Organization (WTO)

WTO is an international organization that deals with global rules of trade between countries. It aims to ensure free and smooth flow of trade between nations. A number of WTO agreements such as the Agreement on Application of Sanitary and Phytosanitary Measures and the Technical Barriers to Trade Agreement contain provisions that are relevant to biosafety. Cartagena Protocol tries to ensure that the checks and balances proposed by it work in a mutually supportive manner with the WTO agreements.

Food and Agriculture Organization of the United Nations (FAO)

FAO is playing an important role in encouraging the countries to take the advantage of advanced technologies in different spheres. It maintains the association with a host of nations as well both national and international standards. It has even developed an international portal on food safety, animal and plant health (http://www.ipfsaph.com)

International Centre for Genetic Engineering and Biotechnology (ICGEB)

ICGEB maintains an informatics tool, the Risk Assessment Searching Mechanism (RASM; http://rasm.icgeb.org), which is an online collection of risk assessment documents related to official government decisions concerning the commercial release of GMOs. The documents cover more than 150 GM crops from around the world.

Organization for Economic Co-operation and Development (OECD)

The mission of OECD is to promote policies and provide forums in which governments can work together to share experiences and seek solutions to problems that relate to economic and social well-being of people around the world. As a part of this initiative, OECD has developed BioTrack Online, a website that provides information on environmental, food and feed safety issues relating to modern biotechnology through various consensus documents, product databas, and the regulatory contacts of OECD member countries and other stakeholders.

Information Systems for Biotechnology (ISB)

ISB (http://www.nbiap.vt.edu/) is maintained by the Agricultural Experiment Station at Virginia Tech, Virginia, USA as part of the National Biological Impact Assessment Program administered by the United States of America's Department of Agriculture (USDA) Cooperative State Research, Education, and Extension Service (CSREES). ISB provides information resources pertaining to the development testing and regulatory review of genetically engineered plants, animals and microorganisms.

Centre for Environmental Risk Assessment (CERA)

Established by the non-profit organization, International Life Sciences Institute Research Foundation in March 2009, CERA works towards application of scientific methods in the assessment of agricultural biotechnologies to ensure that biosafety is maintained while reaping the benefits of GM crops in the sustainable production of fibre, fuel and food. Their website (CERA; http://cera-gmc.org/) gives free access to information on biosafety. They also provide information on GM crop database, which include all GM plant products that have cleared all the regulatory approvals all over the world. Each record describes a transformation event and contains the OECD unique identifier, a descriptor, a synopsis of regulatory approvals and product-specific background information.

Many of these organizations work in collaboration with each other to ensure that the safe practices of biotechnological research are followed and we reap the rewards of biotechnology without compromising on the ecological safety, animal and human health.

Indian Biosafety Framework

Indian regulatory system came in to force in 1989 and has necessary regulatory and institutional mechanisms. India has regulatory framework consisting of six statutory committees prescribed by the DBT to assess and ensure the biosafety of GMOs, which are as follows:

(i) Recombinant DNA Advisory Committee (RDAC) to recommend appropriate safety regulations in recombination research, use and applications
(ii) Institutional Biosafety Committee (IBSC) to prepare site specific plans for use of GMO
(iii) Review Committee on Genetic Manipulation (RCGM) to oversee all research project and field trials on GMO
(iv) Genetic Engineering Approval Committee (GEAC) to consider proposals relating to release of GMOs in to environment
(v) State Biotechnology Coordination Committee (SBCC) to inspect, investigate and to take punitive action in case of violation of safety and control measures in the handling of GMOs
(vi) Six District Level Committees (DLCs) to monitor safety regulations in institutions engaged in the use of GMOs and their application in the environment

All the organizations in India work collectively to ensure the biosafety of an environment, human and animal health. Environmental protection and the conservation of natural resources is the key priority of all the organization. These organizations work in coordination with all the international bodies for effective working and sharing information. All these organizations are discussed in detail in the next chapter.

CHAPTER SUMMARY

Biotechnology is a revolutionary field and emerged as a powerful industry. It has the immense potential to redefine and reshape the world around us. But if proper measures are not being taken, it can lead to tragic changes in the natural world. Our very genetically modified tools organism has to be dealt with biosafe environment to avoid any kind of risks associated with it. The Cartagena Protocol on Biosafety focuses on the biosafety regulations for GMOs, products and crops. There are strict regulations that have to be followed under the guidelines of biosafety, which help avoid release in to the environment, and is a valuable tool for supporting environmental and food risks. Many efforts today are made difficult by different stakeholders and countries engaged in the process. People have different values and expectations; only a transparent respectful and vigorous debate can ensure the positive outcome. The global community has already agreed on the regulatory framework in the development of modern biotechnology. The sciences will continue to advance rapidly. To make sure that it is dealt in biosafe environment; the government will have to review the protocol and its procedure effectively after every five years and also improve the various agreements if required. Biosafety will remain the top priority for the national and international environmental and health agenda for many years to come.

MULTIPLE CHOICE QUESTIONS

1. Which of the following involves preventing transmission of disease in the laboratory?
   (i) Biosafety
   (ii) Biosecurity
   (iii) Biohazard
   (iv) Biofuel
2. Biological material being available only to authorized personnel is one of the aspects of biosafety.
   (i) True
   (ii) False
   (iii) Not always true
   (iv) None of the above
3. The Convention on Biodiversity came in force in the year
   (i) 2000 (ii) 1992
   (iii) 1995 (iv) 2003
4. Which is the nodal center for Indian biosafety framework
   (i) Department of Biotechnology
   (ii) Department of Science and Technology
   (iii) Indian Agriculture Research Institute
   (iv) Ministry of Environment and Protection

REVIEW QUESTIONS

1. What is biosafety? What are the concerns related to biosafety?
2. Elaborate on Cartagena Protocol on Biosafety.
3. Describe various organizations that work in harmony to create a biosafe environment.
4. Define the four levels of biosafety.

GMOs: Concerns and Challenges

9

Chapter Objectives:

Genetic engineering and its application have been the most controversial modern technology for decades. This technology is the vital key to increase the economic competition and one of the only solutions to feed the ever-increasing population but at the same time evoke concerns and challenges about health, safety and environment issues. This chapter throws light on this technology and elaborately discusses one of the major concerns of GMO, which is gene flow and other related concerns and its consequences on the plant, animal and environment.

INTRODUCTION

Agriculture has been the mainstay of Indian economy over the years and can be termed as a major success story in terms of food production capability. In the 1960s the overall food production in India was merely 50 million tons and the nation had to largely depend on the import of large amount of grains to feed the ever-growing population. Then, thanks to the Green Revolution, the production grew from 50 to 242 million tons in the last financial year. This increase in production not only provided food security but also made India the exporter of a lot of food grains to other countries. Development of new breeding methods and the meticulous use of improved agricultural technologies such as irrigation systems, chemical fertilizers and pesticides contributed to the success of Green Revolution. Though Green Revolution was successful in creating food security but nutritional security was still a challenge for the plant breeders. They still faced heavy losses in crop production due to damage by insects, pathogens, weeds and biotic and abiotic stresses during both pre- and post-harvest stages. The only solution to the present problem is the use of transgenic technology. Both the breeders and the biotechnologists—plant biotechnologists, molecular biotechnologists and plant geneticists—together need to make an effort to augment the crop productivity and the nutritional quality with the use of conventional breeding and transgenic biotechnology. This is shown in Figure 9.1.

TRANSGENIC TECHNOLOGY

Molecular biology and biotechnology together enabled identification, isolation, modification and cloning of a gene. The transformation of a cloned gene into an organism to create novel traits and

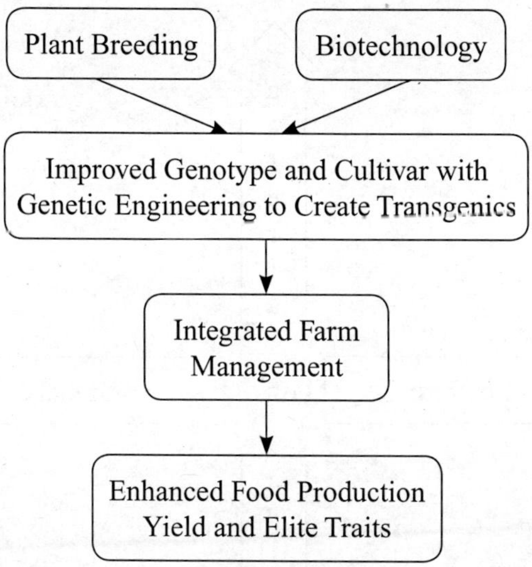

Figure 9.1 *Combined Crop Improvement Programme using Conventional Breeding and Transgenic Technology*

recombinants is called transgenic technology. Transgenic technology enables scientists to transfer one or more gene across species and kingdom barriers. There are five key steps in transgenic technology:

(i) Identification and isolation of desired gene
(ii) Selection of a suitable vector in which the desired gene can be cloned and replicated
(iii) Introduction of the cloned gene into recipient cells
(iv) Stable expression of the introduced gene into functional recipient cells
(v) Regeneration of the stably transformed plant expressing the desired traits.

Heterologous gene transfer that is possible through this technology is shown in Figure 9.2.

Potential of Transgenic Technology

Transgenic technology has opened new horizons in the field of agriculture. It holds great promise to meet the challenges for accelerated and sustainable agriculture production. Transgenic plants have been developed for a variety of purposes like longer shelf-life, pest resistance, disease resistance, biotic and abiotic stress resistance, nutritional improvement, etc. Genetic engineering has helped not only diversification but also genetic restructuring of organisms by which plants can act as bio factories for the production of biologically important molecules, which can be used in diagnostics and therapeutics such as immunoglobulin, interferon, growth factors, recombinant vaccines etc. Transgenic technology has also helped create designer crops with sophisticated and higher level traits. Some such traits are mentioned in Table 9.1.

Plants have been traditionally modified through conventional breeding, which was used to create genetic variability and select desirable genetic combination to develop superior genotypes with higher yield, better tolerance to various biotic and abiotic stresses and enhancing the nutritional quality in crop

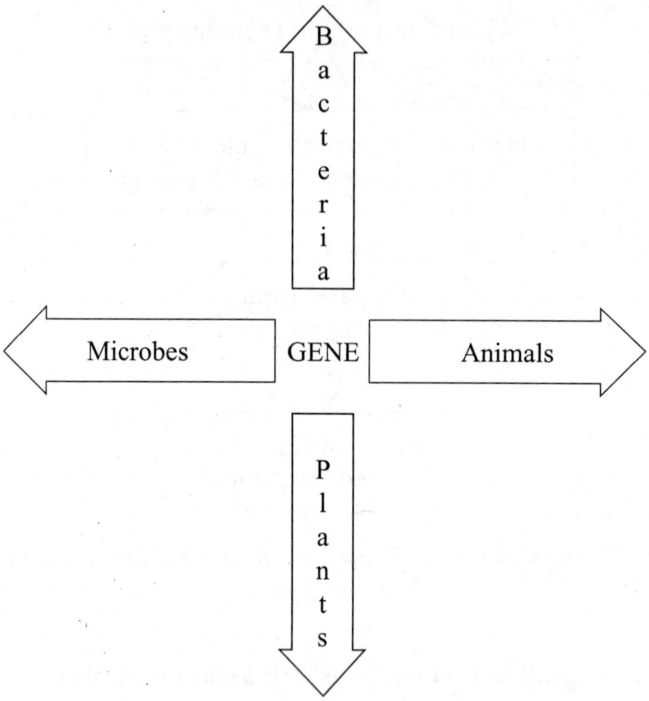

Figure 9.2 *Heterologous Gene Transfer*

plant. However, the limitation of conventional breeding is that one can transfer gene only to the related species. Transgenic approaches, on the other hand, allow for incorporation of the target gene from any genomic background and can be used for crop improvement when no other alternative is possible. However, transgenic approaches are not as biosafe as conventional breeding approaches. A comparative account of biosafety assessment in transgenic and conventionally bred plants is given in Table 9.2.

Table 9.1 *Designer Crops with Elite Traits*

Agronomic trait	Biotic stress like pest resistance Abiotic stress like drought, cold, heat
Reproduction	Sex barrier, male sterility, seedlessness
Quality trait	Yield, postharvest shelf life, nutrient value addition, industrial processing, taste, ornamentals etc.
Novel crop products	Oil, protein and polymers
Renewable resources	Biofuels
Molecular farming through bioreactor plants	Plant bodies, edible vaccine, interferon, herbal medicines, growth factors

Table 9.2 *Comparison of Biosafety Assessment in Transgenic and Conventionally Bred Plants*

Characteristics	Conventional	Transgenic
Gene pool	Restricted to related and sexually compatible species	Genes can be used from any class of organism
Modified phenotype	Potentially thousands of genes can be recombined	Only one or few genes are introduced
	Genetic actions and interactions can be difficult to analyse with accuracy	There is a potential to change plant fundamentally
	Long history of plant breeding means that phenotypic variations usually falls within a familiar range	Change can be analysed with great precision

Concerns and Challenges of GMO

The application of biotechnology offers innumerable benefits to human needs and environment. Advanced biotechnology has generated a series of potential applications in agriculture, animal husbandry, medical applications, environmental management and industrial products. But at the same time there have been growing concerns on the adverse effects of biotechnology. These concerns relate to the harm to the environment, animal and human health as a result of extensive release of GM crops in the ecosystem.

Concerns based on social, ethical and moral standards, beliefs and cultural values will be discussed in a subsequent chapter on bioethics. In this chapter, we will discuss various concerns related to the adverse effect of biotechnology or genetic engineering on environment, animal and plants.

Animal Biotechnology

The research in animal biotechnology can be characterized into four categories:

- Understanding human genetic diseases by producing transgenic animals to provide information on genetic function and regulation
- Producing potential recombinant pharmaceutical proteins from transgenic animals, which can be used for human medicine, e.g. producing transgenic goats or cows to produce protein in their milk, which can be used in pharmaceuticals
- Production of xeno-organs from transgenic pigs for human xenotransplantation
- Manipulation of fertilized eggs and *in vitro* fertilization to help human-assisted reproduction and breeding of endangered animal species.

Concerns Related to Animal Biotechnology Research

The concerns in the field of animal biotechnology are as follows:

- Probable impact on environment
- Concerns over the safety of food produced from genetically modified animals—allergenicity, toxicity, infectious virus or prion causing diseases like mad cow disease

- Xeno transplant of the organs from animals to humans increases the risk of suppression of recipient immunity. Also there is a risk of cross infection due to transmission of pathogens
- If the animal is produced for biopharmaceutical protein, there are the chances of drug residues in animal that can create drug resistance if consumed as food.

Therefore any intentional use of such animals needs tight safety assessments before it can be used for human in any form.

Plant Biotechnology

The rapid progress in transgenic biotechnology has promoted the production of genetically modified crops. The research in plant biotechnology is mainly concerned with the following areas:

- Micro propagation of plants using plant tissue culture techniques
- Production of transgenic plant with elite traits such as resistance to disease, pest and environmental stress
- Production of plants for environment cleanup (phytoremediation)
- Development of plants with enhanced nutritional value like golden rice, transgenic soya with cholesterol-reducing peptide, etc.
- Transgenic crop with higher yield; transgenic crop to remove natural allergens and toxins like allergenic protein in groundnuts.
- Increasing shelf-life to reduce postharvest losses like flavr savr its the first transgenic tomato.
- Using plants as a bioreactor for biopharmaceuticals, edible vaccines for humans and livestock, etc.

Concerns Related to Transgenic Plant Biotechnology

Concerns in the field of plant biotechnology are as follows:

- Presence of allergens and toxins in food
- Unknown results from the transgenic plants, which can harm environment and humans
- Fear of contaminating human food with genetically modified food, which is not meant for humans like in case of starlink maize
- Development of antibiotic resistance due to use of antibiotic resistance marker genes in the gene construct
- Gene flow of transgenic genes to wild species and threat to biodiversity
- Interactions and influences of transgene and GM plants on diversity, ecosystem, soil microbes and target organisms
- Labeling of GM food
- Social and the economic impact of GM crops to the society.

Concerns over introduction of new agriculture and food technologies is not new; each innovation in food production has come with its own set of potential risks ranging from increased pesticide exposure in conventional agriculture to higher pathogen exposure from organic farming. Any attempt to create a better crop plant will be accompanied by potential consequences.

GENE FLOW

Gene flow is the natural process of transfer of genes from one population or one species to the other. This process is key to evolution but in the case of transgenic crops, the flow of one or more transgene could have adverse environmental, socioeconomic or ethical impact. This transgene flow from a GM crop to a non-GM crop or to population of weedy/wild relative has been one of the central ecological or environmental risk associated with the trangene technology. Such environmental risk includes potential adverse effect on natural biodiversity and survival of wild population as plants that will continue to evolve irrespective of natural or selective pressure.

There are two types of gene flow:

(i) **Vertical Gene Flow:** This kind of gene flow occurs through interspecific hybridization mediated by pollen, which results in the transfer of the entire genome. Here the genes are transferred from parents to offspring and express only in the next generation.

(ii) **Horizontal Gene Flow:** This occurs only among unrelated species like plant and microbe or between two distinct microbes without the involvement of sexual reproduction.

Gene flow can be mediated through three ways in the environment:

- *Gene Flow through Pollen*: This occurs when pollen grains travel from one plant to another resulting in fertilization. Here different populations are involved. Wind, animals and water current can serve as a media of transfer.
- *Gene Flow through Seeds*: This occurs through natural dispersal of seeds by animals, wind, water or by some other means from one population to another.
- *Gene Flow through Vegetative Propagule*: This occurs through natural dispersal of vegetative organs like tillers, roots, stems, tuber and rhizomes or by animals, wind or water.

Pollen- and seed-mediated gene flow is more common than vegetative gene flow. When transgenic crops are involved, gene flow can further be categorized into three types based on the flow of transgene from one crop to the other.

- *Crop-to-Crop Gene Flow*: Transgene movement from GM crop to non-GM crop
- *Crop-to-Weed Gene Flow*: Transgene movement from GM crop to conspecific weed
- *Crop-to-Wild Plant Gene Flow*: Transgene movement from GM crop to wild relative species

Such pollination will result in hybridization and entry of transgene into wild population leading to different ecological and evolutionary consequences as shown in Figure 9.3. For example, pollen-mediated gene flow can produce hybrids between one crop like transgenic rice and common wild rice and further backcrosses between the hybrids and wild individual will again stimulate the spread of crop genes in a wild rice population through introgression—movement of genes of one species in to the gene pool of another species by repeated backcrossing of an interspecific hybrid with one of its parent.

Hybridization involves pollination and fertilization of the recipient by a pollen donor. Transgenes that are most likely to be retained in the population of wild relatives are those that have enhanced fitness and they increase the ability of the transgene hybrid to compete in the population under natural condition in the ecosystem, producing superior offspring due to hybrid vigor.

Hybridization between a GM and non-GM crop or a wild relative can occur in one generation from which the escaped transgene may then integrate into the genome of non-GM wild crop relative

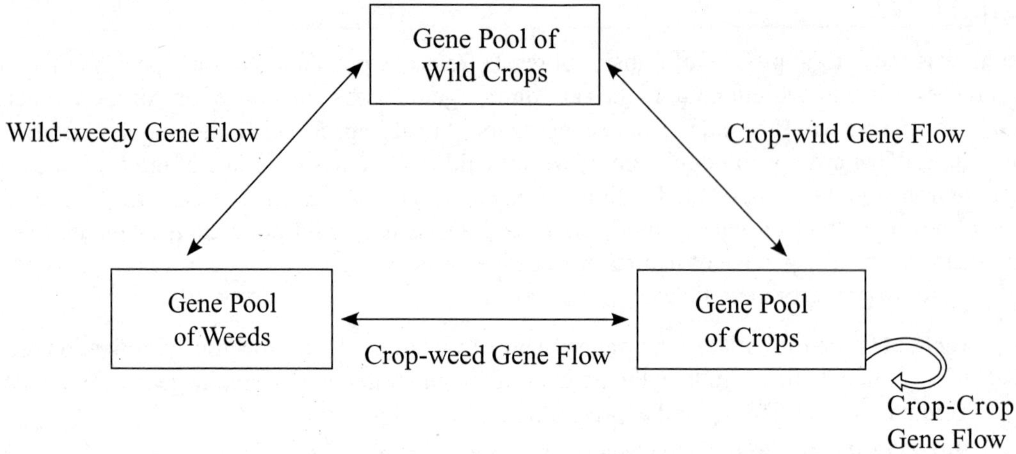

Figure 9.3 *Two Directional Gene Flow Among Cultivated Plant Species, Weedy Types and Wild Relatives*

through further introgression, resulting in the gradual integration of the transgene into plant genome of wild relative through consecutive backcrossing. The hybridization and introgression will promote the long-term persistence and dissemination of transgene in the population of wild and weed and this may cause environmental and ecological adversities as shown in Figure 9.4.

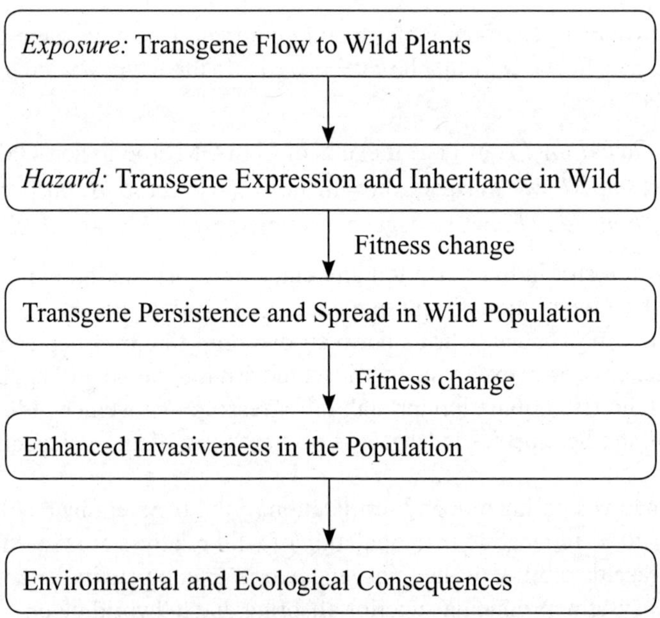

Figure 9.4 *Risk Assessment for the Environmental Consequences caused Transgene Escape through Gene Flow from GM Crop to its Wild Relative Species*

Major Consequences of Gene Flow

Contamination of Non-GM Crops

When transgene moves from GM crops to their non-GM crop counterparts either through seed, pollen or vegetative-mediated gene flow, contamination of GM and non-GM crops happen. If the transgene becomes present in seed or the vegetative part of edible non-GM crop that has to be consumed by human or used as animal feed, it may give rise to food and feed safety concerns, especially if the transgene is designed to alter the composition of food crop.

Change of Genetic Diversity of Traditional Crops

Extensive cultivation of GM crops will pose potential threats to the genetic diversity of traditional crops. The loss of such genetic diversity will reduce the capacity to breed more productive and stress-resistant crops.

Since transgenic crops reinforce genetic homogeneity and are grown in large monocultures—practice of growing only single genetic variant of a food crop—they contribute to loss of biodiversity. 'Novel traits' in transgenic crops could affect dynamics of population and their interactions and may lead to extinction of one or more varieties. These novel traits could also affect the soil and animals who consume them in unknown ways, thus impacting insects, bees and birds that either live in the surrounding soil or consume a plant product directly or indirectly.

Change in Farming Practices

Some GM crops have been engineered using *Bt* toxins to prevent insects from damaging the crops. However, to prevent insects from becoming resistant to the *Bt* toxin, farming practices need to be changed to grow refugee crop (non-*Bt*) adjacent to the fields of transgenic crops to act as hosts for the targeted pest. Such a change helps reduce chances of insects becoming resistant to *Bt* toxins since the likelihood of a toxin-resistant insect mating a non-toxin resistant insect increases, reducing the resistant gene frequency in the insect population.

Another possible change in farming practice could arise if the genetic use restrictiony technolog (GURT) is commercialized. Also known as terminator technology, it causes second generation seeds to be sterile and they cannot be used for the next season. In such cases, farmers would have to buy fresh seeds each year from the company providing the GM seeds.

Due to thefprotest by farmers, NGOs and some governments, the technology has not been commercialized and Monsanto, the largest producer of transgenic seeds, has pledged not to commercialize the same. However, it is worthwhile to understand the two types of terminator technology: V-GURT and T-GURT.

V-GURT: This type of GURT produces sterile seeds, which are restricted at the plant variety level (and hence the name V-GURT), which means farmers cannot save the seeds for further planting.

T-GURT: This type of GURT modifies the crop in such a way that the genetic enhancement engineered into the crop does not work until the crop plant is treated with a chemical that is sold by the company. Farmers can save the seeds for the next year, but the enhanced trait will not be activated in the subsequent year unless the crop is treated with the activator compound. This technology is restricted at the trait level, hence the term T-GURT.

Concerns with Plants used as Bioreactors

Other concerns relate to plant species that are manipulated to produce industrial products, molecules or chemicals. These species are unsuitable as food for human as they have no safe record. Gene flow from such GM crops to general human food chain will create adverse effects and even novel hazards can arise from gene flow because expression of a protein from one food crop may be different from its expression in another crop.

Creation of New Weeds

Transgene flow to wild and weedy species may accentuate the characteristics of weediness, leading to greater persistence and invasiveness of already prevalent weeds. Transgene flow can potentially make weeds tolerant to herbicide. Transgenic herbicide resistance is a trait that can easily be acquired by Bao-Rong Lu wild and weedy species through gene flow. The cultivation of herbicide-resistant crops will certainly complicate the situation of weed control because resistance to different types of herbicides is inherited as a dominant Mendelian trait that easily spreads to weed crops by cross-pollination Figure 9.5 outlines a process of assessment of such environmental risk caused by pollen-mediated gene flow.

Other Concerns Related to Transgenics

Co-Suppression of Endogenous Genes

There are a number of problems associated with transgene integration and expression. Transgenes might not follow Mendelian segregation and their expression can be significantly affected by the integration position of transgenic DNA in host genomes. Transgene could become unstable over generations and might not get expressed (transgene silencing) and this might have negative impact on the expression of endogenous genes through a process called co-suppression. In co-suppression, transgene silencing is accompanied by non-expression of an endogenous gene, which could change the innate properties of the host.

Presence of Antibiotic Marker Gene

As a part of genetic modification processes, antibiotic marker genes are used to selectively identify grow the transformed cells since normal plant cells get killed when the antibiotic or the herbicide is added to the plant culture media. Though essential in the laboratory for selection of transformed cells, the antibiotic marker gene serves no interest after that. However, it remains a part of the genetically modified plant.

As a result, such crops threaten the already growing problem of antibiotic resistance. This can lead to bacteria becoming antibiotic-resistant and infections would become more difficult to treat.

Allergenecity

Another challenge related to food safety with the use of transgenic crops is the potential of GM food to introduce allergens in to food supply. If the gene products have known allergen, then the allergen would be present in the transgenic crop. So, before the transgenic crop is commercialized, it has to undergo strict regulation through various regulatory and a biosafety committee to assess that it is safe for the consumption of humans and the environment.

Various Aspects of Assessment and Evaluation on GMO to Ascertain Biosafety

To comprehend these risks and concerns, it is important to evaluate the risk through risk assessments as already been discussed in Chapter 1. Risk assessment in general indicates a critical and productive exercise that helps to determine the occurrence or magnitude of relevant risks. The objective of risk assessment is to reduce the risk of exposure to the environment to a minimum level. Its assessment depends on the possibility of potential adverse effect from a transgenic plant or GMO. Various biosafety studies needed to ascertain the safety of the transgenic event are listed in the following:

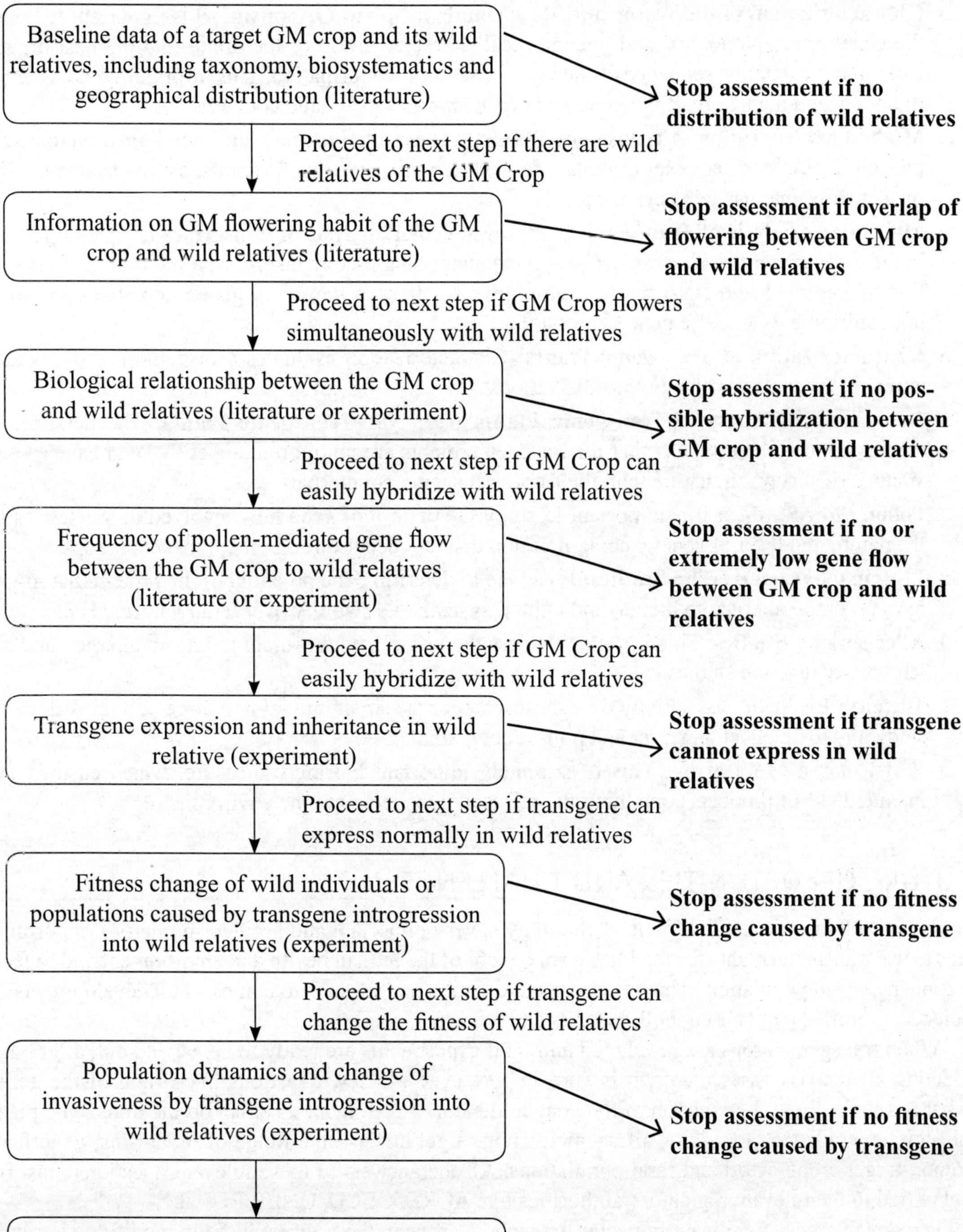

Figure 9.5 *An Outlined Process of Assessment for Environmental Risk Caused by Transgene Escape from a GM Crop to its Wild Relatives Through Pollen-mediated Gene Flow*

- **Characterization of the Vector and Donor and Recipient Organism:** It is important to know the genetic, morphological and phenotypical characterization of the donor and the host organisms, and the detailed sequence of the vector used in transformation. This information is essential to understand the nature of the gene and organisms and its related concerns.
- **Method of Generation of Transgenic Plants:** It is essential to know the technique used to insert plasmid DNA in to recipient organism to generate primary transformants, as this is also one of the concerns and has to be evaluated.
- **Molecular Analysis of Transgenic Plants:** Molecular analysis of transgenics is very important in the evaluation of risk assessments as it evaluates single-copy insertion of the transgene. Insertion of any unwanted DNA might lead to adverse effect of unwanted gene interactions and may not contribute to the false gene expression.
- **Characterization of Transgenic Plants:** Characterization evaluates transgenic plants for any agronomic penalty or phenotypic aberrations.
- **Non-Competitiveness of Transgenic Plants with Non-Transgenic Plants:** The persistence studies are done to establish that the transgenic plants are not more competitive and have an advantage of survival in nature than their non-transgenic counterpart.
- **Pollen Flow Studies:** It is important to study the pattern of gene flow involved in transgenes in the nature and level of genetic contamination that can occur through the transgenic crops.
- **Protein Characterisation Studies:** It is done to determine the potential of the protein that might have potential allergen to human and animal systems, its stability over temperature, pH etc.
- **Allergenicity Studies:** This is done to assess the homology of protein to known allergen and allergenicity reaction studies.
- **Toxicity:** Evaluation of toxicity on fish, insects, birds, small animal and large animal is done to study any toxic effect on target and non-target animal species
- **Post-Release Monitoring:** This is extremely important biosafety measure, which ensures the intended use of products containing the released transgene into the environment.

FUTURE OPPORTUNITIES AND CHALLENGES

It is very well known that transgenic technology is very important and provides numerous opportunities to use transgenic plants for the long-term benefit of the human health and environment and to feed a growing world population, which is expected to double in the years to come. As all developments in science, modified plants bring both benefits and concerns.

When transgenic crops are developed and field experiments are ready to be carried out, after considering all the risk assessments, it is very important to ask few questions like origin of the gene, what is known about the function of the gene in the donor organism, its effect on the transgenic plant phenotype, evidence of toxicity, allergenicity, non-target effects on a range of organisms, gene flow to non-target crops, weed and feral populations. All the answers to these relevant questions must be submitted to the relevant regulatory authorities like ACRE, OECD, UNEP, EU, etc.

Perhaps the most significant impact of transgenic crops in the future will be in modifying agricultural strategies. Many of the principles that will need to be applied to guide the use of several different herbicide-tolerant genes in the same species or similar insect-resistant strategy in different crops will present important challenges to manage the agricultural environment in new ways and all of this advancement requires some concerted action in future.

CHAPTER SUMMARY

Various risks associated with GM crops may pose potential biosafety problems for food and health, environmental, socioeconomics and ethics. Potential environmental consequences from transgene escape through gene flow essentially depend on whether or not the transgene will express normally in wild relative through introgression and invasiveness. It is possible to significantly reduce transgene outflow by the use of proper regulatory strategies and methodologies so as to protect our environment and ecology, human and animal health from any kind of adverse effect of transgenic technology.

MULTIPLE CHOICE QUESTIONS

1. What do you understand by elite traits?
   a. Novel traits
   b. Advanced traits
   c. Traits not present in the crops
   d. All the above
2. Xenotransplantation is a
   a. Biosafety issue
   b. Bioethical issue
   c. Social issue
   d. All the above
3. Gene flow refers to
   a. Movement of transgenic gene to non-transgenics
   b. Movement of gene within the same species
   c. Genes present in the gene pool
   d. All the above
4. V-GURT and T-GURT technology is used by
   a. Mayhco seeds
   b. Biocon
   c. Shantha Biotech
   d. Monsanto
5. Contamination of crops means
   a. Gene flow from the target crop to non-target crop
   b. Crops are contaminated with pollutants
   c. Low pesticides
   d. High doses of *Bt* toxins

REVIEW QUESTIONS

1. What is transgenic technology and how is it beneficial to mankind?
2. What are the different risk assessments associated with genetically modified plants?
3. What is gene flow and how is it mediated in the environment and what hazards are associated with it?
4. Write a short note on
   a. Terminator technology
   b. Loss of biodiversity because of GM crops
   c. Use of antibiotic marker gene
   d. Development of insect-resistant pests

National and International Regulatory Mechanism for GMO

10

Chapter Objective:

It is well known that the applications of biotechnology are ever-expanding. The production and release of the resulting genetically engineered organism have raised concern about possible risk to human and to the environment. Accordingly all biotechnological research has to be carried within a regulatory biosafety framework to conform to the establishment of national and international regulatory structure and biosafety guidelines, as it will ensure the GMO continues to be safe and does not expose employees, the communities and the environment to any possible hazard. Keeping this in mind this chapter will take students to different national and international regulatory bodies and their framework, rules and guidelines and its management.

INTRODUCTION

Biotechnology is a technique that has the potential to modify the product or to improve plants, animals and also to develop microorganisms, which produce unique molecules. It uses cell and tissue culture, recombinant DNA technology, and molecular and cell biology to create a new organism with desired traits. This technology focuses on cloning, overexpression, purification and biopharmaceuticals such as insulin, somatotropin etc. Along with its numerous benefits in health care and agriculture, processing industry, environmental cleanup, there are also concerns regarding its possible risks and the hazards arising from genetically engineered organisms. The main areas of its impact are environment, human and animal health. It is very important to control the safety, efficacy and regulation of GM products, which includes pharmaceuticals, veterinary medicines, medical devices, agrochemicals, cosmetics etc, also to promote safe lab practices, procedures, and proper use of containment, equipment facilities, risk assessment and risk management, evaluation of GMO, etc.

All the new development using recombinant DNA technology (RDT) and genetic engineering requires the mandatory approval from the different regulatory systems for the assessment of probable risk, which is followed by the adherence to biosafety guidelines before the product can be commercialized. The regulatory affairs committees keep the track of all the scientific research, they advice all legal and scientific restraints and requirements, they collect, collate, evaluate all the scientific data that is obtained from the various research and development departments and institute.

To address the concerns, biosafety regulations have been developed, which involve research in transgenic crops, genetically modified organism and transgenic animal and their commercialization. The

Convention on Biological Diversity (CBD) has developed a legally binding international instrument to address the issue of biosafety. A protocol on biosafety addressing transboundary movements of GMOs was adopted by CBD and came in to force in the name of Cartagena Protocol on Biosafety.

According to the protocol, it carries out negotiation necessary to obtain marketing authorization for genetically engineered products. They give strategic and technical advice right from the start of the development of the product. They also build a link between the company and the worldwide regulatory agencies like United States Food and Drug administration (USFDA) and European Union of Drug Regulatory Affairs (EUDRA). All the companies employ associates to review goods manufacturing practices documents, which are one of the legal regulations by FDA to ensure effectiveness of the product developed. All the risks associated with research and development of new bioengineered product requires realistic legislative policy at national and international levels, as it is a very critical and important issues for biotech enterprises.

In almost every country in the world, each type of product is regulated by a different body and often has its own distinct regulation. In some countries, the regulations and procedures are very liberal while in some countries they are very stringent, and in some countries the regulations are yet to be developed. Here we will discuss various international and national regulatory organizations to ensure biosafe environment, human and animal health.

INTERNATIONAL REGULATORY BODIES

World Trade Organization

World Trade Organization (WTO) is mainly involved in establishing international trade in genetically modified food. It plays a vital role in the biosafety of the food products derived from genetic manipulations. Its main features are two agreements. The first is the Sanitary and Phytosanitary Measures (SPS). This agreement deals with the application of food safety , animal and plant health regulation. The second agreement is technical barrier to trade (TBT). It deals with the possibility that no domestic testing, regulation and standards and other procedure create unnecessary obstacle to trade.

Organization for Economic Cooperation and Development (OECD)

This organization is the pivotal organization for the interaction and coordination of the biotechnology regulations. It deals with the assessments of safety of GMO. It focuses on the information related to the regulation of the product of modern biotechnology. It ensures that the GMO is environmentally safe, safe as food and feed. It contains various consensus, documents, guidelines, database etc. OECD is working on the two areas in creating harmonization in different countries to promote and develop the beneficial regulation to safeguard research. It also addresses the various important aspects, on environment, risk assessment of GMO, plant, animal, microbes, food and feed.

Food and Agriculture Organization (FAO)

FAO deals with the assessment of GMO and also guide member countries in building up the technical and institutional information, collaborative regional approaches for harmonization of biosafety procedure, policies and regulations. FAO has taken a lead in expanding knowledge in areas of post-release monitoring, environmental and sociological impact, and consumer issue of modern biotechnology. This is done by the active participation of both national and international organizations.

Codex Alimentarious Commission (CAC)

The CAC is a joint body of the Food and Agriculture Organization and World Health Organization. It looks at the development, collection of food safety standards and guidelines. The main aim of CAC is to protect the consumers and to facilitate international food trade through the harmonization of science-based standards. The working principles are designed as a framework for undertaking risk analysis on the safety and the nutritional aspects of food derived from modern biotechnology. It deals with the hazard identification, risk management, risk communication and post-marketing monitoring.

Convention on Biological Diversity

Cartagena Protocol was developed under CBD. It provides rules for the safe transfer, handling and disposal of LMO. Two main features of this organization are the Advanced Information Agreement (AIA) and the precautionary approach. The AIA provides prior assessment by the importing country that is intended to introduce GMO in to the environment. It requires the complete documents for the use of LMO, its relevant trait, information regarding handling, storage transport and use along with full report on risk assessment. In the other approach, it deals with making decisions to import, the protocol allow the precautionary approach, which can be used to ban or restrict GMO if there is any kind of lacuna of scientific certainty due to insufficient information on the potential risk of LMO, which can have an adverse effect on biodiversity and human health. Table 10.1 shows all the international organizations with their functions and regulations.

Table 10.1 *Various Regulatory Bodies with Their Working and Specifications*

International Biosafety Organisation	Function	Regulation	Salient Feature
World Trade Organization	The main function of WTO is to develop international trade in GM products	Its regulation is involved in two agreements namely: (1) Technical barrier to trade and (2) sanitary and phytosanitary measures	
Organization for Economic Cooperation and Development (OECD)	Its function is to assess the complete safety of GMO and LMO in the environment, or its food and feed safety to human and animal. It is in collaboration with the other member countries for all the information regarding GMO	Its regulation includes addressing the aspects of environment risks and safety, assessment of GMO plants and animals and microbes and the GMO food	
Food and Agriculture Organization (FAO)	Its function includes the safety assessment of GMOs		

(Continued)

Table 10.1 (*Continued*)

International Biosafety Organisation	Function	Regulation	Salient Feature
Convention of Biological Diversity	Its function is that it provides rules and regulations for safe transfer, handling and waste disposal of LMOs during the experimentation.	It regulates by following a protocol the advance information agreement (AIA) and the precautionary approach	– The AIA provides for a prior assessment by importing country of GMOs intentionally introduced into the environment like seeds for plantation, live fish for release etc. This agreement calls for documentation and identification of LMOs, which includes the relevant trait, information handling, storage, transport and use along with a full report or risk assessment. – In making the decision to import, the protocol allows a precautionary approach to be used to restrict or ban the GMO if there is a lack of scientific certainty due to insufficient information on the potential risks that LMOs can have on biodiversity and human health.
World Health Organization (WHO)	Safety assessment of GMOs		
Codex Alimentarious Commission (CAC)	CAC together with FAO and WHO responsible for the developing guidelines and suggestions for the food derived from biotechnological applications	It regulates the proper guidelines for safety assessment for the research in food technology from genetically modified plants	

NATIONAL REGULATORY BODIES

To ensure safety of the environment, biodiversity, human and animal health from the use of GMO and its product, the governments all over the world framed their own specific regulatory mechanism and the guidelines on the use of modern biotechnology. Government of India has evolved its regulatory mechanism for development, evaluation and release of biotechnology product. The Ministry of Environment and Forests has notified rules for manufacture, use, import, export, storage of hazardous microorganisms and genetically engineered organisms under Environment Protection Act, 1986.

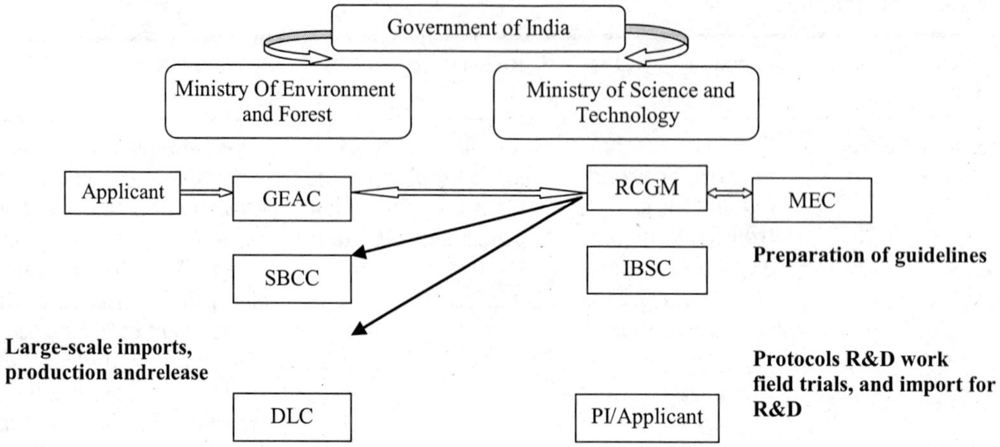

Figure 10.1 *General Procedure for the Approval of Environmental Release of Transgenic Crops after Evaluation of Different Committees*

Six competent authorities have been established as the regulatory bodies for dealing GMO in research and in commercial applications as can be seen in Figure 10.1. These are as follows:

- Institutional Biosafety Committee (IBSC)
- Review Committee on Genetic Manipulation (RCGM)
- Genetic Engineering Approval Committee (GEAC)
- State Biotechnology Coordination Committee (SBCC)
- District Level Committee (DLC)
- Monitoring cum Evaluation Committee (MEC).

Institutional Biosafety Committee (IBSC)

The ISBC is constituted in the organization or an institute where recombinant DNA work has been conducted. One of the nominees in the department acts as the chairman and DBT nominates one nominee from its department. They ensure the adherence of biosafety guideline on research and development product using recombinant DNA techniques. There are the investigators who are required to inform the IBSC about the status and the result of the experiments being conducted. The institutions involved in research process are required to prepare along with the assistance of ISBC, and an advanced onsite emergency plan according to the manual and guidelines of RCGM. IBSC also ensures experimentation at the designated location, adherence to the approved protocols and containment facilities, etc.

Review Committee on Genetic Manipulation (RCGM)

The RCGM is constituted by DBT and functions in the DBT, Ministry in Science and Technology, to monitor the safety aspects of research projects involved in GMO. The purpose of this committee is to review all ongoing research and development projects involving high-risk category and controlled field experiments being conducted by applicant to bring out guidelines, manuals procedures, etc. on handling GMO for production, sale import for research with a view to ensure environmental safety.

RCGM can authorize imports of transgenic germplasm for research and development work, experiments with biosafety level three (BSL3) with appropriate containment measures and generation of relevant biosafety data on the recombinant products.

Genetic Engineering Approval Committee

The GEAC is constituted and based in the Ministry of Environment and Forests (MOEF). It is responsible for the approval of activities involving large-scale use of GMOs in research and in industrial production and application. GEAC permits the use of GMOs and its product and then its commercial applications. It can also authorize large-scale production and release of GMOs and products in to the environment. GEAC can adopt the procedures for restriction and even prohibition production, sale or import and the use of GMO both for research and application under Environmental Protection Act.

State Biotechnology Coordination Committee (SBCC)

The SBCC is located at the state level constituted by the respective state government. It acts as the nodal agency at the state level to assess damages if any from the release of GMO. It has the power to inspect, investigate and take required action in case of violation of statutory provisions through the nodal department of the state pollution control board, directorate of health and medical services. The committee is required to periodically review the safety and control measures in various industries and institutions handling GMO and hazardous microbes and also take onsite control measures.

District Level Committee (DLC)

The DLC is constituted below the state government level in the district where the biotechnology product functions. It is headed by the district collector who also monitors safety regulations in the use of GMO and hazardous microbes. The committee investigates and report violation to the SBCC and GEAC.

Monitoring cum Evaluation Committee

This committee has been constituted in the DBT under RCGM to monitor and evaluate the field trials of transgenic crops approved either by RCGM or GEAC. The committee consists of agricultural scientist, molecular biologist and environmental scientist. MEC evaluates the field trials form the view of agronomic advantage of transgenic crop and environmental safety. It can recommend RCGM, GEAC for further consideration for studies or release of transgenic crops before releasing them in to the environment. In Table 10.2, we can see all the agencies involved in the implementation of biosafety under rules 1989 of EPA 1986.

The applicant involved in the research on the transgenic crop first needs to inform IBSC about the research work intended to be carried out. The IBSC notes the intension of the work at the institutional level and assess its risk category. Then it recommends to RCGM for the approval to conduct the research. Then the RCGM instructs the applicant to generate data about the toxicity, allergenicity and the environmental and agronomic advantage of the GMOs and products. RCGM regularly reviews the progress of the work. The applicant is needed to submit the record of all the data generated on transgenic at the lab and greenhouse level. After RCGM satisfies about the safety of the GMO and recombinant DNA products, it recommends the GEAC for granting approval for environmental clearance for release in to the environment.

To facilitate the regulation and rules, DBT has evolved recombinant DNA guidelines for the research in transgenic plants, regarding its toxicity and allergenicity in plants and guidelines for pre-clinical and clinical for the evaluation of recombinant DNA vaccines, biological and other medical diagnostics. Apart from these guidelines, the Government of India has also amended different Acts and Rules to manufacture and release of GMO and products in to the environment. These include drug and cosmetic rules (8th Amendment), Plant Varieties and Protection and Farmers Rights Act 2001, Drug Policy 2002 and National Seed Policy 2002.

Table 10.2 *Indian Regulatory Framework*

National Organization on Biosafety	Functions of the Organization	Regulation of the Organizations Related to GMOs	Main Features of the Organizations
Ministry of Environment and Forests (MoEF)	All the rules of Environmental Protection Act 1986	It regulates the rule of manufacture, use, import and export and storage of hazardous microorganism	Rules and procedure of handling GMOs and hazardous organisms. It restricts a person from importing, manufacture transport, store, distribute or sale of any food, feed, raw or processed or any ingredient of food, food additives or any food product that contains GM material, without the approval of the GEAC.
Genetic Engineering Approval Committee (GEAC)	GEAC functions as a body under the Department of Environment and Forests and Wildlife for approval of activities involving large-scale use of hazardous microorganisms and recombinants in research and industrial production from the environmental angle. The Committee shall also be responsible for approval of proposals relating to release of genetically engineered organisms and products into the environment including experiment field trials.	A Biotechnology Coordination Committee under the GEAC functions as the legal and statutory body with judicial powers to inspect, investigate and take punitive action in case of violation of statutory provision under EPA. Issues for action include review and control, and monitoring of large scale use of GMOs in R&D and industrial production, environmental release and experimental field trials.	

(*Continued*)

Table 10.2 (*Continued*)

National Organization on Biosafety	Functions of the Organization	Regulation of the Organizations Related to GMOs	Main Features of the Organizations
The Review Committee on Genetic Manipulation (RCGM)	RCGM monitors the safety-related aspects of ongoing research projects involving GMOs. It brings out manuals of guidelines specifying procedures for regulatory process, activities involving GMOs in research, use and application from environmental safety angle (Recombinant DNA Safety Guidelines 1992 and Revised Guidelines for Research in Transgenic Plants 1998).	(Recombinant DNA Safety Guidelines 1992 and Revised Guidelines for Research in Transgenic Plants 1998).	The Review Committee on Genetic Manipulation shall includes representatives of (a) Department of Biotechnology, (b) Indian Council of Medical Research, (c) Indian Council of Agricultural Research, (d) Council of Scientific and Industrial Research (e) Other experts in their individual capacity. Review Committee on Genetic Manipulation may appoint sub-groups. The Review Committee on Genetic Manipulation lays down procedures restricting or prohibiting production sale importation and use of such genetically engineered organisms of cells as are mentioned in the Schedule.
Recombinant DNA Advisory Committee (RDAC) and Institutional Biosafety Committee (IBSC)	The RDAC takes note of development at national and international levels in biotechnology on recombinant research, use and application while the IBSC is the nodal point for interaction within an institute, university, commercial organization included in rDNA research or implementation of rDNA guidelines.	Implementation of two guidelines and Revised Guidelines for Research in Transgenic Plants 1998).	IBSC constituted by an occupier or any person including research institutions handling microorganisms/genetically engineered organisms. The committee shall comprise the heads of the institution scientists engaged in DNA work a medical expert and a nominee of the Department of Biotechnology. The occupier or any person including research institutions having microorganisms/genetically engineered organisms shall prepare the assistance of the Institutional Biosafety Committee (IBSC), an up-to-date on-site emergency plan according to the manuals/ guidelines of the RCGM and make available copies to the District Level Committee/ State Biotechnology Co-ordinating Committee and the Genetic Engineering Approval Committee.

(*Continued*)

Table 10.2 (*Continued*)

National Organization on Biosafety	Functions of the Organization	Regulation of the Organizations Related to GMOs	Main Features of the Organizations
State Biotechnology Coordination Committee (SBCC)		Environmental Protection Act 1986	A State Biotechnology Coordination Committee in the states wherever necessary is established. It has powers to inspect, investigate and take punitive action in case of violations of statutory provisions through the Nodal Department and the State Pollution Control Board/Directorate of Health/Medical Services. The Committee reviews periodically the safety and control measures in the various industries/institutions handling genetically engineered organisms/hazardous microorganisms.
District Level Committee (DLC)		Environmental Protection Act, 1986	A District Level Biotechnology Committee (DLC) in the districts wherever necessary is established under the District Collectors to monitor the safety regulations in installations engaged in the use of genetically modified organisms/hazardous microorganisms and its applications in the environment. The District Level Committee/or any other persons authorized on its behalf shall visit the installation engaged in activity involving genetically engineered organisms, hazardous microorganisms, formulate information chart, find out hazards and risks associated with each of these installations and coordinate activities with a view to meeting any emergency. They also prepare an off-site emergency plan. The District Level Committee shall regularly submit its report to the State Biotechnology Co-ordination Committee/Genetic Engineering Approval Committee.

REGULATORY MEASURES FOR BIOSAFETY

The legal framework that governs GMOs in India is regulated under Environmental Protection Act 1986 (EPA). The Central government formulated the manufacture, export, import, use and storage of harmful and hazardous microbes, genetically engineered organism or cells. These rules are formulated to regulate all spheres of research and large-scale application of GMO and its products in India or imported into India through transboundary movements. These rules are mandatory for risk assessment and regulatory approval for every release of GMO and GMO products.

These rules and guidelines mandate specifically on

- strict prohibition of unintentional release or discharge of GMO and
- prohibition of sale, import and use of substances and products, plants, animals including ingredient in food stuff. Food which contains or derived from genetically engineered organisms and cells or microbes without the prior approval of the authorities.

Revised guidelines also include research in transgenic plants for toxicity and allergenicity evaluation. Thus, the 1998 guidelines demand for a demonstration that the transgenic crop is both environmentally safe and economically viable. Regulatory system comprises of legal binding regulation authority and responsibility between DBT and MoEF. The DBT was constituted under the Ministry of Science and Technology in 1986, for the purpose of planning, promotion and coordination of BT programme. The 1989 Rules constitute regulatory committees under DBT and MoEF for giving one approval for GMO research and development and its commercial use. DBT is responsible for considering GM application for research and small-scale field trials and the commercial use of GMO.

General Procedure for the Approval of Environmental Release of Transgenic Crop

In general, the approval for the release of transgenic crops follows certain steps. First of all, the applicants need to inform the IBSC about the research work intended to be carried out. The IBSC notes the intension of the work at the institutional level and based on the risk category. It recommends RCGM for approval to conduct research. RCGM directs the applicant to generate the biosafety data, which includes environmental, toxicity, allergenicity and agronomic advantage of the GMO and its derived products. RCGM regularly reviews the progress of the work. The applicant needs to submit the information generated on the transgenic crops at the lab and the greenhouse level. After RCGM satisfies itself about the safety of the GMO and its product, it recommends GEAC for granting approval for environmental clearance for release in to the environment. The GEAC, after examination of data and recommendations of the RCGM, may direct the applicant to generate more data on safety of the environment, if necessary. Based on the data available, the GEAC grants approval for the environmental clearance. The applicant has to follow the other statutory requirements applicable to the product for commercialization as stated in the Figure 10.2.

The GEAC after examination of data and recommendations of the RCGM can now direct the applicant to generate more data on the safety of the environment. The applicant has to follow the other statutory requirements applicable to the product for commercialization.

To adhere to the rules, the DBT has evolved recombinant DNA safety guidelines for transgenic plants, testing its toxicity, guidelines for preclinical and clinical evaluation of recombinant DNA vaccines, diagnostics and other biological properties.

Recommended National Regulatory Procedure for Working with New Hybrid Variety with New Gene

Institutional Biosafety Committee (IBSC)

↓

Review Committeeon Genetic Manipulation
(Greenhouse Experiments, Contained Field Trials, Generation of Date on Gene Stability, etc.)

↓

RCGM
(Approval for Conduct on Multilocation Field Trials)

↓

Monitoring cum Evaluation Committee
(Large-scale Field Trials)

↓

Genetic Engineering Approval Committee (GEAC)
(Various Level of Trials)

↓

Environmental Clearancefrom Environmental Safety by MoEF

Figure 10.2 *A Chart Representing a General Procedure for the Approval for Field Trials*

BIOSAFETY GUIDELINES IN INDIA EVOLVED BY DBT

Recombinant safety guidelines and regulations have been prepared by recombinant DNA advisory committee (DBT), New Delhi. Initially started in 1990 and revised in 1994, the salient features of these guidelines and regulations are as follows:

- Every organization involved in research and development using recombinant DNA technique is required to set upon institutional biosafety committee, which has a nominee in DBT.
- RCGM reviews all the approvals of ongoing projects on GMO and several other issues related to RDNA research and development.
- Each state will have state committee and DLC, which monitor and inspect the experiments at the field trial site.
- MOEF has an inter-ministerial committee called GEAC, which is the competent authority to decide on the large-scale use of GMO experiment these are grouped into three categories:
  - Exempt from self-cloning experiments
  - Requiring review and approval from competent authorities for cloning of genes for toxin etc.
  - Requiring intimation of initiation of any kind of work involving GE.
- The biosafety guidelines covers various areas of research containing GE organism, genetic transformation of weed plants and animals, DNA techniques in vaccine development, large-scale

production, and deliberate and accidental release, of organism, plant and animal and all the product derived from RDNA.

- Four biosafety levels have been recognized and containment facility for each level is recommended for necessary safeguard containment, which may be at physical and biological level. These physical containments are required to limit the spread of dangerous microbes by following good lab practices, safety equipments lab design and facilities. Biological containment consists of the use of vectors in such a way that it can limit the infectivity of vectors to a specific host.
- An application to determine, recognize and research facilities to carry out genetic manipulation should be made to the Department of Environment before staring the work. The controlled release of microorganism should be done under appropriate containment area to ensure safety and to prevent unwanted release in the environment.
- Field trials for the transgenic plant are only allowed after the stepwise evaluation in growth chamber or greenhouse to generate data on the promoter sequences, target gene sequences, regulatory sequences, marker gene, and the cell lines used in the production of transgenic plants.
- There should be proper documentation to show that the protein in transgenics are safe for the environment and human being.
- Proper isolation and containment is provided all around the field, which are having transgenic crops.
- Non-target plants should be grown in an isolated area at certain intervals from the transgenic to reduce pollination by wind also to reduce distance of pollen seeds.
- All the vegetative parts and seeds that are left must be destroyed completely by burning once the experiments are finished.
- The field in which trials and transgenic are grown must be checked by the authorized company and all the feedback and records of the visit must be maintained.
- Full account of transgenic seed produced must be taken and well documented.

These are some of the important RDNA guidelines that have to be followed in any research dealing with biosciences. In addition to the rules and guidelines, there are many other important laws and regulations governing food derived from GMO in India. One of the laws is Prevention of Food Adulteration Act (1954).

PREVENTION FOOD ADULTERATION ACT, FOOD AND SAFETY STANDARD BILL AND SEED POLICY

Prevention of Food Adulteration Act, 1954

To ensure safe food to the consumer, the Ministry of Health and Family welfare enacted an act, Prevention of Food Adulteration Act 1954. The main aim of the Act was to ensure pure and wholesome food to the consumer and prevent any kind of deception. The law was made more stringent by amending it thrice. The law regulated the quality of food. Several states framed their own food laws. The central Advisory Board was appointed by the Government of India in 1937 to frame the legislation for the food safety. The Central of food Adulteration Act is a central legislation. Rules and standard under the Act are same throughout the country. Besides framing the rules, various other activities are also handled by the Ministry of Health and Family Welfare, which are as follows:

- Monitoring the activities of state by periodic checkups, investigating working of food law, reports of adulteration

- Arrangement of the training programme for analyst and investigator
- Creating awareness in consumer
- Coordinating with international bodies like ISO/FAO/WHO
- Carrying out survey activities on food contaminants like colour or additive
- Providing technical guidance to the food lab.

This Act does not address risks of transgene or GM food additive, etc. This mandates that every package of food should carry a label, which provides details of the food that includes the ingredients used in the product.

Food and Safety Standard Bill

The Food and Safety Standard Bill has been enacted by Parliament in the year 2006. The Act is called the Food Safety and standard (Amendment) Act 2008, in which Food Safety and Standard Act, 2006 will be referred as the Principal Act. The main features highlights of bill include the following:

- The bill includes eight laws governing food sector and establishes the Food Safety and Standards Authority (FSSA) to regulate the sector.
- FSSA will be supported by central advisory committee to create new standard for food safety. These standards will include specification for ingredients, contaminants, pesticide residue, biological hazards and labels.
- Everyone in the food sector will be required to get a legal license or registration by the authorities.
- The organized as well as unorganized food sectors are required to follow the same law on food. The bill stops the use of food additives, processing aid, heavy metals, insecticides, contaminants, veterinary drug residue etc, unless they are approved by specified regulations and rules under FDA.
- Every packed food product is mandatory to get labelled as per norms and regulations.

The bill gives the power to FSSA and state food safety authorities to monitor and regulate food business operators. The license can be cancelled by these authorities if discrepancy is found. They can prohibit the sale of the product that violates the specified standard. They are responsible for strict inspection and ensuring accuracy about the food and its standard. The Bill also provides for penalty depending upon gravity of violation. The main objective of the Bill is to introduce a statue related to food for scientific development of the food processing industry. The Bill moves from the multilevel departmental control to a single-time command. It is based on international legislation and Codex Alimentarious Commission.

Seed Policy

Seed Policy 2002 states that all GE crops/varieties will be tested for environmental biosfatey before commercialization as per regulations. It will also be mandatory that seeds harvested from transgenic plants for various research purposes are allowed to be imported to the National Bureau of Plant Genetic Resources, according to Environmental Protection Act (EPA), 1986. According to the seed policy, transgenic crops/varieties will be tested for its agronomic importance for at least two seasons under the All India Coordinated Research Project Trials of ICAR in coordination with the test required for biosafety and environment approval by the EPA before any variety is commercially released in the market. It also states that once transgenic plant variety is released commercially, its seeds will be registered and marketed in the country according to the Seed Act. The performance of the transgenic plant after it is released into the environment will be reviewed or monitored for at least 3–5 years by Ministry of Agriculture and Department of Agriculture in the states. The Seed Act also allows protection for transgenic varieties after their release for commercial cultivation.

RULES FOR THE MANUFACTURE AND STORAGE OF HAZARDOUS MICROORGANISM AND GMO

In view of protecting the environment, human and animal health from the potential risk of the application of biotechnology, the Central government and Ministry of Environment and Forests under the Act EPA 1986 have formulated rules to cover the application of hazardous microorganisms, GMO, its storage and manufacture. These rules are called as Rules 1986, which are as follows:

- These rules can be termed as rules for the manufacture and storage export import of hazardous microorganisms and GMO.
- These rules apply to GMO , microorganism and cells and to any substance, product or the food derived from the GMO, and are also applicable in the following cases:
  - Storage for the purpose of sale and the transboundary movements, which include export and import
  - Production, manufacturing, storage packaging and repackaging of GE product
  - In the manufacture of drugs, distilleries, tanneries, which make use of GE microbes
- These rules are applicable when biological agents are used to produce goods and services using biotechnology, when new combination is formed by cell hybridization, which is not present naturally, when gene technology is used for cloning, when there are exotic microbes that are not known to exist.
- All the competent authorities like RDAC, RGGM, IBSC and GEAC under these rules are responsible for reviving development of the safety regulation. They will be in association with other committees to review genetic manipulation. These will take care of all the institutes involved in genetic engineering research. They make sure that all the institutes and organizations follow biosafety guidelines. They will also take care of large-scale use of hazardous microbes and recombinant research from the environmental point of view.
- According to these rules, microbes and genetically engineered organisms will fall under two groups: animal pathogen and plant pest. If any GMO falls in the category of more than one risk, it will then fall into more specific organism.
- No person is allowed to export, import, and transport or manufacture a process or sell any harmful microbes without the approval of approved committees. Proper licence is needed to work with GMO in lab or outside the lab.
- Production in which the genetically engineered organism or cells generated are used will commence only after the consent of proper regulatory bodies. This is also subjected to discharging GMO into the environment.
- The deliberate or unintentional release of GE organism or hazardous microbe for the purpose of experiments strictly not allowed according to these rules.
- All the edibles, ingredients in food stuff containing GMO will not be sold, imported or used without the permission of GE approval committees.
- There are certain guidelines that are determined by GE approval committees to submit information that has to be made by seeing all cases individually.

- In granting approval for the different segments, all the conditions will be stipulated, which include all the terms and conditions that have to be exercised by the applicant under supervision and restrictions, and its submission of the information to the state biotechnology coordination committee. The committee has the power to take back the approval if any kind of discrepancy is noticed in the report submitted.
- There are even some penalties on the person if an order is not complied with DLC or State Biotechnology Coordination Committee. And if there is a need to prevent any damage to the environment and health, the DLC can take necessary steps to see the real fact of the matter.
- It will be the responsibility of a person to notify DLC of any accident that may lead to discharge of GE organism, which will be dangerous to the environment. It will be duty of the DLC to prepare offsite emergency plan, telling that how these major accidents can be dealt with.

BIOSAFETY MANAGEMENT

GMOs raise expectation of enhanced agronomic, nutritional, medicinal, diagnostics, marketing and other benefits. At the same time they also raise concerns about their long-term effect on human health and environment. These concerns have made it a requirement in developed and developing countries to follow and frame guidelines and regulations for the safe use and handling of GMO in the environment. This whole biosafety system requires proper biosafety management and challenges at every step of its growth.

Biosafety is achieved by assessing, managing and evaluating all the environmental risks and their ecological consequences and weighing these against the potential benefits. This whole evaluation requires the biosfatey system in which four elements function altogether to produce environmentally safe decision. These four elements given below are required for the proper management of biosafety:

- The guidelines framed should be transparent and scientific.
- The people involved and their competence.
- There should be a very effective review process.
- There must be the provision of the feedback so that the system can be improved for better.

Scientific and Well Framed Biosafety Guidelines for the Biosafety Management

These guidelines are the backbone of proper regulation and working of biosafety to ensure safe use of biotechnology and its product. It contains all the objectives, scope and responsibilities of all the national and international biosafety review committees. It has the details of applications and review procedures. It has all the details of risk assessment according to the various biosafety levels. Drafting these guidelines includes adaptation of legislation, all the merits and demerits in relation to complexity and time cost. It has all the recommendations for the commercialization of transgenic crops or vaccines, seeds, embryo, livestocks etc, subject to proper regulation on animal, environment and food safety.

People Involved in Decision Making

In managing the biosafe system, both public and private sector involved in research and the different review committees have different roles to play with one objective. These prepare the documents for testing transgenic plants for the field trials. The institutional recombinant committee reviews the research application. Members of national biosafety committee also work for granting the approval after evaluation of risk assessments. These people involved are well familiar with the environmental and legal issues in the review process. They know about the potential risk and its management, which include latest scientific regulatory and biosafety information.

Review Process

The effective part to manage biosafety is the review process, which evaluates the GMOs. It takes into consideration the site where it is released and its potential risk like the nature of the organism that will receive the new trait, the donor of the trait, vector used to transfer, potential toxicity of gene product, environment to which the gene product will be released then the biosafety levels and its containment.

The first level of review is done by the applicant only to reduce risks if any. The second level of review is done by the institutional biosafety committee that evaluates the proposal under all the guidelines and recommends approval risk management procedure if needed.

Feedback Mechanism

The feedback mechanism is very important for the biosafety system. Based on the feedback, reviewers make biosafety decisions. It also helps to improve the biosafety system in a well-designed scientific, procedural feedback that work together to improve the quality of biosafety decisions. Establishing biosafety system requires effective human resource development, which includes lot of capital on biosfety training, framing of guidelines require manpower, inspection and monitoring to perform various management tasks. These training helps to build the competence and confidence of scientist, biosafety review, regulation, increase their awareness on environmental issues and its consequences. These training is conducted by United Nations Industrial Development Organization (UNIDO). This training are important for biosfatey management and should be conducted on a regular basis. Biosafety will have to show the dynamism, as this science will always be challenged by new products, new technologies, new concerns and new targets. There should be more public awareness for its management. There is a need to consult the international experts to access information, monitoring, record track and the complete documentation. This is done to ensure the safe environment, animal, plant and human health.

CHAPTER SUMMARY

All the regulations and guidelines are evolved by the concerned states to protect the environment and also human and animal health. Variations in the regulatory framework, in the present situation, represent the strength of science, necessity of the technology and willingness of the state to adopt goods and services developed through modern biotechnology. It is also important to update mechanisms to meet the current challenges of the society based on the scientific knowledge, which is growing all over the world.

Biosafety regulations have drawn attention from several segments of the society. Transparency, clarity, competency, science-based assessments, effective monitoring, assessment of national and international priorities, trade, cost, effectiveness, coordination among concerned authorities, departments and public participation are some of the desirable attributes of the ideal regulatory framework.

MULTIPLE CHOICE QUESTIONS

1. What is the full form of OECD?
   (i) Organization of Economic Corporation Development
   (ii) Organisation of Equality Economic Corporation Development
   (iii) Organization of Equal and Challenging Development
2. Seed Policy developed in the year
   (i) 2002
   (ii) 1998
   (iii) 2004
   (iv) 2000
3. Food and Safety Standard bill is about
   (i) Adulteration in food
   (ii) Quality of food
   (iii) Feed as animals
   (iv) All of the above
4. Rules for the manufacturer and storage of hazardous microbes and GMO
   (i) Rules 1986
   (ii) Rules 2002
   (iii) Rules 1997
   (iv) Rules 1968

REVIEW QUESTIONS

1. What do you understand by the regulatory affairs? Why do you think there is a need to establish regulatory affairs in the entire research organization dealing with GMO?
2. What are the various national and international regulatory bodies?
3. What are the basic biosafety guidelines of biosafety?
4. Write short notes on
   (i) Prevention Food Adulteration Act
   (ii) Food and Safety Standard Bill
   (iii) Seed Policy
5. What is the general process of releasing transgenics into the environment? What all approvals are required?

Biosafety of Genetically Engineered Products

11

Chapter Objectives:

Recombinant DNA techniques represent a development of advanced procedures. They permit precise alteration, construction, recombination, deletion and translocation of genes that may give the recipient cells a desirable phenotype. Recombinant products and their biosafety are important aspects to look in to before their commercialization. This chapter emphasizes on the biosafety of the newly formed product and its risk assessment keeping in mind human health, environment, food and feed and the other economic and social impacts. Transgenic regulation and the grant of permission for the transboundary movements of GMO are discussed. Few examples are taken of some of the recombinant DNA products and its biosafety.

GENETICALLY ENGINEERED PRODUCTS AND RECOMBINANT DNA TECHNOLOGY

In the last two decades, new developments have already been added to the science of biotechnology using which scientists have discovered biological techniques to recombine DNA from different sources. It has been a subject of intense research and development since then. Genetic engineering in the broader perspective is the manipulation of an organism's nucleic acid. Organisms whose genes have been artificiallyaltered for some desired effect are called genetically modified organisms (GMOs) and the technology used in creating GMOs is recombinant DNA technology (RDT). RDT refers to cutting the DNA sequence from one organism and introducing it into another organism and in this course altering the genotype of the recipient. Collectively these techniques are used to achieve the following aims:

- To study the expressions, regulations and arrangements of the gene.
- Manipulation of genes at the gene level to produce altered or changed protein product.
- Modification of gene expression either to suppress or enhance a particular product.
- Transformation of one gene to another to form a transgenic organism.
- Formation of an organism with new desirable characteristics and traits.

These advances bring new commitments and responsibilities to produce and use them judiciously and safely. The development and implementation of genetically modified products need effective environmental and safety risk assessments in a stringent manner. Modern molecular biotechnology creates lots of concerns about safety and risks as it uses living organisms or material from related or unrelated sources and then modifies it to improve quality and quantity of food, drugs, health care products, vaccines, industrial chemicals and transgenic crops. It also uses altered genetic microbes for controlling pests and weeds in agriculture, cleaning up toxic chemicals at waste site, bioleaching and many more uses. There are significant biosafety and regulatory issues that need to be considered and regulated to ensure safety.

RISK ASSESSMENT OF RDT PRODUCTS

Considerations of risk assessment for recombinant DNA organisms are very important. A recombinant DNA organism is generally constructed by introducing small segment of DNA from donor cell to recipient cell as already discussed. It is important to assess the risk it causes by knowing the properties of the recipient—its origin, classification, genetic makeup, pathogenicity, physiological and ecological characteristics and those of the donor including structure and function of the DNA sequence. Risk assessments rely on the extent to which the properties or traits are altered in the recipient species in terms of increase in degree of expression or expecting some unexpected results. Any probability of novel hazard cannot be ruled out and has to be assessed very meticulously.

These risk assessments fall in the following categories:

- If the living organism or virus used in the GMO has the potential to cause disease in man, animals and plants on its exposure, it has to be treated as an infectious hazard and its assessment needs to be done to the full satisfaction of the regulatory authorities.
- Toxic, allergenic or biological effect on the nontarget organism or cell or its components can also effect naturally occurring metabolic products.
- Environmental effects can affect the food chain, biodiversity and ecosystem as whole.

REGULATING RECOMBINANT DNA TECHNOLOGY

The concerns about RDT safety and its unforeseen results are raised from all communities of the world, whether scientific or non-scientific, by debating on the phrases like 'playing God','manmade evolution' etc. A major concern with RDT is that this science can, knowingly or unknowingly, be used for the purpose of warfare through creation of novel pathogenic microbes, which can cause epidemics and environmental hazards.

In 1976 the National Institutes of Health, which is the primary US grant agency in the area of medical and health sciences, issued a set of guidelines for research in the area of recombinant DNA technology. These rules and regulations defined physical containment levels for RDT experimentation. More stringent rules were brought inby NIH-RAC (Recombinant DNA Advisory Committee of the National Institute of Health, USA), which established the recombinant DNA research guidelines. The United States Department of Agriculture (USDA), the Food and Drug Administration (FDA), the Environment Protection Agency (EPA) and most state governments closely monitor the development and testing of genetically engineered (GE) products. These GE products are being used in the production of pharmaceuticals, gene therapy and in the development of transgenic plants and animals, e.g. human drugs such as insulin for diabetics and tissue plasminogen activator for heart attack victims, animal drugs like bovine growth hormone somatropin are produced in bacteria with the help of RDT techniques. Transgenic animals are designed to help researchers diagnose and treat human diseases through these advanced techniques.

The appropriate administrative divisions of USDA, FDA and EPA regulate the development of animal and human health products including GE vaccines and other pharmaceuticals that are developed through GE. Development of these health-related products have not generated same level of debate as GE food. After the approval from the governing bodies, FDA announces the approval of GE products.

The USDA regulates GE products and food through its division, The Animal and Plant Health Inspection Services (APHIS). This organization regulates interstate movement and field testing of organisms produced through GE. APHIS exercises its regulatory authorities through a permit system. Any company, academic research institute or private scientific organization that wishes to move or field test a GE plant or GE product must obtain necessary permit for further proceedings. Any applicant falsifying any information in the permit will have to pay penalty in terms of either money or imprisonment.

PERMIT FOR MOVEMENT AND IMPORT OF GMOs

In United States, an APHIS permit and approval is required if there is a need to move GE organisms in different parts of the country. In such cases, the applicant must provide details about the nature of the organism like its origin and its intended use. This is followed by an inspection and investigation by APHIS authorities. If the committee members are satisfied, the permit is provided.

APHIS also oversees field testing or environmental release of GE crops. Precautions that are taken care of include prevention of the escape of pollen, plants or plant parts from the field test site. Cross-pollination is blocked by tagging and blocking the flower or growing flowers in a cage where insects cannot take the pollen out. A petition to APHIS is required for commercialization to ensure environmental safety.

SOME OF THE PRODUCTS DEVELOPED FROM RDT AND THEIR BIOSAFETY ISSUES

Recombinant Insulin

Recombinant DNA technology was first used commercially to produce human insulin from bacteria. In 1982, genetically engineered insulin was approved by FDA for use in diabetics. Insulin preparations usually come from the pancreas of slaughtered animals such as pigs or sheep, which are used as a source of insulin though a very difficult process of isolation and purification. To provide a reliable source of human insulin, researchers used genetic engineering techniques to isolate the insulin gene. A copy of DNA carrying this insulin gene was inserted into the bacteria, *E.coli,* to produce insulin that is chemically identical to human insulin. This was world's first FDA-approved recombinant DNA drug manufactured by Eli Lilly and Co. under the name of humulin. Recombinant human insulin proved to be identical to human insulin and proved to be safe and efficient, and as a result, completely replaced the animal source of insulin.

FDA played a key role in ensuring the safety and efficiency of this first genetically engineered product created using RDT technologies.

Post the FDA approval of humulin, a part of the scientific community expressed concern about the use of new technology to manipulate the very essence of life and about the fear of developing mutant genes in the process. With regard to this view, scientists recommended that NIH should provide guidelines for recombinant research. Even though the amino acid sequence of humulin occurs naturally in humans still FDA reviewers chose to consider it as a new molecular entity. Therefore, it was regulated for all kinds of risk assessment under Division of Metabolic and Endocrine Drugs in the Centre for Drug Evaluation and Research (CDER).

Human Growth Hormone

Recombinant human growth hormone is a protein that is identical to the naturally occurring form of human growth hormone. Recombinant growth hormone is administered to increase growth rate. It is also known as somatotropin. Recombinant HGH been produced by some of the largest pharmaceutical companies in the United States. FDA has very strict policy about the usage of human growth hormone and mentions very clearly where it can be used or administered. There are certain diseases where the use of human growth hormone is essential like turner syndrome, chronic renal insufficiency and growth hormone deficiency. It is illegal in the United States to sell it in the drug stores without prescription because of fear of misuse.

Bovine Growth Hormone

The development of recombinant bovine somatotropin (BST), also known as bovine growth hormone, provides an example of a hormone created through recombinant DNA technique. It was shown in the year 1930 that cows injected with BST show significant increase in milk production. Obtaining natural BST is both expensive and difficult to obtain in huge quantities. But with the help of recombinant DNA technology, the gene for BST was cloned and transferred to *E. coli* where it was expressed. The bacteria are then broken up and separated from the rBST, which is purified to produce the injectable hormone. Under trial conditions, cows with BST produced 20% to 25% more milk than normal. As a part of its risk assessment, it was found that the level of BST in milk was not higher for hormone-treated cows compared to normal cows. It was also found that BST is not active in humans and does not have any side effects. Post the risk assessment exercise, FDA approved milk of BST treated cows as safe for human consumption. This conclusion was also approved by the US office of technology assessment after its own analysis.

Some groups of people had their concerns with rBST related to its economic consequences on the dairy industry. It was thought that rBST usage would mean more business for larger dairy farms at the cost of small farms. Usage or rBST was also thought to increase incidents of bacterial infection of the milk glands of dairy cattle. This infection called mastitis could mean large usage of antibiotics for treatment, which could show up in cow's milk and may even correspond to allergic response in consumers. However, the Veterinary Medicine Advisory Committee of the FDA maintained that the frequency of mastitis is no greater in rBST cows as compared to the cows that were not treated with BST. Some groups also campaigned against rBST mentioning that the hormone laced milk could cause cancer in humans.

Finally, recombinant BST was given license for its use in dairy in United States in 1994.

Recombinant Tryptophan

Tryptophan is one of the 20 aminoacids, as well as an essential aminoacid in the human diet. This means that it cannot be synthesized by the human body and therefore must be a part of human diet. Tryptophan synthesizes serotonin, a neurotransmitter; niacin, an essential nutrient; and auxin, a phytohormone. Deficiency of tryptophan leads to emotional and behavioural problems ranging from PMS, anxiety, insomnia, violence, aggression and even suicide. So it is very important for normal brain function. Although tryptophan can be produced from plant and animal proteins, but its production from the fermentation of tryptophan producing bacteria is more economical. This bacterium is genetically modified to enhance the production of tryptophan.

In 1989, people consuming high doses of tryptophan started showing symptoms of eosinophilia myalgia syndrome (EMS), a new disease which was characterized by painful and swollen muscles, rashes and gastrointestinal problems. In the United States, 37 people died, 1500 were disabled and around 5000 affected in all. This group of people was taking tryptophan supplements produced from genetically modified bacteria, produced at a facility in Japan. That tryptophan batch was tested and was found to contain 60 contaminants, of which six were responsible for causing EMS. Hence, the US council decided that it was the manufacturing process rather than the genetic modification of bacteria to produce tryptophan that was responsible for causing the disease. But still the US council called off all the dietarysupplements containing manufactured tryptophan. This restriction was loosened later in 2001 when marketing of US-manufactured tryptophan was allowed.

One of the lessons learnt from tryptophan manufacturing is that extreme precautions are needed in the entire manufacturing process of genetically altered products since even slight traces of impurities could cause adverse reactions in the human body.

BIOSAFETY IN GENE THERAPY

Gene therapy is the insertion of genes into an individual's cells and tissues to treat diseases, especially genetic diseases that occur when the innate gene malfunctions. A common technique used in gene therapy is to identify the malfunctioning gene and then replace it with the functional copy of that gene. Other approaches of gene therapy include gene regulation by switching genes on and off or introducing a gene to kill diseased cells or to suppress tumour cells by inhibiting blood supply.

There are two types of gene therapy, germline gene therapy and somatic cell gene therapy. In germline gene therapy, germ cells like sperms and eggs are modified by the introduction of functional gene; therefore any modification or change due to this type of therapy is heritable. This type of gene therapy is very useful for treating genetic disorders, but many groups prohibit using germline genetherapy on humans for technical and ethical reasons. In somatic cell genetherapy, the therapeutic gene is transferred into the somatic cells and this kind of change is not heritable.

Many scientists are in favour of somatic cell gene therapy as this change is restricted to the patient and not passed to the subsequent generations. Regulatory bodies have restricted gene therapy only to the life-threatening disorders. Researchers involved in gene therapy must obtain approval from Gene Therapy Advisory Committee (GTAC). Taking into account the scientific merits and potential risks, different phases of clinical trials are needed before the actual approval.

Different Issues Related to Gene Therapy

Though gene therapy is only used to treat dreadful diseases, which include single gene disorders or complex disease disorders like cancer, the therapy offers hope for various other diseases. But at the same time, there are various concerns related to its safety, effectiveness, durability and commercialization like the following.

Gene Delivery

Targeting a gene to the correct cells is the key to success of any gene therapy. At the same time, it is very important to ensure that the gene is not incorporated in the wrong cells. Gene delivered to a wrong tissue could cause a lot of health problems for the patient. Challenges to successful gene delivery could be many; it could be presence of mucus while delivering gene targeted to the lungs or need for multisite delivery in case of cancer.

Durability and Integration

Before gene therapy can become a permanent cure for any disease, the DNA that is introduced in to the target cell must remain functional and the cell containing that DNA must be long lived and stable. Problems with integrating therapeutic DNA into the genome and dividing nature of many cells prevent gene therapy from achieving any long-term benefit. As a result, patients need to go through multiple rounds of gene therapy.

Immune Response

When a viral vector is used to deliver the gene, the immune response of the body recognizes it as foreign and prepares the immune system. Gene delivery vectors must be able to escape the body's natural immune systems. Failure to do so can cause serious illness or even death.

Use of Viral Vectors

Viruses are most likely to be used as vectors to carry the gene in most gene therapy cases. However, use of viruses can be accompanied with various problems in the patient like toxicity, immune and inflammatory responses and gene control and targeting issues. It is also feared that once virus is inside the patient, it may recover the ability to cause disease.

Chances of Inducing a Tumour

If the DNA is integrated at a wrong place in the genome, for example in the tumour-suppressing gene, it could induce a tumor in the patient. Few deaths caused due to gene therapy can be attributed to this.

The regulatory system considers all gene therapy research proposals and studies them on case-by-case basis taking all ethical and scientific studies into account. Some cases require more open and transparent assessments. Also, technical development needs to have more stringent regulatory framework required to separate therapies derived from human gene, stem cell and tissues.

ECOLOGICAL SAFETY ASSESSMENT OF RECOMBINANT ORGANISMS

There are serious ecological concerns of releasing genetically engineered organisms to the environment. When a novel trait is transformed, it is very difficult to screen for ecological safety. The unknown species is more likely to present the greatest challenges for risk assessment of plants and animals. The ecologically competent GMOs, with new adaptive features, which can be compared to the exotic or introduced species, have to be assessed to ensure the biosafety of the environment.

Transfer of Genes to Ecologically Competent Relative

The transgenic plant or animal species can pass novel gene to a nontarget relative and hence increase competitiveness of these wild relatives, which can cross anywhere in the world. This wild population can give its progeny large competitive advantage – its genotype can sweep the population, eliminate other genotypes, reduce the amount of genetic variation and can create practical implications for plant breeders in future who might have had important uses for the genes that are eliminated from natural germ plasma.

Risk with Plants that are Altered for Bioactive Molecules rather than for Food

There are many crop plants that are genetically engineered not for food purposes but to produce drugs and industrial chemicals in large amounts. In such cases, the challenge is to anticipate any effect of chemical residue in the fields on wild life, soil or water quality. Regulators should be alert that there is a possibility that these chemicals could enter the food supply if pollens from such fields get blown or carried by insect into the fields where food crops are being grown. Therefore, higher containment and quality standards are desired when food safety is concerned.

Ecological Pleiotropic Effect of Genetically Engineered Organism

Pleiotropy is described as the genetic effect of a single gene on multiple phenotypic traits. It is possible that the introduced gene affects an unknown phenotypic trait apart from the trait for which it was inserted for.This can raise potential risks related to food safety, toxicity and allergens. In the natural state, plants have their own systemic resistance to fight against insects, pathogens or mammalian herbivores with their own biochemicals. The concern with transgenic plants is that biochemical modification can sometimes alter a biosynthetic pathway, which can altogether change or produce a completely new bioactive compound, which may be toxic to humans.

Pleiotropic Effect is Enhanced in Transgenic Organisms Which is an Ecological Concern

Many scientists argue that pleiotropic effect is also shown in traditional breeding and so it should not be treated differently with transgenic organisms, but there is evidence to prove that pleiotropic expression is often greater in transgenic organisms and hence there is a need for strict observation to assure food and ecological safety.

Ecological Risk by Field Trials

Ecological problems are more likely to occur within the biological and physical interactions that take place on soil in the vicinity of transgenic plants. A casual observation of the field cannot resolve such ecological concerns. Organized studies of transgenic plants are very important and essential to draw any conclusion of potential risk and hazards from transgenic release to the environment. Valuable information can be gathered from field trials about seed dormancy, vegetative reproduction, seed dispersal, pollination biology, water and mineral requirement, growth and germination responses to changes in weather, resistance to natural diseases etc. This information can provide potential data to regulate, frame and implement the required decisions for the safety of environment, plant and animal health.

CHAPTER SUMMARY

Significant technological advances in biotechnology are rarely implemented without controversies. The issues and concerns raised by the ability of scientists to genetically engineer organisms have far-reaching implications both in the establishment of the guidelines for the conduct of research and the formulation of requirements for the introduction of recombinant DNA products. In this chapter, various aspects of the regulation of recombinant DNA technology, the release of the genetically engineered organism in to the environment, approval and the production of various genetically engineered products like insulin, bovine growth hormone, somatotropin, tryptophan and biosafety issues associated with commercialization have been discussed. The possibility of being able to genetically engineer human beings has always been a cause of concern. Technically, human gene therapy has two aspects—somatic cell gene therapy and germ line gene therapy.

Because germ line gene therapy has genetic consequences for future generations, it is currently not permitted. In contrast, somatic cell gene therapy is rapidly becoming potentially important mode of treatment for a number of dreadful diseases. It is very important to know about the ecological safety assessment of genetically engineered organisms to ensure complete safety to the environment, plant and human health.

MULTIPLE CHOICE QUESTIONS

1. Bovine growth hormone is sold under the name
   (i) POSILAC
   (ii) Bovine RDT
   (iii) Recombinant growth hormone
   (iv) Milk enhancer
2. Human growth hormone is also called
   (i) Somatotropin
   (ii) Humulin
   (iii) Recombinant hormone
   (iv) All the above
3. Tryptophan is an
   (i) Protein
   (ii) Essential amino acid
   (iii) Non-essential amino acid
   (iv) Gene
4. Gene therapy has more of
   (i) Biosafety issues
   (ii) Bioethical issues
   (iii) Social issues
   (iv) Public acceptance issues

REVIEW QUESTIONS

1. Discuss the quote "Genetic engineering a new technology that violates the fundamental laws of nature."
2. Discuss why human germ line gene therapy research is prohibited.
3. What are the various concerns and risks related to gene therapy?
4. Discuss the positive and negative aspects of recombinant bovine somatotropin.
5. Discuss various genetically modified organisms and related biosafety issues.

Allergenicity: Assessment of Genetically Modified Food

12

Chapter Objectives:

Millions of people all over the world have acute allergic reactions to various foods. It is important to know what are these allergen and their causes. Through this chapter, students will learn about the different food allergens that are plant- and animal-based. They will also learn a relation between GMO and allergens and what are the different methods to assess whether the newly formed chimera is toxic or not by using different methods to check their allergenicity.

INTRODUCTION

Genetically transformed plants have the potential to feed the ever-growing population of the world. They are produced to have desirable traits for improving quality and quantity of food. These characteristics include resistance against, biotic and abiotic diseases like herbicides, insects, fungal and bacterial diseases, tolerance to different environmental stresses and nutritional quality. Even fruits and vegetables are modified to produce human vaccines against infectious diseases like hepatitis B. Despite such immense benefits, there are concerns regarding possible adverse effects of these GM foods on the health of animals, humans and the environment. Due to their adverse effects, there is an intense need to assess safety aspects of genetically modified food before it enters into the food chain.

FOOD ALLERGY

Food allergy is an abnormal immune response when certain food is ingested. Most of the food allergies have IgE antibodies and have a quick manifestation, within few minutes of exposure. Immunoglobulin E (IgE) is a protein antibody that recognizes an allergen. It circulates in the blood, and becomes fixed on the surfaces of specific cells (basophils and mast cells). When IgE on the cell surface binds to an allergen, it triggers the release of chemical mediators that provoke the symptoms associated with allergic reactions. Some of the allergic food reactions are food intolerance, which is an abnormal physiological response to an ingested food; food poisoning, which is a toxic reaction; and pharmacologic reactions, which are manifested due to different chemicals present in the food that produce a drug like effect. These food-related allergies can prove fatal and require proper management. The Codex Alimentarius Commission has listed common allergenic food which accounts for 90% of all kinds of severe and moderate allergic reactions. The list of such food is mentioned in Figure 12.1.

Most of the food contains different proteins to which an individual can react. It is still not understood completely what makes some proteins in the food cause an allergic response. These include both

Common Allergy Causing Foods
Cereals containing gluten (wheat, rice, barley, oats etc)
Crustacea and products of these
Egg and egg products
Fish and fist products
Peanuts, soyabeans and their products
Milk and milk products (lactose included)
Tree nuts (and nut products)
Presence of sulphite in concentration of 10 mg/kg or more

Figure 12.1 *The Codex Alimentarious Commission on Food Labeling has Listed the Foods and Ingredients that Cause Food Hypersensitive Reactions*

animal- and plant-derived food allergens. There are several recommendations that are relative to the allergenicity of GM food, which are as follows:

- Until and unless the gene to be transferred is well documented to not code for any allergen, its use should be discouraged.
- Food found to contain an allergen should go through proper assessment and should not be considered for marketing and distribution.
- Proper action must be taken if the food contains new protein and has traits of allergens even if there is no patient population that suffers from allergy to the new gene product is known to exist .
- Identification of various food allergens and their characteristics related to an immunological response should be encouraged.

Animal-Derived Food Allergens

There are many foods from animal sources that show allergic reaction like milk, egg, fish, etc. Several milk proteins are found to be allergic to humans. Many people are allergic to more than one milk protein. Casein and beta-lactoglobulin are the most involved allergens in cow's milk. Egg allergy is one of the most common allergies in small children; hen's protein is more allergic than those of duck eggs. In egg itself, egg white is more allergic than the yolk proteins. It is been studied that phosvitin and livetins are the potent allergens in some egg-sensitive individuals. The consumption of fish most of the time causes IgE-mediated allergic reactions. The protein involved in the allergic reactions is parvalbumins. This protein is found only in the muscles of amphibians and fish. Some of the sea food belongs to class crustacean that include prawns, shrimps, crabs, lobster, which causes food hypersensitivity in some individuals. The potent allergen protein is tropomyosin in crustacean species.

Food Allergens Derived from Plant Origin

Plants are consumed by a larger population of the world. Several plant foods constitute major food allergens. Theses involve fruits, vegetables, grains, seeds, nuts and legumes like peanut and soybean. Peanut is a very popular food product but at the same time known for acute and severe reactions. Its

Table 12.1 *List of Allergens Derived from Plant and Animal Origin*

Allergic food	Potent allergen involved
Brassica juncea (oriental mustard)	Albumin
Hordeum vulgare (barley)	Hor v1
Sinapis alpa9 (yellow mustard)	Albumin
Arachis hypogeal (peanut)	Ara h1
Penaeus aztecus	Tropomyosin
Gallus domesticus (chicken)	Ovomucoid
Penaeus indicu (Indian shrimp)	Tropomyosin
Metapenaeus (greasyback shrimp)	Tropomyosin
Penaeus aztecus	Tropomyosin

proteins, albumins and globulins generally cause dermatitis reactions. There are certain tree nuts that cause serious systemic anaphylaxis in certain individuals. Systemic anaphylaxis typically results in a number of symptoms including throat swelling, itchy rashes and low blood pressure. Such reactions are rapid in onset and may even cause death. Allergic reactions are confirmed by taking samples—serum of allergic hypersensitive individual—and by performing many immune assays like immunoblotting and ELISA, to find the protein involved by comparing the homology with the preexisting data.

Table 12.1 shows a list of allergens that correspond to common allergic food and food products derived from plant and animal origin.

General Traits of Food as Allergens

- Generally all food allergens are glycoproteins with acidic isoelectric points.
- Many known allergens have 10 and 70 kDa molecular weight.
- All allergens contain two IgE antibody reactive sites to trigger the hypersensitive reaction.
- Allergens are resistant to heat or acid treatment, proteolysis and digestion so they reach the intestinal tracts in an immunologically active form for their allergic manifestation. However, there could be some exceptions to the above.

ALLERGENS AND GMOs

Genetically modified organisms used as food/food products could carry the same allergen that the non-genetically altered organism had. In some cases, the expression of such allergens can be altered for reducing their allergenicity. However, as a part of the genetic transformation process, expression of new proteins may result in new allergens, which may result in significant food allergy.

So, it is important to carefully assess any new transgenic food product for its allergic activity to ensure that a harmless food has not been turned into a serious allergic threat due to genetic modification.

Assessing Allergenicity in GMO Food

Assessing allergenicity is an integral part of safety of GM food for possible human consumption and avoiding any unwanted health effects. The International Food Biotechnology Council (IFBC), in collaboration with the Allergy and Immunology Institute of International Life Sciences Institute (ILSI), has developed approaches for the assessment of potential allergenicity of GM foods. This assessment focuses on sequence homology between the novel proteins and already known allergenic proteins followed by assessment of immune reactivity with the sera from the allergic patient.

Allergenicity Assessment Methods

Gene Sources

The gene used for genetic transformation can come either from a source known to be allergenic or non-allergenic or of an unknown allergenic potential. If a gene is taken from a known allergic source, sequence homology (explained below as a separate section) of expressed protein is undertaken. If sequence homology to a known allergen is demonstrated, no more testing is undertaken and the product is considered allergenic. If no sequence homology to a known allergen is found, the expressed protein is tested with the sera of patients allergic to the source material.

When the gene used for transformation is taken from a source not known to be allergic, the final product still needs to be tested for allergenicity because some novel proteins might be expressed during the transformation process. This is shown as a pictorial representation in Figure 12.2

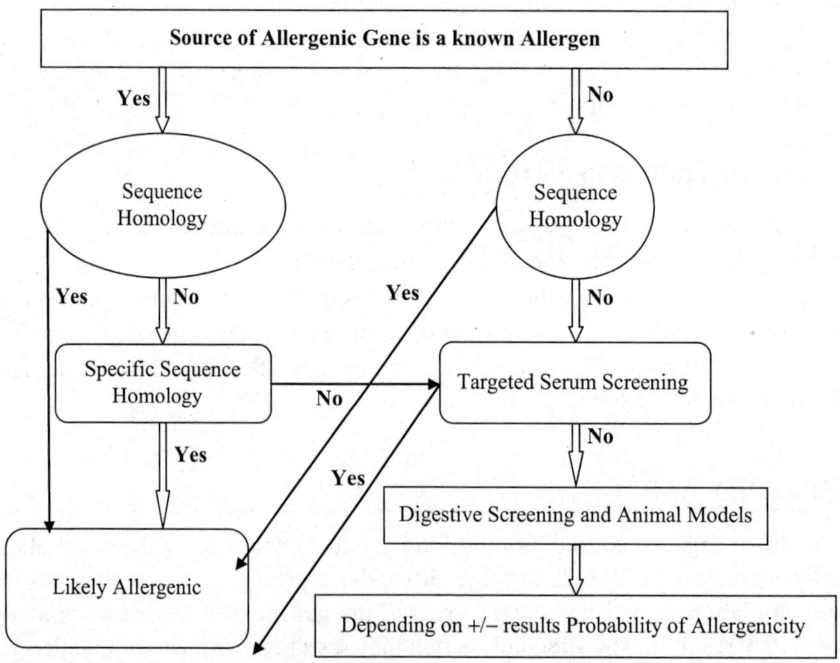

Figure 12.2 *Assessment of the Allergenic Potential of the Food Derived from Biotechnology FAO/WHO 2001*

Allergenicity is tested by multiple methods as given below:

1. Sequence homology to known allergens
2. Cross reactivity testing with serum of patients allergic to products related to the source
3. In vitro studies of physiochemical and biological characteristics
4. Immunogenicity testing in animal models

Screening Homology with Known Allergens

Allergens from food and non-food sources can cross react, so it is important to compare the amino acid sequences of the genetically engineered food with all known allergens. Over 200 allergens have been identified, characterized and sequenced and their information is available in public databases like genebank, swiss-prot etc. Comparison of the amino acid sequence of the expressed protein to the amino acid sequences of known allergens is one of the important methods used to assess product safety. Homology in sequence to known allergens suggests that the transferred protein may be allergenic and a failure to match any homology suggests that the introduced protein does not share any similarity with known allergens. FAO/WHO experts recommend 35% identical amino acids in 80 amino acid segments as a threshold for comparison. Demonstration of homology with known allergens alone does not mean that the product will not be allergenic as there might be three dimensional conformational similarities between the novel protein and already known allergenic proteins.

In Vitro Studies of Physicochemical and Biological Characteristics

All the food allergens share physicochemical and biological characteristics that include molecular size, stability and solubility. Thus it is worthwhile to compare these characteristics in novel proteins in the transgenic with known allergens

In Vitro Digestibility Study

Stability to digestive processes is an important factor when assessing potential allergenicity. Proteins that are stable under acidic and proteolytic conditions of the digestive tract are more likely to invoke immunologic response compared to proteins that are digested. So, if the novel protein in genetically engineered food is digestible or degrades in acidic or proteolytic conditions, chances of the protein being an allergen are low.

Allergens of plant-derived foods like peanut and soybean remain stable for as long as 60 minutes in simulated gastric fluid while non-allergenic food proteins like those in spinach get digested within 15 seconds. Similarly, the Cry9c proteins from transgenic corn are stable for up to 4 hours and thus have the potential to create immunogenic response compared to choline oxidase in transgenic mustard which shows complete digestion within few seconds. Thus stability to digestion is a significant and important parameter to distinguish food allergens from non-allergens.

In Vitro Digestibility through Thermal Stability

Thermal stability of newly expressed proteins in transgenic food is a weight-of-evidence approach to assess potential allergenicity. All known protein allergens tend to be stable to heat while non-allergens tend to degrade. Retention of biological activity after incubation under high temperature may indicate that there are chances that the protein is allergenic and hence further investigation should be carried out.

Animal Models for Testing Potential Allergenicity

Animal models are appropriate for testing novel proteins from the transformed or genetically altered food, which has no earlier history of exposure to the gastrointestinal tract. The designed model for this purpose must meet certain criteria:

(a) The model should not involve the use of adjuvants as this can initiate antigen-specific immunity and can influence the type of immune response shown.
(b) There should be preferential oral administration of novel food in assessment; any test done must detect the presence of an IgE response to the protein as well as other associated immune response.
(c) The clinical response should mimic that of humans with the food allergy.
(d) The model should be easy to conduct, reproducible and should develop allergen-specific IgE antibodies to known allergens.

Examples of such models already developed are Brown Norway rat, dogs and pigs. It is also well understood that this is not the only method to detect potential allergens as it is complex process in humans that depends on number of factors. So, in addition to this, other sensitive methods need to be used to identify the potential hazard of the GM food.

CHAPTER SUMMARY

Agriculture biotechnology can provide new ways to improve the quality and yield of GM crops. In India, there are many labs that are engaged in creating transgenic crops with improved characteristics. Creating plants with elite traits is the only answer to the question of food security for future generations but all these crops need proper assessment before they are ready to enter the food chain owing to the health challenges they may cause. So in order to have their safe distribution, their allergenicity and toxicity assessment is needed prior to their commercialization. Proper guidelines need to be followed for their commercial release as per Indian and international norms.

MULTIPLE CHOICE QUESTIONS

1. The characteristics of allergenic proteins are
   (i) Thermal stability
   (ii) Stability to digestive processes
   (iii) Both of the above
2. Genetically modified organisms are not always accompanied with a new protein because
   (i) An existing gene is simply switched off by means of incorporating a reversed copy of the gene, cancelling out the existing version.
   (ii) Transgene does not express
   (iii) Transgenic gene does not produce new proteins
3. What do we use as a model for assessing plant allergenicity
   (i) An animal
   (ii) A plant
   (iii) Both a and b
   (iv) Microbes
4. An allergen invokes
   (i) IgM response
   (ii) IgE response
   (iii) Both IgM and IgE response
   (iv) None of the above

REVIEW QUESTIONS

1. What are allergens and how are they associated with GMOs?
2. Discuss plant and animal allergens by giving their examples.
3. What are the different methods of assessing allergenicity?
4. What are the different biochemical and molecular strategies for assessing allergenicity in GMOs?

Introduction to Bioethics

13

Chapter Objectives:

Biotechnology applications have many concerns that are not necessarily scientific. There are numerous ethical, legal and social implications of biotechnology and other biosciences. There has been strong pressure to regulate the technology to address these concerns. This chapter deals with the ethical, legal, social, philosophical issues pertaining to biological research, medicine, health care and other areas of biotechnology. Students would be knowing about different theories and approaches to bioethics and its associated conflicts with GMO. They will know about how human cloning is surrounded by different bioethical issues. This chapter gives the insight of different perceptions about consumer acceptance. Different bioethical committees and their important guidelines are presented. This chapter also provides a brief overview of biological weapons and its ethical implications.

BIOETHICS AND ITS SCOPE

Ethics refers to the moral value of what is good or what is bad and the individual judgements on values. These judgements are based on cultural and religious beliefs. Bioethics is a compound word: bio represents life and therefore bioethics means concerning life with ethics. The purpose of bioethics is to deal with the ethical and value issues that have surfaced due to the rapid development of science, technology and biomedicine during the last two decades. It is a new 'supra-interdisciplinary' study; it presents serious issues for all of us living in an era of life manipulation and genetic engineering. Its study deals with all the complex and integrated aspects of life beginning, ending and its quality.

Origin of Bioethics

It was Van Rensselaer Potter in 1970 who used the term 'bioethics' for the first time for the protection of earth from the high pollution growth and wastage of natural resources, thus defining global ethics as a discipline representing a link between biology, ecology, medicine and human values in order to ensure the survival of both human beings and other animal species. Initially it was thought that bioethics only deals with the discussion on medical treatment, transplantation, *in vitro* fertilization etc. but now the field of study has expanded to include daily medical examination, diagnosis, matters of informing diseases and the matters of environment that concern human life. Biotechnology issues related to ethics include:

- Cloning
- Stem cell research
- Drug trials

- Use of pharmaceuticals
- Xenotransplantations
- Safety of the nanoparticles
- Genomic studies
- Release of transgenicorganisms
- New reproductive strategies.

There is a growing recognition all over the world that development of biological scientific knowledge must be accompanied by public debate on societal choices and informed participation of people. Bioethics states that there is a difference between what is scientifically possible and ethically acceptable.

Branches or Theories of Bioethics

There are three main branches of bioethics namely normative (prescriptive ethics), non-normative (descriptive/metaethics) and interactive bioethics. The branch of ethics that prescribes the moral standards that need to be followed so that the action may be considered morally right is called normative/prescriptive ethics. Normative ethics sets up a value system that tells that how human beings are supposed to behave. Non-normative ethics includes the analysis of the meaning of the term used in moral discourse and debates where moral beliefs can be shown to be true or false. Interactive bioethics debates about the other two forms of ethics between people, groups, societies and communities as a whole. It increases the communication within the society to debate and clarify doubts and creates a universal acceptability on safe handling of the application of biotechnology.

DIFFERENT APPROACHES TO ETHICS

There are various approaches to ethics and these are the following:

- The utility approach
- The rights approach
- The fairness and justice approach
- The common good approach
- The virtue approach.

In the utility approach, multiple courses of action are identified and evaluated for effectiveness and the harms and benefits that can be derived from these actions. It finally narrows down to the action that will produce more benefit and least harm.

The rights approach talks about the right of an individual to make a choice. It focuses on different rights of a person, like the right to the truth according to which one has a right to know about the things that affects one by making some choice, the right to privacy as long as it does not violate the rights of others, the right not to be punished until proven guilty and the right to speak if there is a breach in an agreed contract.

In the fairness and justice approach, it is stated that everyone should be treated equally. It deals with the fairness of action that should treat everyone in a same way and should not show any kind of discrimination.

The common good approach deals with the community as a whole and not as individuals. It ensures that all social policies and systems are designed in a manner so as to benefit all the people rather than a select set of people.

The virtue approach to ethics talks about virtues like honesty, courage, compassion, generosity, integrity, fairness etc. while dealing with ethical problems.

Bioethical issues are evaluated using the above approaches and are taken care by the bioethical advisory community.

Bioethical Issues and Conflicts in the Development of GMOs

Bioethics addresseses the impact of GM technology on individual and on society as a whole. Various bioethical issues regarding GMOs are listed below:

- Interference with nature and effect of transgenic organisms on the environment.
- Mixing of DNA to form chimeras that are not present in nature
- Risk of altering the ecosystem through gene flow
- Lack of consumer choice as most of the GMO products are sold without labelling.
- Mass destruction of non-target insect population, loss of balance of nature and adverse effect on individuals who consume crops that are genetically modified by the use of bio-pesticides
- High cost of transgenic seeds, non-availability of seeds to farmers in case a crop is raised from seeds using terminator gene technology
- Use of animals in GMO experiments
- Manipulation of genetic traits of the children to produce designer babies
- Unnatural, immoral acts of violation of God's law by crossing species by creating transgenic combinations from different sources and putting the entire species concept at risk resulting in loss of biological, ecological and morphological diversity
- Mass production of pharmaceuticals using cloned genes in plants as bioreactors imposing the risk of toxicity and allergenicity
- Premature death of most cloned animals due to illness and other complications arising out of cloning
- Possibility of introduction of new diseases in humans by xenotransplantation Long-term adverse effects on the environment when transgenics are released in the field
- Risk of creating new diseases/disease agents for which there is no medical treatment through DNA combinations used in transgenic research.

Bioethical Issues in Transgenic, Gene Therapy and Human Cloning and Its Bioethical Implications andsConflicts

Bioethics is related to various queries about the basic human values like right to life and health, advanced developments in medicines and diagnosis and life technologies. It also involves various issues related to the beginning and end of human life. Some of other such issues are summarized in Table 13.1

Subsequent sections of this chapter discuss some of the important bioethical issues.

Bioethical Issues in Genetically Modified Organisms (Plants, Animals, Microbes)

Biotechnologists all over the world claim that this science and the products created through this science will increase the production of crop and animals to feed the ever-increasing population of the world. The modification of crops and animal at the gene level can contribute to the sustainability of

Table 13.1 *Areas Subject to Ethical Issues*

❑ Abortion	❑ Gene therapy	❑ Population control
❑ Animal Rights	❑ GMO	❑ Prescription drugs
❑ Artificial insemination	❑ Genetically modified food	❑ Professional ethics
❑ Artificial womb	❑ Human cloning	❑ Recreational drug use
❑ Biorisk	❑ Human genetic engineering	❑ Reproductive rights
❑ Brain-computer interface	❑ Infertility treatments	❑ Reprogenetics
❑ Chimeras	❑ Medical malpractices	❑ Sperm and egg donations
❑ Cloning	❑ Moral obligation	❑ Stem cell research
❑ Confidentiality of medical records	❑ Organ donation	❑ Spiritual drug use
❑ Euthanasia	❑ Parthenogenesis	❑ Surrogacy
❑ Gene theft	❑ Placebo	❑ Transsexuality
❑ Genomics		❑ Transplant trade
		❑ Xenotransplantation

the environment and reduce the use of fertilizers in farming. But scientists must realize that there is a debate over GMOs and a substantial public distrust in the products developed by manipulation of life through genetic engineering.

GMOs Contain Altered Gene from Other Varied Sources

Genetically engineered organisms are produced by gene cloning methods in which a gene from a different origin is introduced and expressed in the host organism and the newly produced protein is further manipulated for enhanced expression in the host. The cloned gene is then combined with other genes to form a chimera, which is introduced in another organism to create a transgenic. This chimera has genes that are introduced by different gene transfer methods using different biotechniques rather than the conventional method of selective breeding.

Transgenics have Traits that are Conventionally Not Present in the Species

Researchers today develop organisms that express a novel trait by transferring a gene that is originally not present in the organism. For example, golden rice that has increased level of provitamin A, sunflower that is resistant to mildew and transgenic cotton, which is resistant to insect damage. Such gene transfers can be done in various combinations like a plant—animal—human combination. For example, a DNA of mouse and human tumour fragment is inserted in tobacco DNA, and the plant produced now contains the potential vaccine against non-Hodgkin's lymphoma. This combination can be used to produce edible vaccines by incorporating human protein into fruits like banana, potato and tomatoes, which get engineered to secrete human protein, which can then be used as edible vaccines. In animal—animal gene transfer combinations, a private company in Montreal isolated a gene responsible for silk protein from a spider and inserted it into a genome of goat egg before fertilization. The milk of the resulting transgenic goat produced a protein from which spider silk is made. Animal human combination proves to be promising and of great potential. Animals like pigs can be used as transgenic animals as there physiology and organ size is very much similar to human. The motto behind this is that the organ of pigs can be used in human organ transplantation, which will lessen the crisis of shortage of human heart and kidney available for the transplant. Transgenic animals can also be used as temporary skin substitute for healing wounds and burns. Therapeutic proteins like monoclonal antibodies can also be extracted from the milk of transgenic animals, which can be used in the treatment of various ailments.

By the use of genetic engineering, superbugs are created. These are genetically modified microorganisms created for bioremediation to clean up the environment by tolerating extreme conditions and rapidly breaking down complex nonbiodegradable toxic chemicals to simpler form that can be degraded by nature. However, the issues of controlling the spread of these superbugs have hampered their development.

Bioethical Issues in Gene Therapy

Advancements in understanding and manipulating genes have allowed scientists to alter an individual genetic material to fight and prevent diseases and to replace the malfunctioned gene by the correct gene. The overall aim of gene therapy is to sustain the normal function in cells which have been affected by genetic disorders. Ethical issues in gene therapy are around

(a) differentiating good and bad uses of gene therapy,
(b) availability only to the super rich due to the high costs involved,
(c) change in social behaviour to people who are different (and need gene therapy) and
(d) using gene therapy not for malfunctioning genes but for improving basic human traits like intelligence, etc.

Ethical Issues in Human Cloning

With the successful production of embryonic stem cell cultures, it is possible to grow any type of human tissues that can be used to repair damaged heart, pancreas, blood vessels or brains, clone animals and humans. These techniques have attracted the attention of people worldwide. Dolly was a Finnish Dorset sheep (cross between Finn sheep and Dorset breed), the world's first clone of an adult animal very identical to the adult sheep whose DNA (from a single cell) was used by Dr. Ian Wilmut from Roslin Institute in the UK. Dolly was a breakthrough as it bypassed the need for sperm in procreation, a process similar to parthenogenesis.

After the success of Dolly, scientists have aimed to clone more and more animals for:

- desirable traits and for producing large quantity of less costly pharmaceutical protein in milk,
- analysis and therapy development for genetic disorder,
- producing human organs that can be implanted to a person,
- finding treatment for diseases like cancer and
- reviving species who are on the verge of extinction.

Social and Ethical Implications of Cloning

Cloning experiments have created anxiety and fear in everybody's mind. The history of eugenics has already again and again shown that the economic, social stress can lower our sensitivity to each other and to moral and ethical values and this is what cloning of animals and humans will do. So far, God was supposed to be the creator of life but now scientists and their success is about to put human beings in the position of God, which is not acceptable to many religions and cultures.

Some ethical issues related to cloning are as follows:

(a) Religious objections—man's effort to become immortal and play God
(b) Cloning contradicts human nature and dignity
(c) Producing children without fertilization
(d) Exploitation of animals during research on cloning
(e) Death of more than 90% of the offspring from cloning
(f) Higher chances of cancer, infections and other disabilities in cloned animals
(g) Cloned organisms are often biologically damaged.

Transgenic Animals and Bioethical Issues

Transgenic animal research includes alteration of genome so that the altered animal can be used to serve man. These animals are altered to produce animal models like disease model to understand a disease more effectively, to produce pharmaceutical molecules in the blood or milk of animals, for xenotransplant to produce donor organs and as the scientific model to study metabolic biology. Depending on the need of the experiment, different types of animals are made using the genetic engineering aspects.

Types of Transgenic Animals Produced

The first type of transgenic animals are disease models for knowing and curing diseases that currently have no cure like cancer, AIDS, Parkinson's disease etc. An example of such type of animal is oncomouse. As we know that cancer is caused by the damage to DNA where there is an uncontrollable replication of cells in the body. Oncogenes lead to uncontrollable cell growth. Oncomouse was first created at Harvard University in 1980 by inserting human oncogenes into mouse genome so that the mouse shows symptoms of cancer and then investigation and potential therapeutics research can be carried out on the tumorigenesis. Similarly, scientists are making new animal models with HIV receptors so that some therapeutics related to AIDS can be found. Professor Dave Adams and his colleagues had created an Alzheimer disease's mouse model in the same way. Their vaccine is currently in human clinical trial.

The other types of transgenic animals include the transpharmers and xenotranslanters. Transpharmers are engineered to produce various drugs and medicine in their blood from where they can be secreted and purified. A mouse producing tPA was the first transpharmer. This protein is an important clot-dissolving drug used to open arteries following heart attack. First transgenic bull called herman was engineered to pass on the genes required to create human lactoferrin, an antimicrobial protein. Xenotransplanters on the other hand are made as organ donors. Pigs were chosen for these experiments as their physiology closely matches that of humans. These transgenic pigs can donate liver, kidney, lungs etc. There are other transgenic animals that are created as a food source by adding growth hormones to make them grow faster. Super pigs and super fishes are two animals that scientists are trying to create.

Ethics and Morals Associated with Transgenic Animals

Many groups of people and many organizations profess strong opinions on such topics as transgenic animals. Some think that the world biomass might shift following the release of transgenic animals and plants while others debate on the ethics of harming animals for research. There are debates on the ethical, spiritual and cultural impact of this science.

One way to decide what is ethical is to consider the benefits of the experiment to the society against the determents to animals. Take for example the xenotransplanter pig whose cells are being genetically altered not to express any specific glycoprotein residue on the surface that is viewed as foreign by the human immune system. This type of animal is called knockout transgenic animal as the alteration is done to delete the expression of its own gene instead of expressing immune response against foreign gene. The ethical issue here is that the animals have to sacrifice their life to provide its organ to save human life. In a similar way, Harvard mouse is also an ethical concern as it induces the disease in mouse, which is unethical, but at the same time this is the only means to measure and find cure for many important diseases. In summary, the following ethical concerns exist in working on transgenic animals.

(a) Violation of animal rights—their treatment as a human property rather than beings in their own right
(b) Dangers that transgenic animals may pose to human health
(c) Poor quality of life for genetically engineered animals, e.g. fast growing pigs have discomfort in their heart when they are too active

Other Major Issues Related to Bioethics

Socioeconomic Issues

There are various social issues that are raised by the use of biotechnology:

- Will the benefits of genetic engineering and molecular biotechnology be available only to rich people or will it be universal?
- With the advancement in research in the area of agriculture, will these new techniques overlook the conventional farming practices?
- Will it be the case in future that medicinal therapies that are based on molecular biotechnology will surpass the equally potential and effective conventional treatments?
- Finance to such advanced areas of biotechnology will cause hindrance to funding of important and useful technologies in other areas. More money today is being spent on rare genetic disorders than on more prevalent diseases like malaria.

Sociolegal Issues

As the science of biotechnology is product-oriented, it is important to have supervisions, regulations and legal boundaries in place. The release of GMOs in the environment or farm trials must be adequately monitored because lack of supervision and regulation can lead to illegal practices around them.

- Erosion of public accountability due to the transfer of novel technology from public sector to the private sector.
- No legal binding from the FDA for mandatory labelling of GM food.
- Genetic engineering is being used for creation of biological warfare through the development of dreadful virus and bacteria, which can cause an epidemic and initiate a genetic arms race. There has to be legal ban to stop such kind of inhumane applications of biotechnology.

Environmental Issues

A summary of environmental issues related to bioethics is given below.

- Careless release of genetically engineered micro-organisms can cause damage to the ecology. Different organizations under biosafety have made it mandatory to the release of GMO under proper regulations.
- GM products are live entities. They pose danger to the environment because they can reproduce, mutate, migrate and spread.

- Introduction of novel types into foreign habitats may disturb the natural equilibrium. Carp, salmon etc. have been transformed with a number of genes from human, cattle and rats to increase their growth and reproduction. If released into the environment the novel mutant fish can mate with the native species, mixing and polluting the gene pool of native species.
- Unforeseen and undesirable characteristics can occur in novel species through genetic engineering.
- Unacceptable transmission of gene as genetic material to other hosts.
- The production of genetically engineered organisms in large scale will reduce natural genetic diversity. Genetic diversity found in animal breeds and plant breeds is the foundation of on-going continuous evolution and selection of stocks by farmers and breeders will inhibit this natural evolution process.

Health and Safety Issues

Genetic engineering has proved to be unsafe in some of the projects, which have been abandoned due to negative results.

- Bovine growth hormone has resulted in the increased occurrence of diseases like mastitis in cows.
- There are reports of users of genetically engineered insulin collapsing to unconsciousness.
- Use of synthetic tryptophan resulted in various symptoms like severe muscle pain. It was banned later but this has questioned the risks of bioengineered products.
- Use of recombinant human growth hormone in children has been linked to incidence of leukaemia and melanoma.
- Use of BT endotoxin gene for pest resistance in crops has been linked to stunted growth in plants.
- Possibility of antibiotic marker gene and known allergens getting passed to the human food chain.

Bioethics and Consumer Acceptance

Bioethics is about moral choices arising from the assessment of risks and benefits related to human progress in biotechnology. Bioethics is also about a range of social and ethical factors and concerns related to the consumption and development of genetically engineered food and products. Different people have different perceptions related to this area of research. One group of people who supports the well-being of animals does not want animals to be experimented because these techniques and manipulations inflict suffering on them Vegetarians are debating on the transfer of animal genes to plants. However, something unethical for one group of people may not be unethical to the other group and this disparity opens up a difficult challenge to the regulatory authorities to frame guidelines for the use and development of GM food.

To reap the benefits of the technology, it is important to have public perception and acceptance through trust building. If there is no trust and willingness to accept the technology, there is no use of it in the welfare of mankind. It is very well quoted by Dan Glickman, former US Secretary of Agriculture. 'With all that biotech has to offer, it is nothing if it is not accepted.' This boils down to the matter of trust in the science and regulatory processes to ensure thorough assessment and review.

For public acceptance, it is very important to have the right understanding and awareness on all aspects of biotechnology. Failure to do so will surely result in lower degree of public acceptance of GMOs and agricultural products. It is also important to consider that public may not be interested in the fine technicalities involved in the development of the GMO but in the more relevant direct outcome—how GM food is going to benefit an individual, what potential it holds as a whole, what impact will it have on human health and the protection of the environment and freedom of choice to the consumer. Besides this, all queries related to moral actions need to be answered to individual satisfaction.

It is highly likely that the consumer is not able to decide between the risks associated to health and environment and the huge benefits of GM food-enhanced nutritive and therapeutic value. At this point, scientific and non-scientific organizations are needed to guide the consumer to make the right choices. However, this will help only if these organizations are not driven by their personal gains. Once the ground is set, it is important to label the GE product. Labeling is under discussion in the European Union. Labeling GE products is consistent with bioethics as long as it represents the truth in full details—what all is present in the product—which will enable the consumer to choose according to their own ethical principle. This freedom of choice has an implication for national policy in technology assessment, education and other information campaigns and openness about where and what decisions are taken. The scientific community, government, industry and the media are together responsible for providing all the relevant information in the public interest.

Bioethics Advisory Committees

International Bioethics Committee (IBC) of UNESCO

In 1993, UNESCO created the International Bioethics Committee (IBC) amid concerns about the social, cultural, legal and economic issues arising out of the advancements of research and commercialization in the field of biotechnology. Since, the discovery of DNA, humanity has learned a lot about the vital function and mechanism of genes. But a few questions have also been thrown up—how can we protect ourselves against the possible abuse of the powers of biomedical research like cloning and how can we make sure that the progress resulting from this research will benefit everyone. This is the main task that IBC has undertaken since inception as it tracks the progress of scientific research and defines the principle of dignity and individual liberty against the threat of unethical practices in bioethical research. The various tasks of IBC are as follows:

- To promote reflection on the ethical and legal issues raised by research in the area of life sciences and their applications
- To encourage action to increase awareness among the general public, specialized groups and public-and-private decision makers involved in bioethics
- To cooperate with the international government and the various NGOs concerned by the issues raised in the field of bioethics
- To contribute in spreading the principle set out in the universal declaration on the human genome and human rights
- To make necessary recommendations to the general conference on the practices that can oppose human dignity
- To spread public awareness of genetic testing, gene therapy, genetic counselling neuroscience, population genetics etc.
- To focus on problems such as confidentiality of genetic data, pre-implementation of genetic diagnosis and patenting of genes.

All debates on ethical issues between the scientific community and public are discussed under this forum with the motto that the progress of science cannot be stopped but the direction can be questioned and debated upon.

IBC is the only constitutive body that focuses on bioethics. It has 36 members appointed by UNESCO Director General for a four-year term. These members are from diverse areas like doctors, geneticists, chemists, legal experts, anthropologists, philosophers and historians. The forum enables exchange of ideas and information and identified universal values in order to reconcile scientific progress with human rights and freedom.

International Association of Bioethics (IAB)

IAB is associated with the study of ethical, social, legal, philosophical and other related issues arising in the area of health care and biological sciences. IAB is a leading international organization bringing together researchers in all area of bioethics.

Objectives of IAB

- To facilitate contacts and information exchange between professionals and organizations engaged in the area of bioethics
- To encourage research and teaching in bioethics and to enable free and open discussions on various issues on bioethics through international conferences.

International Bioethics Survey (IBS)

The International Bioethics Survey conducts various surveys to gauge people's opinion about how they feel about the ethical and moral issues related to the advancement in biotechnology—issues ranging from global warming to *in vitro* fertilization to screening genes to predict the future possibility of diseases.

In 1993, a survey was performed across ten countries of the world that include Australia, Hong Kong, India, Israel, Japan, New Zealand, Russia and Singapore. The main objective was to find out how the layman thinks and feels about the diseases, life, nature, genetic engineering its related products, gene therapy etc. To do this study, IBS chose three samples of population from public, university students and school teachers. A questionnaire was prepared and sent to the three samples across countries and the answers were analysed. The results showed that people in different countries shared more or less similar views on most of the issues mentioned in the survey.

Also, the results clearly showed that people do show the ability to balance benefits and risk of science and technology. This is very important for bioethics—to balance good and harm and the survey showed that people are capable of doing this. Support was seen in favour of disease-resistant crops and bacteria to clean oil spills while most people were against genetic engineering for fun, like the creation of sport fish.

It is the responsibility of each nation to develop social and educational systems that allow this division of individual perception.

EuropaBio

EuropaBio is a non-profitable organization created in 1996 to provide a voice to the biotech industry at the European Union level. It is an association of bio-industries that has 62 corporate and 7 associate members operating worldwide. Members of EuropaBio are involved in research and development, manufacturing and commercialization of biotechnology. The corporate members have a wide range of activities like human and animal health care, diagnostics, crop protection, agricultural food and environmental products and services.

The main objectives of the organization are as follows:

- Promotion of the novel and dynamic biotech industry
- Contributing to responsible use of this science and its potential for humans and the environment.
- Fostering good bioethics practices among the European biotechnology industry.

EuropaBio's Core Ethical Values Charter

The core ethical values charter adopted by EuropaBio highlights the following:

- Priority to health, safety and environment during research and development, manufacture and distribution of product and services
- Commitment to socially responsible use of biotechnology, use of biotechnology with respect to human dignity and human respect
- Treatment of animals with minimal pain and distress their usage only when scientifically necessary
- No support for human cloning
- Protection of confidentiality of medical information of patients, including genetic information
- Provision of applicable information to patients before and after genetic testing
- Support for improvement of crops by genetic engineering for better quality of food and to enhance world's food supply
- Sustainable use of plant material for production of bio-based products
- Support for the current bans on human germ line gene therapy.

Convention on Human Rights and Biomedicine

The Convention on Human Rights and Biomedicine covers all medical and biological areas concerning human beings: right to live, right to information, prevention and diagnostics and other research areas. The right to respect for their personal lives and the right to information about ill health are some of the agendas covered in various articles of the convention.

- Non-discrimination—There should not be any form of discrimination against any person on the grounds of his or her genetic heritage.
- Predictive genetic tests—Genetic tests that can predict genetic diseases or find out a gene responsible for a disease or genetic hindrance to a disease can only be performed for health purposes only after proper genetic counselling.
- Interventions on the human genome—Interventions on the human genome are only allowed for preventive diagnostics or therapeutic purposes. Such modifications are not allowed if the purpose is to introduce modifications in the genome of descendants.
- General rule of scientific research—All the scientific research in relation to medicine, whether therapeutic or diagnostic, can be carried out freely, subject to provisions in the convention, ensuring the protection of rights of the human being.
- Protection of individuals undergoing research—Research should be done on a person only if there is no alternative of equal effectiveness. The research has been approved by the competent authorities after examining its merit, person undergoing research has been informed about his rights and safeguards and consent has been provided by the individual for the same.
- Researches on embryo culture—Research on *in vitro* embryo culture is allowed only if there is a surety of adequate protection of the embryo. The development of human embryo for research purposes is strictly prohibited.
- Organ or tissue removal from a living donor—Transplantation of organs from a living person can only be done if there is no organ available from a deceased person and there is no other alternative for the recipient.

Bioethics Guidelines from European Nutrigenomics Organization (NuGO)

There are several bioethics guidelines from NuGo, which are as follows:

Guideline 1—Human studies, genetic or other, should only be carried out after the research volunteer has provided free and informed consent to the process. It is preferable to seek advice of a sociologist or psychologist to optimize the information process. The consent process has to assure

- voluntary nature of participation,
- difference between research and medical treatment and limitation of the personal benefits,
- necessary commitments arising from the participation in research projects and
- right to withdraw the consent at any point of time without any linked consequences.

Guideline 2—Content of the consent form for the nutrigenomic study. The signed consent form should serve as a record of the information conveyed to the participant. It should therefore include all the information mentioned in the guideline 1.

Guideline 3—Informed consent from the volunteer who cannot give consent. The consent process needs to be adapted to the comprehension of the research volunteer and must take place in front of one witness who is legally authorized to sign the consent form.

Guideline 4—Informed consent for biobanks. The collection of biological material and personal data from an individual, including the routine samples must be subjected to donor's consent. Different consents are required for the collection and subsequent use of samples.

Guideline 5—Extent of informed consent for biobanking. The consent should cover the duration for which the sample can be retained and the purposes for which the same can be used.

Guideline 6—Disclosure of genotype test results. The extent, form and timing of the disclosure of genotype test results should be consistent with what was agreed upon in the informed consent.

Guideline 7—Whenever there is a disclosure of an individual's result, the concerned should be offered full information about the implication of the test results.

Guideline 8—Ownership agreements of the samples and the data should be established prior to biobanking. Usually the institution is the owner of biobank and scientist in-charge of the biobank is the curator. These two have to take all the steps to protect the samples, data, its storage, its use and access.

Guideline 9—Samples need to be stored by coding the biological material and the key for the code to be stored separately. Strict rules for storage and use must be established so that personal identifiers are removed from the data.

Guideline 10—Independent review of research using material stored in biobank. Review by the bioethics committee must be conducted on regular bases.

Guideline 11—Benefit sharing. According to international law, the donation must not be paid for because of the ethical reasons as body parts are not for sale and also to avoid the exploitation of an individual for benefit sharing.

Guideline 12—Fate of sample and associated data if consent is withdrawn. If there is a case where the volunteer needs to withdraw her consent, she has a right to decide whether her samples must be unlinked, anonymized or obliterated.

Guideline 13—Samples from deceased persons. Samples from deceased persons can be collected and stored for biobanks and subsequently used in research on the same conditions as for living research volunteers. If the deceased has not given consent during his life time, his relatives can do the formalities. In this way ethical approval can be obtained.

Guideline 14—Quality control. Biobanks should have adequate quality control procedures. This includes proper systems for storage, coding and registration.

Guideline 15—Legal successors. In case of the hosting institution closedown, the scientists and the institution involved should seek the advice and approval of an ethics committee.

Guideline 16—Access to biobanks. Access to the biobanks for use of its samples by third parties should be in the form of research contracts and all access should be recorded.

Guideline 17—Disclosure of personal data. Any form of personal data cannot be transferred to the third party without the consent of the volunteer.

Guideline 18—Use of biological materials and data in further research projects. If there is a use of biological data in any form other than the core research it was volunteered for, it should be subjected to ethical approval.

Guideline 19—Transfer of a biobank. The transfer of an entire biobank can only be permitted if the recipient institution or organization maintains the same level of protection and quality assurance in comparison with the original institution.

BIOLOGICAL WEAPONS AND THEIR SOCIAL AND ETHICAL IMPLICATIONS

Biological weapons are harmful materials produced from critically pathogenic microorganisms. They can also be genetically engineered microorganisms that are intentionally used to cause harm. These weapons are used to target living organisms like humans, animals or vegetation and can also be used to contaminate non-living substances like air, water, soil, which will ultimately be consumed by living organisms. There are many microbes that can be used as bioweapons because they are highly toxic, easy to obtain, easy to multiply and easily transferable from person to person.

These microbes are used as weapons by attaching the toxin to the bomb so that they may be released upon explosion. They can also be dreadful pests that can be released easily into the environment to destroy the agriculture. Biological weapons are far more dangerous than nuclear, chemical or conventional weapons.

Genetic engineering can alter microorganisms like microbes to make them resistant to antibiotics, harder to detect, more stable in the environment and more lethal. In 1990, some Russian researchers succeeded in altering the immunological properties of *anthrax* making existing vaccines and their detection methods ineffective against the new genetic engineered type. The German Army Institute of Microbiology created tularemia bacteria genetically altered to withstand antibiotic treatment.

The Biological and Toxin Weapons Convention (BTWC) outlaws any development, production and stockpiling of bioweapons and has contributed to biological weapon disarmament and the prevention of biological arms race. The Geneva Protocol prohibits the use of bioweapons but the BTWC goes a step forward in prohibiting the development and stockpiling of bioweapons as well. The scope of biological weapons under this convention includes all microbial and other biological agents and toxins and their means of delivery.

Potential Biological Weapons

A list of a few biological organisms that may potentially be used as biological weapons are given in Table 13.2.

Table 13.2 *Biological Organisms that can be used as Biological Weapons*

Microbe	Diseases/Symptoms
Anthrax (Bacillus anthracis)	*Pulmonary anthrax septicemia, flu-like symptoms*
Clostridium perfringens	*Gas gangrene, severe abdominal Cramps, Diarrhoea*
RICIN (Protein Toxin)	*Severe abdominal pain, watery and bloody diarrhoea, vomiting, weakness, fever, cough, and pulmonary edema*
Variola virus	*Persistent fever, vomiting, rash on tongue and in mouth, rash and bumps on skin*

CHAPTER SUMMARY

Transgenic technology and genetic engineering present intriguing and difficult challenges for 21st-century scientists and ethicists. Until we as a society or, perhaps, as a global entity can agree on what beings, human or otherwise, are worthy of moral and legal status and respect, we can expect intense cross-disciplinary debate and discussion as new intelligent life is created through science and medicine. Questions around what level of risk is acceptable, who bears the risk, who decides what is moral and ethical, who decides if the benefits outweigh the risks, for what purposes should genetic modification be allowed form the basis of intense debate.

In this chapter, we have tried to study both perspectives on the debate. The 'for' perspective—GM crops are needed to feed the growing population of the world, genetic research can find cure to diseases, xenotransplants can reduce human organ shortages saving large number of lives—and the 'against' perspective about animals being involved in research, loss of biodiversity and man trying to play God were discussed.

We cannot abandon scientific research and advancements in biotechnology. At the same time, we need to make sure that ethics and morals pertaining to the commercial use of this research are observed and there is public acceptance at large for the use of this technology for the betterment of life on the planet.

MULTIPLE CHOICE QUESTIONS

1. Bioethics is the philosophical study of ethical controversies concerned to
   (i) Life sciences and biotechnology
   (ii) Medicine
   (iii) Politics law and theology
   (iv) All the above
2. Which are the below is used for the creation of bioweapons
   (i) Colastridium
   (ii) Anthrax
   (iii) Small pox
   (iv) All of the above
3. Human cloning is one of the concerns in bioethics where people call it as
   (i) Playing God
   (ii) Against nature
   (iii) Creator of basic essence of life
   (iv) All the above

REVIEW QUESTIONS

1. What is bioethics? What is its scope and approaches?
2. Discuss the ethical and practical issues surrounding the use of animal organs as xenotransplants.
3. Discuss the various ethical issues surrounding gene therapy.
4. What do you understand by bio weapons? Discuss the concerns in the use of biotechnology for warfare.
5. Discuss the role of various bioethical committees in solving the debate on bioethics.

NGOs for Biosafety and Bioethics

14

Chapter Objectives:

It is not only government which plays an important role in securing international and national rights but a major role is also played by the various non-governmental organizations, in the country and abroad, for the liability and redressal of damage caused by genetically modified organisms (GMO) and its related work. In this chapter, students will be knowing what are these different organizations, their activities and their campaigns, their socioeconomic and cultural considerations related to the use and release of GMO.

INTRODUCTION TO NGOs

The main goal of biosafety in relation to genetically modified products is to ensure that all possible risks arising out of such research and commercialization is properly assessed and evaluated under various regulatory bodies to ensure that there are no adverse effects on the environment, animal and human health.

The integral part of most biosafety frameworks include administrative structure, risk assessments, methodologies and program to access information and public awareness, education and participation related to the safe transfer, handling and use of GMOs. It is also the responsibility of the government to engage in awareness-raising activities about GMOs and related products. Without public consent and decision making, the commercialization of GM crops might be dangerous. Till now, public acceptance related to GMOs has not received enough focus.

The GM debate belongs to either government or scientists in public or private sector organizations. Various NGOs who represent the concerns of the consumers and the environment talk about farmer rights. The concerns of the various organizations involved are based on the following:

- Technical, ecological, ethical and economical grounds
- Highly favourable nature of GM technology towards multinational agribusiness corporations at the cost and rights of small-scale farmers
- Biotechnology's interference with the laws of nature
- Public acceptance about the choice and acceptance and GMOs used by consumers
- Adverse consequences arising from unplanned combinations of the transferred gene with the host genome
- Adverse effect on native germplasm due to the use of transgenics leading to loss of important innate properties.

In the debate on the use of GM crops, many NGO activists have argued that it should be left with the farmers and consumers to decide on the use of this advanced technology. On the other side, private multinationals want to lock in their profits through the use of terminator technology on seeds where the farmers would have to buy fresh seeds every season. Also, parallel developments in IPR help them create larger control on the agriculture sector.

Organizations, both public and private, government and NGOs play an important role in raising all these issues pertaining to biosafety and bioethics. These issues are being discussed at different forums both at the national and international levels.

The following sections cover some Indian organizations that are stakeholders in the debate on the safe use of GM technology—either as research institutions working on better understanding of the genome or as companies entrusted by the government for the safe commercialization of biotechnology or NGOs working for farmer rights and ethical issues.

PUBLIC SECTOR ORGANIZATIONS

In the public sector, Department of Biotechnology (DBT) promoted several autonomous biotechnology research institutes, e.g. National Centre for Plant Genome Research (NCPBGR) and National Bioresource Development Board. In 1990, DBT established an autonomous body Biotechnology Consortium India Limited (BCIL) to establish the links between research, financial and industrial institutions related to biotechnology research and development. BCIL is involved in capacity building activities in biosafety related to genetically modified organisms (GMOs) including preparation of research documents and reports and organizing national and international conferences, workshops on key policy issues and state and district level events for various stakeholders and farmers welfare.

Other than DBT, many other institutions funded and supported by the government are also involved in the research and safe commercialization of biotechnology. Some of them are Indian Council of Agriculture Research (ICAR), Central Plantation Plant Research Institution (CPCRI), Directorate of Wheat Research (DWR), National Bureau of Plant Genetic Resources (NBPGR), Indian Agriculture Research Institute (IARI) and Indian Institute of Vegetable Research (IIVR). Since 1980, the government has been consistently putting efforts to create collaborative ventures with national and international organizations.

PRIVATE SECTOR ORGANIZATIONS

Most private sector organizations in biotechnology are focused on its industrial potential like production of enzymes, bioactive compounds, vaccines (recombinant Hepatitis B), diagnostic immunological kits and development of novel microorganisms with the help of genetic manipulation. The new laws on patents and IPR are also responsible for private investments and the involvement of private sector organizations in biotechnology research.

Biocon, Bharat Biotech, Dr Reddy's, Reliance Life Sciences, Zydus Cadila, Myco and Monsanto are some of the private sector organizations working in the field of biotechnology research and development. Monsanto is especially known in this field for the development of transgenic seeds.

Two important industry bodies that play an active role along with the government to promote the interest of the biotech industry as a whole are Confederation of Indian Industry (CII) and Federation of Indian Chamber of Commerce and Industry (FICCI).

NATIONAL NGOs

There are several NGOs at the national and the state levels engaged in generating wider public participation and public debate on the various issues on GM crop and GM food. Some of the more popular NGOs are the following.

Gene Campaign

Gene Campaign is a grass root level organization with presence in almost 17 states in India. It was started by Dr. Suman Sahai in 1993. Gene Campaign is a leading research and advisory organization working in the field of bioresources, farmers and community rights, IPR, biopiracy and on the debate and issue related to GM crops and food. Since its establishment, it has been working to empower local communities to retain control over the genetic resources in order to ensure food security. Its work also includes involvement in policy making and legislation with respect to biological resources.

Apart from the above, gene campaign works for the recognition of native or the innate knowledge of the resources and its potential for increasing incomes for the rural and the tribal communities. Their aim is to provide these communities with the legal rights over their own native resources. Their effort is to keep medicines and products derived from the native resources and knowledge, out of the shackles of patents. Gene campaign has been largely responsible for raising the national debate on the danger of seed patents and its threat to food. It has set an example fighting against the patent on basmati rice and turmeric. Apart from this, they have also campaigned to protect biodiversity and provided the first draft of the biodiversity legislation in 1997; the law was finally passed in 2001. They have also raised voice in concern to transgenic crops and demanded transparency and public participation and greater competence in regulatory systems. They have put a lot of effort in disseminating public awareness, which was supported by simple literature in all possible regional languages explaining the process of globalization and the national and international development that could threaten food and security. The campaign is still working together with wide range of people including farmer advisory committees, academic institutions, government sector, political and activist group, various NGOs and students. It is linked with the larger network of national and international organizations which enables it to have varied and diverse out reach.

Research Foundation for Science, Technology and Ecology (RFSTE)

It was a research initiative founded in India in 1982 by the world-renowned scientist and environmentalist Dr. Vandana Shiva to provide direction and support to environmental activism. It works for the conservation of biodiversity and protecting people's rights from the threats to their livelihoods and environment by the centralized system of monoculture in forestry, agriculture and fisheries.

This trust started the program 'Navdanya' for nonviolent farming, which protects biodiversity. The main aim of this program is to support local farmers to conserve crops and plants that are been under the verge of extinction; it spreads native knowledge and culture. It has created awareness on possible harmful effects of GMOs. This movement has now spread throughout the country along with the other organizations and farmer network. Navdanya has trained many batches of men and women farmers, students, government officials, representatives of national and international NGOs on conservation of biodiversity and organic farming. RFSTE has its own seed bank and organic farm over an area of two acres.

In May 2001, Navdanya launched its campaign on food rights and food sovereignty with the local communities to take a pledge to save their food and food culture from the malicious intent of the corporate world. They even declared the launch of 'Bija Satyagriha' against the seed and patent laws to keep seeds in the RFSTE even challenged a patent against a fungicidal product derived from seeds of neem tree since the fungicidal properties of the neem tree had long been in public knowledge in India for centuries and the patent law had been misused to transfer biological wealth from India to the hands of a private corporate. The patent was finally rejected on the grounds of traditional knowledge and biopiracy. This case in particular was inspiring for a lot of developing countries who suffer the same kind of theft.

Farmers Movement and its NGO

There are two groups of farmers, one supporting the GM technology in agriculture and the other opposing it. There have been allegations and counter-allegations between these groups. The ones who support biotechnology allege that the group that opposes GM crops are mentored and financed by the lobby of the companies engaged in pesticide production. On the other hand, the group in favour of GM crops is supposed to be backed by the biotechnology companies. It is already known that there are both advantages and disadvantages of the use of GM crops and hence both groups, even if financed from the industry, seem to have a valid stand.

Some movements in relation to farmer rights are discussed below.

- Karnataka Rajya Raitha Sangha (KRRS; Karnataka State Farmers' Association) is a farmer movement from the southern state of Karnataka. This farmer group strongly opposes the introduction of GM crops. It was associated with the NGO RFSTE while protesting against Monsanto's field trials on *Bt* cotton in 1998.
- Shetkari Sanghatana is a farmer's movement in western India. This group, led by prominent farm leader Sharad Joshi, is in favour of GM crops due to the advantages they have over normal crops. But at the same time, they are also of the view that farmers should have the right to choose.

MEDIA

Media plays a very vital role in spreading information on GM crops and discusses the ongoing debate on GMOs. Media is the best way to reach out to people to make them more aware of the facts about biosafety and bioethics so that they can understand both the benefits and also the concerns related to GM technology is safety of environment, human and animal health.

- *Down to Earth*: This magazine is published by the NGO Centre for Science and Environment. It regularly covers a lot of contemporary issues about GM crops, their introduction, assessment etc.
- *Newspapers*: There are different national level journals and newspapers like *The Hindu Business Line*, *Financial Express*, and *Times of India* that cover GM-related issues.

IMPORTANT ROLES THAT NGOs PLAY

- *NGOs Act as Voice of the People*: NGOs speak to the government and its organizations on behalf of people on policy matters. Being in constant touch with the local population of an area, NGOs can better empathize with the people and understand local capabilities, culture and challenges better.
- *NGOs Provide Technical Assistance and Training*: NGOs arrange and develop technical assistance with the help of government and other supporting organizations to make people aware of the environmental issues that may arise from new advancements in technology.

- *NGOs Gather Independent Data on Monitoring, Research and Evaluation*: Most NGOs try to gather independent data on the pros and cons of a research, which is to be commercialized, thereby empowering people with the pros and cons of such activity. This helps people take an informed stand and draw a conclusion.
- *Advisor for Indigenous People*: NGOs are playing an increasing role in spreading awareness about biodiversity, its conservation, and the innate properties of indigenous plants and trees that are in existence since ages and are being used by people for various purposes.

CHAPTER SUMMARY

Integration of socio-economic considerations into biotechnology and biosafety decisions is a difficult subject. But a practical approach and transparent and participatory processes can make this challenge easier to handle. Some groups of people support GMOs and its products while others are against it. This difference of opinion arises due to the fundamental difference in people's thought processes, the direct and indirect impact of commercialization of GM technology and their economic status. There are various campaigns that raise the issues about GMOs and their social, economic, ethical and environmental impact. NGOs have an emancipator potential in the promotion of public acceptance and can act a bridge between the people and the government.

MULTIPLE CHOICE QUESTIONS

1. NGO Stands for
   (i) Non-Government Organization
   (ii) Non-Geographic Organization
   (iii) National Government Organization
   (iv) New Government Organization
2. Private sector is mainly focused on
   (i) Bioactive compounds for industry
   (ii) Enzymes for industrial use
   (iii) Diagnostic kits
   (iv) All of the above
3. FICCI is a
   (i) Private NGO
   (ii) Public NGO
   (iii) Government NGO
   (iv) Autonomous Body
4. Gene Campaign was initiated by
   (i) Dr. Suman Sahai
   (ii) Dr. VandanaiRai
   (iii) Dr. Vandana Shiva
   (iv) Dr. Shri Krishnan

REVIEW QUESTIONS

1. What are non-governmental organizations (NGOs)? Why are they important in the context of biosafety?
2. Discuss Gene Campaign.
3. How can NGOs be the voice of the people?
4. What can the NGOs do to spread awareness among people about GMOs?
5. Give an account of various NGOs—public and private.

Web-based Information of Biosafety on GMO

15

Chapter Objectives:

This chapter gives students the insight on all databases present nationally and internationally on biosafety on what factors these databases contain information and all the organizations associated with it. In the end there is an elementary introduction of role of bioinformatics in creating these valuable databases.

INTRODUCTION

Ever since the first transgenic crop was released for commercial cultivation, various scientific and non-scientific organizations have shown serious concerns regarding the risks posed by genetically modified organisms (GMOs) to human and animal health and to the environment. The impact of biotechnology covers diverse areas like research, industrial, public sector, private sector enterprises and hence GMO research produces and requires a vast amount of information to assess biosafety risks around GMOs. The basic objective of risk assessment of GM plants is to identify and evaluate the risks associated with the release and cultivation of these plants and products compared to their non-transgenic counterparts. Detailed information on the host and donor organisms needs to be documented for creating awareness among public and scientific communities. Considering that more than 58.7 million hectare area worldwide is under transgenic crops (http://www.isaaa.org), a comprehensive and detailed database of GM crops released or to be released is very essential for the successful commercialization of these crops in various part of the world. To accomplish this goal, a growing number of databases are available that collect and store information related to GMOs. These databases deal with information on field trials, environmental releases, transgenes, regulation, risk assessments, documentation and other literature available worldwide on GMOs.

Several important factors explain the need of collecting such database and sharing information created by different tools. Some of these factors are the following:

- Biosafety includes risk analysis and risk management and its regulation includes biosafety framework and taking informed decisions. Information from across the world is needed to enable such decisions.
- Consumers need information on safety clearance of recombinant DNA products to start using them.
- Risk communication and its explanation play a major role in ensuring a higher participation of public in biosafety assessment. Enriched databases support such initiatives.
- Under different national and international regulatory bodies, there are various obligations related to GMO transfer and usage that need to be fulfilled. For the development of various policies and treaties around trans-boundary movements, right information in the form of a database is required.

These databases are maintained by various national and international organizations.

BIOSAFETY DATABASE

Most of the information on biotechnology and biosafety of GMO research and science can be accessed through Internet, which is considered as the main source of information. The list of websites available to consult is present on the website of Information System for Biotechnology (ISB), http://www.nbiap.vt.edu/guidance-resources.aspx

This site gives link to various important websites for agriculture and environment biotechnology. It also has a retrieval system that allows easy and efficient access to data. It has the information on proteins, DNA sequences, germplasm, genetic maps, food safety and allergenicity. It also has data on all the regulations and quality assurance. It must be noted that all the published reports helped initially to develop the database related to biotechnology and the safety of GMO.

Recombinant DNA technology is used for manipulation of the genome of an organism. It requires various gene sequences for transformation and expression, like sequences of marker gene, promoters and terminators. Concerns related to transfer of these sequences from plants to microbes have increased the need of information on nucleotide sequences. Databases also provide information about the nucleotide sequence, encoded polypeptides, restriction maps, transcription and translation start and stop codons, multiple cloning sites and putative glycosylation sites.

These databases have different files from which data can be retrieved for experimentation and evaluation of different factors. These files have been named as gene files, botanical files and food files. Some examples of these files are provided in Table 15.1.

Table 15.1 *Useful Scientific Information Available from Major Databases*

Character	Site/URL	Description
Genes, gene elements	www.biosafety.nl	Provides data on the species of the inserted DNA, biological function of the gene product, probability of physiological impact to the host
Toxins	www.glfc.forestry.ca/bacillus	*Bt* toxin specificity database
Food Safety	http://www.iit.edu/ifsh/resources_and_tools/links.shtml	Food Safety organization directory
Methods for risk identification and assessment	http://gmo-crl.jrc.ec.europa.eu/gmomethods/	Gives general information on GMO, specific and technical information about the constructs used in GMO
Biological data	http://www.fao.org/biotech/index.asp http://www.tolweb.org/tree/phylogeny.html http://www.biosafety.nl	Provides glossary of various terms and definitions and details of phylogenetic information Data on the native plant species, ability to outcross the given GM crops
Environmental Releases	http://www.olis.oecd.org/biotrack.nsf http://www.isb.vt.edu/search-release-data.aspx	Record of field trials on GMO under OECD, it also has data from other countries as well
Food safety	Food files http://www.biosafety.nl	Data on safety test on food and feed as GM and the list of product from GM.

- Gene files have data with information on genes, promoters and selection sequences.
- Food files contain information on food safety aspects of GMO, animal allergenicity tests, probability of occurrence of novel proteins etc.
- Botanical files give information about the chances of crops to out-cross with the wild and weedy relatives. It gives the possibility of gene flow and its potential risk.

The process of risk assessment of food, especially for allergenicity, is done by searching the sequence of the suspected protein against a known allergen database. The objective of this exercise is to identify proteins that may require additional tests such as serum IgE binding or *in vivo* challenge to evaluate potential cross-reactivity. AllergenOnline.org provides one such database (http://www.allergenonline.org/)

Databases from National and International Organizations

Several databases are being developed by national and international organizations involved in biosafety aspects of GMOs (Table 15.2). Participation of international organizations plays a vital role in collecting and harmonizing the information from different countries. The harmonization of regulatory oversight in biotechnology was established in 1997–1999 through an effort of the OECD programme; its aim is to bring together information of different countries on environment health and safety aspects. The on-line data base site http://www.oecd.org/biotech has been established for field trials database. Another organization is the Biosafety Information Network and Advisory Services (BINAS) to monitor the global development on regulatory issues.

Convention on Biological Diversity (CBD) and Biosafety Clearing House (BCH) also play an important role in conservation and sustainable use of biological diversity. Its aim is to enable the exchange of scientific, environmental, legal and technical information and experiences with LMOs and to promote use of databases to national and international organizations.

FAO is also involved in spreading and sharing information on animal and plant health and food safety for different sectors. Through its specialized portal system it enables Internet-based exchange of information on national and international regulatory policies framework along with alerts, warning system, capacity building and access to other sources and links. Their database not only stores information on GMOs but also on other biotechnological products like micro propagation and *in vitro* germplasm.

Different countries have their own databases generated in systematic methods, which provide all information about GMOs and their products and such database are openly shared with all other countries as well.

Table 15.2 *Useful Databases with Potential Applications in Biosafety Research and Regulation*

Website URL	Brief Description of the Database
Biosafety clearing house (BCH) http://bch.cbd.int/	It contains all the rules, regulations, guidelines, agreements and risk assessments etc.
OECD product database http://www.oecd.org/biotech	Database for the product derived from genetic engineering, which are being approved of Commercialization
ICEGBs risk assessment searching mechanism htpp://www.icgeb.org/~bsafesrv/rasm.html	Database for official and technical documents of risk assessment on LMOs, authored by biosafety regulatory authorities.

Other Databases

Some other databases, not especially designed to address biosafety issues and concerns, provide important information useful in decision-making process. EMBL (http://www.ebi.ac.uk/Databases/), Swissprot (www.expasy.org), NCBI (www.ncbi.nlm.nih.gov), DNA data bank of Japan (http://www.ddbj.nig.ac.jp/) provide vital data for sequence retrieval for detection identification or risk assessment of GMO. A database to address toxicology issue is established by US National Library of Medicine (www.toxnet.nlm.nih.gov)

Another source of data that can be very important in today's research and can be used by scientists and risk assessors is related to the number of GM crops that are resistant to insects and to the role played by *Bt* toxin genes in the development of GM crops. This information is available on the URL www.glfc.forestry.ca/bacillus/.

Role of Bioinformatics in Creating Databases

Bioinformatics provides various algorithms and computational tools to collect, store and retrieve information for scientific use. Such algorithms have now become indispensible and crucial tools in biotechnological research and application. For the efficient and optimal use of published data generated on GMOs and transgenic crops, construction of an integrated database (data collection, storage, retrieval and data query) would be of great importance. Such integrated databases would serve as a catalyst for the identification of potential risks involved in the release of such organisms in the nature. In this direction, an effort has been made in India to construct a complete database consisting of all the information on genes and promoters used for the generation of GMO through a dedicated website www.nrcpb.org specifically designed for this purpose.

CHAPTER SUMMARY

The recent trend in database development has made it easy to gather data for risk assessment and biosafety evaluation of products derived from modern scientific research. There are various information portals worldwide that provide information through the web. The major databases are on regulations, commercial release, food safety, nucleotide sequences, etc. Databases support the three important aspects of dissemination of information, capacity building and transparency, which are important both for new scientific growth and public faith in the biosafety of GMOs.

REVIEW QUESTIONS

1. Why there is a need for web-based information on GMOs?
2. Which are the major organizations involved in the development of the biotech-related web-based information?
3. What are the factors required for the development of databases?
4. What information is available through important databases on the Internet?

16

Good Laboratory Biosafety Practices

Chapter Objectives:

Biosafety itself is a measure to reduce or eliminate accidental exposure to infectious agents and prevent the release of infectious agents into the environment. This objective of biosafety can only be achieved in the real sense by the good and safe laboratory practices while handling GMOs. In this chapter students will learn what are the good laboratory practices. They will learn about the different levels of biosafety, its possibility of pathogenicity and measure of its gravity at each level. It will also tell how to avoid accidental spillage of pathogenic organisms. At the end of the chapter, they will be fully aware of the safety, precautions and the importance of good laboratory practices.

IMPORTANCE OF GOOD LABORATORY PRACTICES

Biosafety itself means safe laboratory practices that are very important to ensure potential risk to human, animal and environment and eliminate the potential for exposure to biological hazard. Most of the information and guidelines in this chapter are taken from the book *Biosafety in Microbiology and Biomedical Laboratories* (US Health and Human Services), which is the standard book on the laboratory manual on safe practices of biosafety.

In all the advanced research in biotechnology and genetic engineering in various spheres at various institutions, organizations, academics, private or government, there is a need to follow the safe laboratory practices that may involve exposure to biohazardous organisms like different bacterial species, fungal agents and research animals carrying bio hazardous agents. There are different methods and areas that need to be taken care for the safe laboratory practices, these methods include the following:

- Containment area method
- Precautions at each biosafety level
- Unintentional spillage of biological agents
- Use of infectious material
- Research involving recombinant DNA and animal studies
- Management of biological waste.

Containment Methods

The term containment is used for a specific zone of work within limits for safe methods for managing infectious agent escape to the environment and also to reduce exposure of the worker to these hazardous agents. There are three containment areas and the principles of biosafety, which include the following:

- Laboratory procedure and technique
- Safety equipment
- Facility design.

Laboratory Procedure and Technique: This containment area follows the strict adherence to the potential standard of microbiological practices, person working should be fully aware of the potential hazard from the agent used and should be trained properly to handle such agent. When this is not enough to ensure safety other safety equipments are designed to meet the required need and safety.

Safety Equipment and Facility Design: These safety equipments include biological cabinet, enclosed container, especially designed devices to control or minimize the exposure to the hazardous agent. These equipments are designed in such a way that provides containment of infectious splashes or aerosols they have the potential to capture microbial contaminants and infectious agent using specialized filters called HEPA.

Certain Guidelines to be Followed Using This Containment Equipment

- The biological safety cabinet should be used properly; its blower should be on for a few minutes before it is used for the next experimentation.
- Turning off the UV lights is very important as UV lights can damage the eyes very quickly.
- The working area should always be wiped off with 70% alcohol before and after the use.
- The waste container should always be covered.
- It is important to remove all the glassware and equipments once the work is finished.
- One has to wash the hands thoroughly with the soap and the disinfectant before and after the work is finished.

Facility Design

These facility designs work as a secondary barriers to protect the environment from the exposure of infectious agent. In this particular type of containment, all the biosafety levels are taken care of according to the potential hazard it can cause. If strict adherence to the guidelines is followed; it contributes to a healthier and safer work environment for the laboratory and their workers.

Different Containment Levels and Their Safety Practices

The objective of physical containment is to confine the organisms containing recombinant DNA molecules. Combination of laboratory practices, containment equipments and special lab designs can be made to achieve different level of physical containment. The four levels of physical containment, namely BL1, BL2, BL3 and BL4, are described earlier. These levels were used called as P1, P2, P3 and P4. All the precautionary measures and safety is taken in to consideration according to the biosafety levels.

Practices for Biosafety level 1 (BL1)

In this level, there is work with well characterized agents. These agents are not known to cause disease in a healthy adult. Its prophylactic treatment is also available. Risk agent of group includes *E. coli*

K12, transgenic plants, plasmid, fungi, mould etc. The good biosafety practices for this level include the following:

- Bench top work is allowed in this level
- One needs to do daily decontamination of the work surfaces
- All contaminated liquid or solid wastes are decontaminated before disposal
- Manual pipetting is allowed, mouth pipetting is prohibited
- Eating, drinking, smoking and applying cosmetics are not permitted in the work area. Food may be stored in the cabinets designed for this purpose only
- Person need to wash their hands after handling the recombinant DNA or other experimental organisms
- All procedures are performed carefully to minimize the creation of aerosols.
- Red bag is kept as waste disposal bag.
- Special biocabinet not required unless creating aerosols.

Practices of Biosafety (BL2)

Access to the laboratory is limited or restricted by the laboratory investigator when the work with organism containing recombinant DNA molecules is in progress. Risk agents involved in BSL2 are human primate cells, *Herpes simplex* virus, HIV viruses, patient specimen, etc.

- In this level, there is a limited access to the laboratory.
- Daily decontamination of work surfaces at least twice a day.
- All contaminated liquid or solid wastes are decontaminated before disposal.
- Mechanical pipetting is recommended, experiments of lesser biohazard potential can be carried out carefully in a demarcated area in the same laboratory.
- Lab coat, gloves and safety glasses required.
- Red bag and sharp container required for the contaminated material that need to be decontaminated at a site away from the laboratory.
- The investigator must establish the policies and procedures where only person who have been advised of the potential hazard and meets any specific requirements like immunization is allowed to enter the laboratory or the animal house.
- When the organism containing recombinant DNA molecule is in use in the laboratory, then it requires special provision for entry, a hazard warning sign must be there
- Special training must be given to the workers.
- A biosafety manual is prepared or adopted. Person working are advised of special hazards and are required to read instructions on practices and procedure and to follow them.
- Biological cabinets or any other physical containment is required if there is a high potential for creating aerosols.

Standard Practices Biosafety Level 3 (BL3)

Agents involves in the biosafety group 3 are HIV virus, *Mycobacterium tuberculosis*, *Coxiella, Burnetti,* etc. This requires working in high containment area.

- One needs to do daily decontamination of the work surfaces.
- All contaminated liquid or solid wastes are decontaminated before disposal.

- Manual pipetting is allowed mouth pipetting is prohibited.
- Eating, drinking, smoking and applying cosmetics are not permitted in the work area. Food may be stored in the cabinets designed for this purpose only.
- Person need to wash their hands after handling the recombinant DNA or other experimental organisms.
- Person under 16 years of age shall not enter the laboratory.
- In special practices at BL3, laboratory doors are always closed when work is in progress.
- Red bag and sharp container required for the contaminated material that need to be decontaminated at a site away from the laboratory.
- The investigator must establish the policies and procedures where only person who have been advised of the potential hazard and meets any specific requirements like immunization is allowed to enter the laboratory or the animal house.
- When the organism containing recombinant DNA molecule in use in the laboratory that requires special provision for entry, a hazard warning sign should be visibly displayed.
- All the activities involving organisms containing recombinant DNA molecule are conducted in biological safety cabinets or other physical containment devices within the containment module. No work is conducted in the open.
- Autoclave required; waste is disposed only after the treatment and decontamination.
- Requires foot activity in hand washing sink and other control, to minimize the exposure to risk.
- No sharp instruments or tools are used unless required urgently.
- Aerosol minimization procedure required.
- Wrap around and scrub suits disposable clothes required that covers all.
- Special care is taken to avoid skin contamination with contaminated material, gloves should be worn while handing the material or infected animals.
- Moulded surgical masks or respirators are worn in rooms containing experimental animals.
- Animals and plants not related to the work are not allowed in the laboratory.
- Animals held in BL3 area need to be caged in partial containment system.
- Biohazard signs and labels are mandatory.
- Documented training and competency certification is required by the worker.
- If spills occurs it has to be reported to the biosafety officers for the cleanup procedure.
- Special containment equipments are required such as special protective clothing, masks, gloves, respirators, sealed centrifuge rotors and containment caging for animals etc.

Practices of the BL4

Agents involved in this group are *Lessa fever* virus, *Marburg virus*, *Herpes* virus. The agents are exotic, dangerous and life-threatening, agent of unknown risk of transmission, or health effect, no known treatments are available. This group is under major risk.

- Maximum containment facilities are required.
- Work surface are decontaminated at least twice a day and immediately after any kind of spill.
- All procedures are performed carefully to minimize the creation of aerosols.
- Eating, drinking, smoking and applying cosmetics are not permitted in the work area. Food may be stored in the cabinets designed for this purpose only.

- Biological materials are to be removed from the cabinet or from the maximum containment laboratory in a viable state are transferred to non breakable, sealed secondary container which is removed from the facility through disinfectant dunk tank.
- Equipment or material, which might be damaged by high temperature or steam is decontaminated by gaseous and vapour methods in an airlock or specially designed chamber.
- Only person who is working in the facility can enter the experimentation area.
- Access to the facility is limited by means of locked doors and all other physical security.
- Before entering, the person is informed of all the potential biohazard and instructed about all the safeguards that needs to be followed.
- A logbook is maintained and signed by all their personnel indicating the date and time of each entry and exit.
- People leaving the room will only come and go through the air shower and clothing changing room.
- When the organism containing recombinant DNA molecule in use in the laboratory that requires special provision for entry, a hazard warning sign must be affixed on all access doors. The sign identifies the agent, indicates any special requirement like respirator or immunization an insect, and identifies the name of the principal investigator for any kind of emergency information.
- All the plastic glassware should be disposed after decontaminating it.
- A record is maintained about all the accidents, absentee, medical surveillance of potential lab-associated illness.
- Lab animals involved in experiments requires physical containment kept in special designed cages.
- If the risk of agent used in experimentation is too high, then the alternative selection of containment equipment is required for the safeguard.
- Pressurized containment area is also required at times according to the pathogenicity of the biological agent used.
- Certain specialized laboratory facilities are constructed, which contain either the separate building or the clearly demarcated isolated zone within the building. Outer and inner change room separated by the showers are provided.
- The internal surfaces are resistant to water thus helping in cleaning and decontamination of the area.
- Any drains in the floor contains trap filled with chemical disinfectant, which have the potential efficacy against the target agents; they are connected directly to liquid waste decontamination system. Sewer and other ventilation lines contain HEPA filters.
- Windows are breakage resistant.

Biological Spillage

Biological spills are the dangerous if they happen. Proper measures have to be taken. The degree of risk when spillage occurs depends on amount of spillage, concentration of the organism spilled, organism with hazard, route of infection of the organism and the disease caused by the organism.

Biological spillage can contaminate areas and can lead to severe infection. Prevention from the spillage is the primary goal. If an accident generates droplets or aerosol in the lab and if agent belongs to BSL2 the room shall be evacuated immediately. Even if the spillage occurs in public area evacuation of the area should be done and there should be a call for the biological safety officer to supervise the clean up. Anyone who is cleaning the spillage shall wear protective clothes to prevent exposure to organism. If required an air purifier negative pressure respirator is adequate for the protection against any kind of harmful inhalation. Appropriate disinfectant should be chosen for the cleanup activity like sodium hypochlorite, hydrogen peroxide, mercuric chloride etc.

If the spillage has occurred within the biological safety cabinet, immediately chemical disinfectant procedure should be followed. It is important to spray, wipe the wall, and work surface area and equipment with the disinfectant. If the spillage occurs in the centrifuge or any other equipment, it can have the potential for producing large volume of aerosol; it is important to first switch off the equipment and let the aerosol settle down and then decontaminate with the appropriate disinfectant.

If a spillage occurred on a person then the emergency response is based on the potential infectivity and hazard of biological agent. If aerosol formation is associated with the spill, the person should immediately leave the area, and clothing be removed and placed in the red or orange bag. Skin should be washed with water and then with disinfectant.

Precaution When the Use of Human Blood or Other Infectious Material

If the worker or the scientist is involved in the use of human blood or either fluid tissue like semen, amniotic fluid, vaginal secretion, saliva, cerebrospinal fluid etc tissues like from the organ of living or dead, HIV-containing cells, where there is a risk of blood-borne pathogen and disease-causing microbes, certain biosafety measures have to be followed to avoid any kind of risk. These methods involve appropriate clothing, masks and inhalers to avoid any kind of exposure to the infectious agent. If a person is involved in animal research where exposure to handling of animals are inevitable, then caution must be taken from allergens, zoonoses, physical hazards like bites and scratches.

Managing Biological Waste

Life sciences research creates a lot of biological waste that is both hazardous and non-hazardous; managing the disposal of this biological waste is very important. Biological waste means solid or liquid biological waste that is hazardous because of its biological and physical nature. This includes waste from infectious animals, microbiological waste, pathological waste, hazardous products of recombinant DNA research and genetic manipulations. Treatment of all laboratories biological waste before its disposal is a good practice and highly recommended but the bio hazardous waste must be treated with thermal, chemical disinfection, encapsulation or incineration before its disposal. This waste must be separated from the other waste, separately packed, labelled, transported to the site of treatment for the removal of the biological hazard.

Treatment of the Biological Waste

- Animal carcasses and body parts are sent to the commercial plant for their incineration and these cannot be disposed in the landfills.
- Discarded metal sharps are disposed in such a manner that it should not pose injury to the workers, needles, blades; these all are considered biohazardous even if they are sterile—never put these sharps in plastic or container.
- All the Pasteur pipettes or the broken glassware, which contains the biohazardous material, should be disinfected thermally and chemically before they are disposed.
- All the plastic waste containing bio-hazardous material should be disinfected thermally and chemically, and if the plastic waste is not contaminated it can simply be thrown in a trash can.

- All the microbiological waste solid and liquid, first disinfected through the thermal treatment followed by the chemical treatment.
- All the genetic material involved in genetic manipulation must be applicable with the NIH guidelines.
- Biological waste that is treated with radioactive substance or contains radioactive substance must be treated as radioactive waste.
- Bio-hazardous waste, which contains hazardous chemicals, must be managed as hazardous chemical waste.

GENERAL GOOD LABORATORY PRACTICES

- Hygienic practices—no smoking, no eating, application of cosmetic or lip balm in the working area, that is, labs.
- Washing of hands with soap after and before the work.
- Water lab coat, safety glasses and gloves.
- Plan the work in advance and read all the precautionary measures.
- Always keep first aid and give the immediate aid when required.
- Maintain the safety laboratory manual about all the safety practices.
- Safety manual must be read by the workers for the safe practices of laboratory work.

MULTIPLE CHOICE QUESTIONS

1. What is meant by the term exposure incident?
   (i) an exposure to mucus membrane such as eyes and nose
   (ii) a stick from a contaminated needle or sharp
   (iii) an exposure to non-intact skin such as skin that has a rash or is chapped
   (iv) a b and c
2. Any spill on the floor can cause an accident. Always clean it up
   (i) at once
   (ii) during clean up time
   (iii) when you have time
   (iv) at the end of the work
3. If you see a fire in an apparatus, or a burning liquid, it is best to put it out with
   (i) the fire blanket
   (ii) water from the sink
   (iii) your coat
   (iv) the fire extinguisher
4. most dangerous level among all the biosafety levels are
   (i) BL1
   (ii) BL2
   (iii) BL3
   (iv) BL4

REVIEW QUESTIONS

1. Describe in detail the practices followed in all the four biosafety levels.
2. What are the basic good laboratory practices?
3. What do you understand by the term containment? Why it is required?
4. How will one manage the spillage of biohazardous agents?

5. How the biological waste can be managed?
6. How do you approach risks when addressing a particular organism?
7. Based on what you know about biosafety levels, practices and operational controls, what are some discussion issues for conducting biohazard risk assessments?

17

Case Studies in IPR and Biosafety

Chapter Objectives:

In this chapter we will discuss briefly some of the very important and famous case studies related to intellectual property rights and biosafety issues. The study of cases helps us to understand the subject matter deeply and in a better way. The case studies discussed are as follows:

- *Diamond vs Chakraborty* Case (1980)
- *Dimminaco A.G.* Case (2002)
- Neem Patent Case
- Turmeric Patent Case
- *Asgrow Seed Co. vs Winterboer* Case
- *Harward College vs Canada* Case
- *Delta Pineland Co. vs the Sinker's Corporation* Case
- Myriad's Case on Gene Patenting
- *Bt* Brinjal
- *Bt* Cotton
- Golden Rice

There are several court cases related to biotechnology patents, which have generated controversies or have been rejected by the court at some point of time but are important to study in order to understand the subject better. We come to know the complexities of patent grant and types of oppositions that can be faced by an inventor. We have summarized below a few such important case studies.

DIAMOND VS CHAKRABORTY CASE

Diamond vs Chakraborty, 447 U.S. 303, was a US Supreme Court case dealing with whether genetically modified organisms can be patented. Genetic engineer Anand Mohan Chakraborty working for General Electric had developed a bacterium from *Pseudomonas* genus capable of breaking down crude oil, which is used in treating oil spills. He requested a patent for the bacterium in United States but the request was turned down by a patent examiner, because the law dictated that living things were not patentable. The Supreme Court case was argued on 17 March 1980. After 4-5 ruling, the court ruled in favour of Chakraborty and upheld the patent, holding that a live, human made microorganism is patentable. Final decision was made on 16 June 1980.

DIMMINACO A.G. CASE

The applicant in this case was a Swiss company named Dimminaco A.G., which filed an application for the process of preparation of a live vaccine against the Bursitis virus, which infects poultry. The Patent Office rejected the application giving a reason that statutory definition of 'manufacture' did not include a process that resulted in 'living organism' and hence the claim did not fall within Section 2(1)(j) of the Patent Act 1970. The patenting of a process relating to manufacture of a product containing living organism was strictly not considered patentable in India until 2001. The case was then directed to Calcutta High Court, which stated that in the absence of a definition, the normal dictionary meaning of these words should be accepted. There is no statutory bar in the Act to accept a manner of manufacture as patentable even if the end product contains a living organism.

Calcutta High Court directed the Patent Office to reconsider the patent application in light of court's observation and the patent was finally granted to the company.

NEEM PATENT CASE

The multinational agribusiness corporation W.R. Grace of New York and the United States department of Agriculture, Washington D.C., filed a European patent application in EPO on the method for controlling fungi on plants by the aid of hydrophobically extracted neem oil.

After very difficult and highly controversial examination procedure, the grant of a European patent for this application was published on 14 September 1994.

But, In June 1995, a legal opposition against the grant of this patent was filed by two, Magda Aelvoet, MEP on behalf of the Research Green group in the European parliament, Brussels, and Dr. Vandana Shiva on behalf of Research Foundation for Science and Technology & Natural Resource Policy, New Delhi and International Federation of Organic Agriculture Movements based in Germany.

The opponents submitted evidence to the EPO that the fungicidal effect of hydrophobic extracts of neem seeds was known before and used for centuries on a broad scale in India, both in Ayurvedic medicine to cure dermatological diseases and in traditional Indian agriculture practice to protect crops, so the patent application in question lacked two basic requirements for the grant of European patent, namely 'novelty' and 'inventive step'. The first preliminary statement by the opposition board of EPO on 30 September 1997 held that the present patent cannot be maintained. The EPO, which administers patents under European Patent Treaty, has acted to revoke a patent granted earlier to fungicide derived from Indian medicinal tree, Neem. India won the case against the European Patent Office. The European Patents Office accepted the arguments offered by Indian scientists and rejected the order of the US Patents Office to award the patent to W R Grace, a US-based company, at the last hearing of the case.

The victory in this case was a result of a four-year-long effort by the Research Foundation for Science, Technology and Environment. According to information gathered, the Indian scientists argued that the people of India have known the medicinal properties of neem for thousands of years and hence no other company can patent its properties. The EPO accepted the argument.

TURMERIC PATENT CASE

Turmeric is a tropical herb grown in East India and the powdered product made from the rhizoids of its flower has several popular uses worldwide. Turmeric powder, which has a distinctive deep yellow colour, is used as a dye, a cooking ingredient and has medicinal uses. In mid 1990s, this product became the subject of a patent dispute when a US patent was awarded to two US-based Indians on turmeric in the University of Mississippi Medical Centre in 1995 specifically for the 'use of turmeric in wound healing'. The patent claimed that the administration of an effective amount of turmeric locally or orally to enhance the wound healing process was a novel finding. This patent also granted them the exclusive right to sell and distribute turmeric.

Two years later, a complaint was filed by India's Council of Scientific and Industrial Research, which challenged the novelty of the university's 'discovery, and cited 32 references (some were more than 10 years old) showing that the invention was well known in India prior to the patent filing date. The US patent office investigated the validity of this patent. In 1997, the patent was revoked. India woke up late but for two years the patent on turmeric had stood, although the process was non-novel and had in fact been traditionally practiced in India for thousands of years, as was eventually proven by ancient Sanskrit writings that documented turmeric's extensive and varied use throughout India's history.

India, where turmeric has been used medicinally for thousands of years, was concerned about the economic and social devastating impact of this legal 'biopiracy'. This was the first time when a patent based on traditional knowledge of a developing country was challenged successfully. The two interesting thing about this case was that there were loud protests against 'biopiracy' and 'theft' of India's biodiversity by foreign nationals and the two patentees of this case, Suman K Das and Hari Har P Cohley, were US-based Indians.

ASGROW SEED CO. VS WINTERBOER CASE

Asgrow Seed Company of the United States (manufacturer of soybean, corn, sorghum, sunflower, and alfalfa seed products, operates as a subsidiary of Monsanto Co.) obtained two certificates under Plant Variety Protection Act (PVPA) for protecting two different novel varieties of soybean seed, which it calls A1937 and A2234. These certificates are like patents in order to promote research in agriculture, especially to protect the owners of new varieties of plants and seeds from unauthorized use. However, it excludes the farmers who sell seeds to the other farmers whose primary occupation is growing crops for sale.

In 1990, Winterboer (operating and owning a farm in Clay County, Iowa grows corn and soybeans and sells harvested soybean seed to other farmers who use their seeds to plant future crops) planted and harvested 265 acres of land with two Asgrow soybean varieties. He then sold enough plant 10,000 acres to other farmers for use as seed. Asgrow claimed that PVPA prohibits anyone from selling of seed more than it is needed to replant his own field, an amount greatly exceeded by Winterboer's sale. Winterboer argued that the exemptions in the statute protect sales of unlimited amounts of seed as long as both seller and buyer grow crops primarily for 'other than reproductive purposes'. The District Court ruled in favour of Asgrow, but the US Court of Appeals for the federal circuit reversed and denied Asgrow's petition for rehearing.

Finally the court held that farmer may sell only such seeds for reproductive purposes that they have saved for the purpose of replanting in their own fields, while statue followed farmers to save seeds to replant and then sell that saved seeds to other farmers for planting.

HARWARD COLLEGE VS CANADA CASE

In 2002, Harvard researchers developed a process by which it could breed genetically altered (transgenic) mice that would possess a cancer-promoting gene. The school applied for a patent for the genetically altered mouse, 'Oncomouse'. The patent was to cover both the 'process' for producing these mice or any similar animals and the 'product'(the mice or other animals).

The patent authorities allowed the patent on the process but disallowed it on the transgenic animals themselves, finding that a higher life form is not a 'manufacture' or 'composition of matter', under Section 2 of Canadian Patent Act. According to the authorities, the Patent Act was not designed to apply to higher life forms and cannot easily be applied to them. They said that they have separate rules for plants (the Plant Breeders' Rights Act), which suggests that living inventions or discoveries can also be protected without needing them to be patentable. Because if the Patent Act was made applicable to higher life forms, then, it would be very difficult to stop the patent application for creating transgenic human beings. Finally it was concluded that the Patent Commissioner should forbid this kind of patent until Parliament creates applicable legislation.

DELTA PINELAND CO. VS THE SINKERS CORPORATION CASE

Delta Pineland Co. (cottonseed producer) is the owner of numerous certificates (PVP certificates) of cotton plant variety protection issued by the Plant Variety Protection office of US Department of Agriculture. The cottonseeds from the producers are first taken to a gin where most of the fibre or lint is separated from the seed. Seeds are then taken to de-linter. The de-linting process removes the remaining lint. In 1992, Delta obtained information that led them to believe that cottonseed of their PVPA-protected varieties was being de-linted at Sinkers's de-linting facility in Kennett, Missouri, and was being sold in violation of Delta's rights under the PVPA. In essence, Delta believed that suspected sales by Sinkers, which were certainly unauthorized by Delta, did not fall within any of the statutory exemptions to the PVPA. After further investigation, Delta filed their complaint on 29 April 1993, alleging violations of the PVPA, 7 U.S.C. 2321-2581, and demanding financial compensation for damages and injunctive relief.

Delta's instant action in District Court claiming infringement of its IPR under PVPA, specifically presented three claims that Sinkers infringed:

- The Sinkers transferred possession of protected seeds without Delta's authority.
- The Sinkers did not put mark on the bags with a notice that they contained protected seeds.
- The Sinkers funnelled massive quantities of Delta's protected varieties with knowing or reckless indifference on Sinker's part regarding the absence of authorization or exemption, thereby actively inducing others to infringe Delta's PVPA rights.

The District Court found, at the conclusion of a bench trial, that Delta had failed to prove by a preponderance of the evidence that Sinkers committed any violations of Delta's PVPA rights. In essence, the court found that as a passive conduit of seed that it transferred according to the instructions of its customer, Sinkers had no liability under the PVPA, as construed by the District Court. All injunctive relief and damages were therefore, denied. The District Court found no infringement and dismissed all three Delta claims on 5 March 1998.

MYRIAD'S CASE ON GENE PATENTING

The patents for genes were controversial for decades but the controversy peeked in 2009 when the American Civil Liberties Union (ACLU) and the Public Patent Foundation filed a suit against Myriad Genetics, a genetic testing company. The lawsuit was filed against the US Patent and Trademark Office, and Myriad Genetics (a molecular diagnostics company based in Salt Lake City, Utah) and the University of Utah Research Foundation, for holding patents on the human genes, BRCA1 and

BRCA2 that are very reliable in predicting breast and ovarian cancers, and the genetic test for detecting the genes. The lawsuit charges that patents on human genes violate the First Amendment and patent law because genes are 'products of nature' and therefore cannot be patented.

The American Civil Liberties Union and the Public Patent Foundation in New York joined with individual patients and medical organizations to challenge the patents and argued that genes are the products of nature and fall outside the patentable criteria; they also argued that patents stifle research and innovation and limit testing options. Myriad Genetics, the company that holds the patents with the University of Utah Research Foundation, claimed that the work of isolating the DNA from the body transforms it and makes it patentable. Such patents, it said, have been granted for decades and the Supreme Court also upheld patents on living organisms in 1980. There were debates between the parties, the opponent and the defendant. The opponent lawyer said: 'The human genome, like the structure of blood, air or water, was discovered, not created. There is an endless amount of information on genes that begs for further discovery, and gene patents put up unacceptable barriers to the free exchange of ideas'.

In March 2010, Judge Robert W. Sweet of the US District Court in New York ruled that the patents were invalid. He found that isolating a molecule did not make it novel, which is a pre-requisite for patentability. However on 29 July 2011, the Federal Appeals Court in New York overturned Sweet's ruling. The three-judge panel ruled that complementary DNA (cDNA), an altered type of DNA, is patentable (3-0 votes); isolated DNA is patentable (2-1 votes); and that Myriad's methods for therapeutic screening of breast and ovarian cancer genes are patentable (3-0 votes). Finally, in July 2011, the appeals court ruled that companies can obtain patents on the genes but cannot patent methods to compare those gene sequences.

BT BRINJAL

Bt brinjal is the transgenic brinjal created by inserting a gene (*cryIAC*) from the soil bacteria *Bacillus thuringiensis*. This gives brinjal plant resistance against *Lepidopteran* insects like the brinjal fruit and shoot borer *Leucinodes orbonalis* and fruit borer *Helicoverpa armigera*. When the insect injects the *Bt* toxin, there is a disruption of digestive process resulting in the death of insects.

Bt brinjal is been developed in India by the collaboration of Maharashtra Hybrids (Mahyco), a hybrid seed company, and Monsanto. This project started in year 2000. Its biosafety assessments include pollen flow test, test for acute oral toxicity, allergenicity etc. All these tests were performed in 2002. After two years of green house evaluation in 2004, field trials were conducted in 11 locations with five hybrids of brinjal. Under strict evaluation field trials were conducted. In addition to this, Mayhco even got sublicensed technology by the USAID support. When the transgenic *Bt* brinjal was created, it had both positive and negative view from different group of people.

Positive view of the Company

- It was reported that the average shoot damage in *Bt* brinjal was less than the non-*Bt* brinjal.
- The percentage of damaged fruit was more in non-*Bt* brinjal.
- No substantial difference was noted between *Bt* brinjal and non-*Bt* brinjal on the test like toxicity allergenicity.
- This will be helpful for the marginal farmers, which otherwise used to use 25–80 sprays of pesticide, which too was ineffective.
- The price used would be cost-effective for all farmers.
- Farmers will be able to save and reuse their seeds.

Negative view from the Opposition Group

- Several studies on *Bt* crops and GM crops showed many potential health problems in foods bio-engineered in this manner.
- GM-fed animals showed various health problems like growth, organ development and less immune responsiveness.
- Itching, eruption in body and swollen faces were reported on exposure to high levels of *Bt* toxins.
- In Philippines, people living next to or nearby *Bt* corn field were found to have some strange allergies.
- *Bt* toxin had caused immune response and abnormal cell growth in mice.
- Cry protein in *Bt* crop have amino acid sequence similar to known allergens.

The Controversy Surrounding Bt Brinjal

Bt Brinjal has generated much debate in India. Some activists say that it is good for small-scale farmers, insect-resistant, increases yield, more cost-effective and has minimum environmental impact. On the other hand, there are concerns that *Bt* Brinjal has an adverse impact on human and animal health, biosafety and biodiversity. Ministry of Environment and Forests (MoEF) has a governing body GEAC, which has recommended the environmental release of *Bt* Brinjal in India based on the recommendations of RCGM. But Ministry of Environment and Forests responded with strong views for both for and against the introduction of the *Bt* Brinjal and has deferred the final decision only after public consultations across the country. Its sequential development is shown in Table 17.1

Table 17.1 *Sequence and Chronology of the Development and Approval of* Bt *Brinjal in India*

Year	Sequential Development
2000	*Commencement of the project transformation and integration of cry1AC gene*
2001–2002	*Preliminary evaluation in green house to study the development and efficacy of* Bt *brinjal*
2002–2004	*Confined field trials to evaluate and study gene flow, weediness, toxicity and allergenecity, etc.*
2004	RCGM *gave approval conducting multi-location research trials of seven* Bt *brinjal hybrids*
2005	Mahyco *under the support of* Agriculture Biotechnology Support Programme *shares transfer technology*
2004–2005	*Biosafety data on the effect of* Bt *brinjal on soil, microflora, efficiency against fruit shoot borer, pollen flow, germination toxicity were well documented and submitted to* RCGM, *which recommends large-scale trials to the* GEAC
2006	*Mahyco submitted biosafety data to* GEAC *to seek permission on large-scale trials; it published the data on the web in response to the concerns raised by civil society*
2007	*Subcommittee submits its report and recommended seven more studies on biosafety to be repeated for conformation.* GEAC *approves large-scale trials.* *Due to the concern raised by the several stakeholders including some national and international experts,* GEAC *constitutes two more sub-committees to look into the biosafety data generated, as well as all the concerns raised by the stakeholders*
14 October 2009	*The* Subcommittee *submits its report based on which* GEAC *approves the environmental release of* Bt Brinjal.
15 October 2009	*Responding to strong views expressed both for and against the release of the* Bt Brinjal, *the Minister of State for Environment and Forests (to whom the* GEAC *reports) announces a nationwide consultation in January and February of* 2010 *pending a final decision on This issue.*

BT COTTON

Biosafety study conducted on *Bt* cotton expressing the *cry1Ac* gene. Various studies on risk assessment was done on gene flow, aggressiveness, effect on target and non-target organism, effect on soil micro flora and agronomic advantage. Further studies were conducted on toxicity of *Bt* cotton seed on goats, bird, fish, allergenicity in rats, food and feed safety studies in cows and buffaloes. In all the studies and evaluation conducted on *Bt* cotton, it found to be safe and very much similar to non-*Bt* cotton. As on date 62 *Bt* cotton hybrids have been approved for commercial cultivation in India. Till now the only approach to engineer the crop for insect tolerance has been the addition of ***Bt*** toxin from soil bacteria. These toxins have no effect on the non-target species and are environment friendly. *Bt* cotton is the only crop commercialized in India. Three hybrids containing ***cry1Ac*** gene approved in 2002. Various biosafety studies were done on environmental safety, food safety and all risk assessments.

Environmental Risk Assessments

- *Pollen Escape or Out Cross Evaluation*: This evaluation was conducted on multiple locations and it was found that the pollen transfer is very limited because of stickiness, its travel is limited and pollen does not escape the confinement.
- *Weediness and Aggressiveness*: For evaluating this, the rate of germination and vigour were compared with non *Bt* counterparts, and it resulted in no significant difference hence no weediness and aggressiveness.
- *Effect of Bt on Non Target Organisms*: *Bt* cotton does not show any on toxic effect on the non-target species. Beneficial insects remained active in both transgenic and non-transgenic.
- *Presence of Bt Protein in Soil*: It was evaluated that if there was an accumulation of *Bt* toxin in the soil. *Bt* toxin was not present in the soil sample that suggest that this toxin is degraded by the soil.

Food Safety Risk Assessments

- *Compositional Analysis*: All the studies conducted reveals that there is no change in composition in *Bt* and non-*Bt* plants with respect to proteins, oil, carbohydrates and calories.
- *Allergenicity Test*: Allergenicity was tested on brown Norway rats with *Bt* and non-*Bt* seeds and the results showed that there was no significant differences in consumption, weight gain and general health; also there was no change in endogenous allergens of *Bt* seeds compared to non-*Bt* seeds.
- *Toxicological Studies*: Goat feeding studies were conducted for understanding the toxicological effect of *Bt* seeds. The animals were tested for gross pathology and histopathology. No significant differences were found in animals fed with *Bt* and non *Bt* seeds.
- *Feeding Studies*: On cows, buffaloes, poultry and fish-feeding, experiments using *Bt* seeds as free to different animals at different research institutes conducted showed that *Bt* cotton seed mean was nutritionally wholesome and safe as the non-*Bt* seed as feed.

Figure 17.1 shows the development of *Bt* cotton processed in India from its commencement to its commercialization. *Bt* cotton went through all the risk assessments and proved to be safe for the environment, animals and plants. All the regulations were followed to get the approval for commercializing *Bt* cotton.

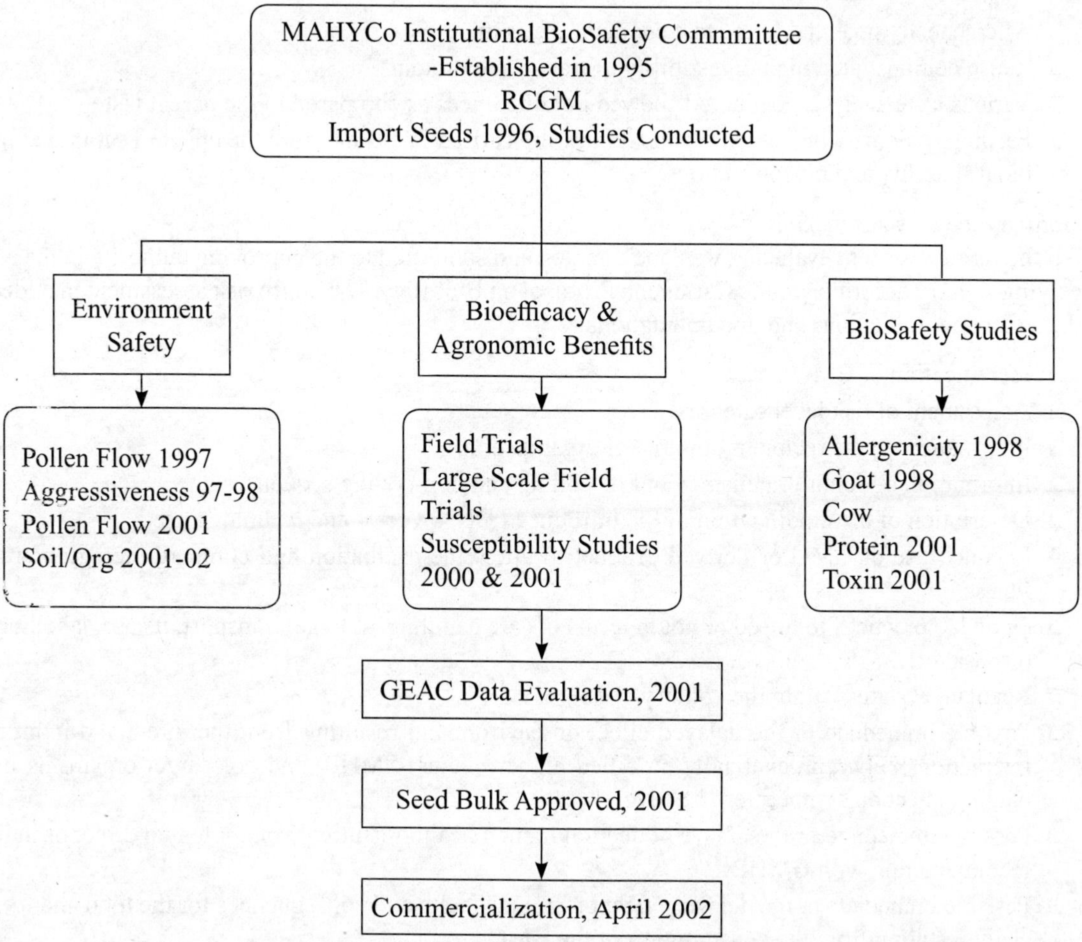

Figure 17.1 Bt *Cotton Development Process in India*

GOLDEN RICE

The development of golden rice faced with both technological challenges and ethical issues. The rice has been modified to contain the precursor of vitamin A, a vital constituent missing in the diet of millions of impoverished people in various developing countries. In July 2000 *Science* magazine announced the solution to the vitamin A deficiency and that was golden rice. The announcement came with the global controversy. Various anti-GM protesters campaigned against it. Golden rice has been researched under all biosafety norms and regulations. Few of the tests performed are as follows:

- Molecular tests which looked in to the biosynthetic pathway and its bioconversions.
- Gene expression profiling of genes were done showing no abnormal changes in the expression profile compared to the parent gene.

- Allergenecity potential in the test conducted was nil.
- It also demonstrated high digestibility of transgenic protein.
- Various taste analysis conducted showed no differences as compared to the parent taste.
- Feeding trials with human adults in China were carried out to measure the effect of fat in diet on bioavailability and bioconversions.

Golden Rice Risk Assessments

All the risk assessment evaluated was documented and submitted to the approving authority in the receiving country according to the Cartagena Protocol on Biosafety. The entire risk assessment included the following evaluations and documentations:

- Identification of GMOs.
- Assessment of risk level category.
- Information on the recipient or parental organization.
- Information of donor organism about its coding and non-coding sequences.
- Description of the modification of the introduced DNA, vector and technique used.
- Intended use of GMO or derived product to allow the evaluation and compare the agronomic fitness.
- Good lab practices followed or not in terms of safe handling, storage, transport, its use, labelling, disposal etc.
- Regulatory status within the country.
- Possible immediate or the delayed effect on environment resulting from the direct and indirect interactions between genetically modified higher plants (GMHP) and non-target organisms including effect on competition, herbivore, etc.
- Possible immediate or the delayed effect on human health resulting from potential direct or indirect interaction with GMHP.
- Possible immediate or the delayed effect on animal health and consequences for the food and feed chain resulting from the consumption of the GMO.

Other assessments were done during the evaluation of golden rice, which include the following:

- Its specific composition and distribution.
- Environmental safety considerations that include weediness and out crossing potential.
- Food and feed safety includes presence of anti-nutrients in rice.
- Allergen assessment evaluation on the possibility of any kind of known and unknown allergen.

Assessments of all the possible risks are shown in Figure 17.2. All the details of all the data are well documented and monitored by all the competent authorities before they were submitted for commercialization approval. It was on 21 June 1998 that golden rice got the approval from Food and Drug Administration (FDA). Initially the approval was given to the adult consumption and then on 11 September 1998 approval for children was given as well.

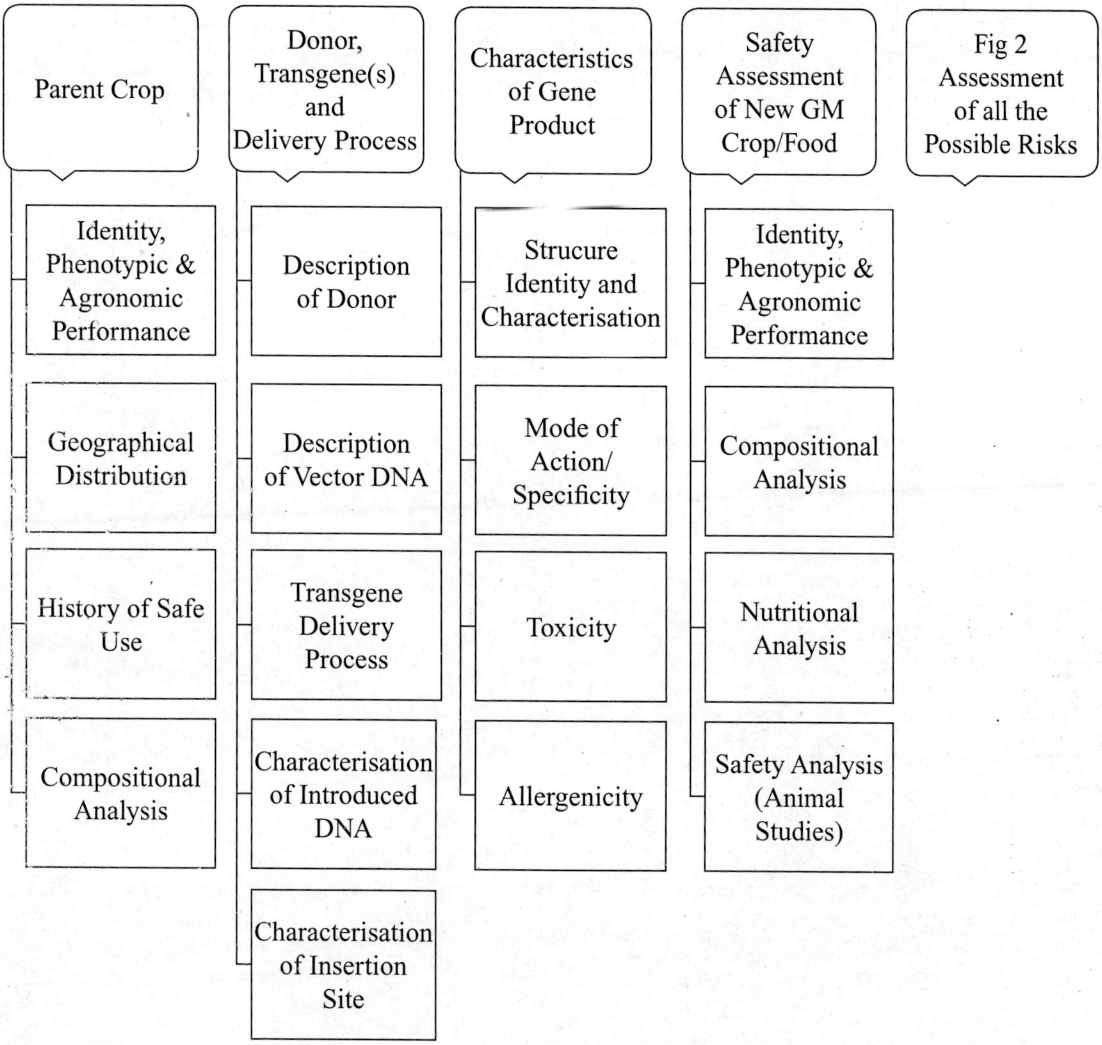

Figure 17.2 *Assessment of all the Possible Risks*

Glossary

Allergenicity: Degree of measure of the capacity of causing allergy.

Amendment: The formal process of altering or making changes in the earlier manuscript for improvement.

Anticipation: The condition results when the prior act indicates that a patent application lacks novelty.

Anti-dumping: Dumping means export of goods by a country to another country at a price lower than its normal domestic value. It is harmful for the domestic industry as it results in reduced sales volume and market shares, as well as job losses. Thus, anti-dumping is a measure to rectify the situation arising out of the dumping of goods and its trade distortive effect.

Appropriation of the invention: The act of keeping the money aside for invention/research by a company, organization, government or a research institution. In other words, it can also be called 'capital allocation'.

Arbitrarily: Determined by chance or by impulse, not by necessity, reason, or any principle.

Biohazard: Material of biological origin that is hazardous to humans, especially in biological research or experimentation.

Black-box system: It is a system that enables the developing countries to preserve their applications and filing dates for the grant of patents on pharmaceutical and agriculture chemical products once the transition period is over. TRIPS grants 10-year transition period to developing countries during which patents are filed in black box.

Burden of proof: The duty placed upon either on plaintiff or on defendant to prove or disprove a disputed case, or it can define which party bears this burden. In criminal cases, the burden of proof is placed on the prosecution while in civil cases, it is on the defendant.

Capacity building: Establishing the ability of individuals, institutions, organizations and societies to perform functions, solve problems, and set and achieve developmental objectives in a sustainable manner. Or ongoing process through which individuals, groups, organizations and societies enhance their ability to identify and meet development challenges.

Claim: Claim in the patent document defines the scope of protection of an invention granted in the form of patent in a specific legal style.

Comprehensive agreement: It is the detailed agreement.

Compulsory License: It is mandatory license or a patent-use license granted on court orders, by the government to the third parties (such as a company or the government itself) for the manufacture or use of a product or intellectual property, when the patent holder fails to make use of it.

Convention country: The countries/ states that sign some conventions such as Paris Convention. These are member countries to a convention.

Counterfeit goods: These are the goods or products that are not authorized to carry on business because they are forged or created to look real, and intended to pass for real. Product counterfeiting is a form of consumer fraud as the product is sold as a copy of the real.

Defendant: The party on which the case is filed.

Deferred examination: It is an examination that has been postponed to a later date.

Endogenous genes: DNA/RNA sequences developing or originating within a concerned organism or part of an organism.

Euthanasia: The act of assisting a chronically ill person to die.

***ex parte*:** Latin term meaning 'from one party'. It is a legal proceeding brought by one person in the absence of and without representing or notifying the other parties. It is also known as without-notice proceedings. It can be a hearing between the patent office and a single party (patent applicant)

Exclusive Marketing Rights (EMR): EMR is the exclusive right given to a person to market, i.e., to sell or distribute, the article or substance covered in a patent or patent application in the country, in order to ensure that the innovator can market free copies of his product.

Field trials: Trials of transgenic plants and its method in the natural environment rather than in the green house or in the laboratory.

Forfeited application: The application whose maintenance fees or other fee has not been paid within the prescribed time period.

Gen bank: Genetic sequence database, an annotated collection of all publicly available DNA sequences.

Genetic engineering: Alteration of an organism's genetic, or hereditary, material to eliminate undesirable characteristics or to produce desirable new ones.

Genetically modified organism: Organisms that have had genes from other species inserted into their genome.

Genome: The total hereditary material of a cell.

Heterologous gene transfer: Type of gene transfer where there is a transfer of traits from species possessing different genome(s).

Humanistic: Concerning human nature and the welfare and dignity of humans.

Immunosuppression: The prevention of or interference with an immune response, either by disease or drugs. After receiving an organ transplant, a patient must be immunosuppressed by drugs to prevent the body from rejecting the organ.

***In vitro*:** Performed in a test tube or other laboratory apparatus. The term literally means 'in glass'.

Infringements: It is the violation or encroachment of a law or legal agreement, which is someone's right or privilege.

Ingenuity: Skills of invention or imagination. Imaginative and clever design or construction of any article.

Injunction: It is a judicial remedy against infringement of rights, given in the form of court order, which restricts the infringing party to do or refrain from doing specific acts. If any such party fails to comply with an injunction, it has to face criminal or civil penalties and may have to pay damages or accept sanctions.

International application: The application which leads to the grant of a patent in any of the states contracting to the PCT in order to centralize the formalities of filing patent application and avoiding the need to repeat the steps in all countries in which a patent may ultimately be granted.

International search report: The report provided to the applicant by the International Search Authority (ISA) nine months after filing the first international patent application. ISA finds the most relevant prior art documents regarding the claimed subject matter at the international level.

Jurisprudence: Pertaining to law; a system or body of law. It is the branch of philosophy concerned with the laws and principles that lead courts to make the decisions.

Multilateral agreement: An agreement among many nations at one time, which as a result it becomes complicated to negotiate but once signed by all nations, it becomes very powerful.

National patents: The patent whose applications are generally filed at a national patent office to obtain a patent in the country of that office.

Obscure: Not clearly known till now. Anything which is ambiguous or vague.

Parallel import: A parallel import is a non-counterfeit product imported from two or more countries without the permission of the intellectual property owner in order to get competitive prises. Parallel imports are often referred to as grey product.

Patent Litigation: It is a legal process of filing charge against someone for infringement and bringing the case to court. In this process, there is a plaintiff (one who brings the charge) and a defendant (one against whom the charge is brought).

Patent of addition: It is the patent additional to the main patent with a view to improve or modify an existing main patented invention. It can only be granted after the grant of main patent.

Patents of importation: It is a patent granted to an invention that is imported from one country to another. The person seeking the patent may not actually have invented the subject of the patent but may simply have discovered it.

Patents of improvement: It is a patent that adds to the technology of the pioneer or parent patent. It is an improvement over the basic patent.

PCT: Patent Co-operation Treaty is a treaty by which a single patent application can be filed in many countries at once. Initially at the receiving office and later a series of national applications are formed in different countries.

***Per se*:** It is a Latin phrase, usually italicized. It means 'by itself", oneself' or 'by themselves' intrinsically.

Petition: A written document addressed to some official and signed by numerous individuals requesting to do some legal act.

Phytosanitary: The inspection intended to prevent the spread and the introduction across national boundaries of pests of plants and plant products.

Plaintiff: It is the term used in some jurisdictions for the party who initiates a lawsuit before a court for seeking legal remedy. The one who complaints first, who is also known as claimant.

Plaintiff: The party who files the case.

Preliminary examination: The basic examination of the patent application to check that the application meets all formal requirements. The inventions will be classified by their technical content using a refined international classification scheme, IPC (International Patent Classification). After this preliminary examination, the substantive examination, the actual patent examination, may start.

Preliminary Search Report: The report prepared by the officer of the Patent Office after initial study of the patent application i.e. after preliminary examination.

Prima facie: This Latin word literally means 'at first face'. It means something that is self-explanatory or true at first sight itself and does not require any evidence to prove its authenticity.

Prior art: It is previously known or published technology or literature that has to be examined by the examiner before granting the patent.

Priority date: The date of priority is the date on which the patent application either with provisional specification or with complete specification is filed at the Patent Office.

Proprietors: It is the one who holds the legal right to do something. He can be the owner of a patent or a copyright.

Provisional specification: The initial application filed at the Patent Office to specify that the invention is only at a conceptual stage and a delay is expected in submitting full and specific description of the invention. It is filed in order to get the priority date.

Ratified: To approve and give formal sanction, to confirm something.

Recombinant DNA: DNA molecules that have been created by combining DNA from more than one source.

Regional patents: The patent granted within a range of countries. For example, the European Patent Office (EPO) grants patents in some or all countries contracting to the EPC. It allows patents in a number of countries to be obtained without having to process applications in all of those countries. The cost and complexity of obtaining patent is therefore reduced.

Regulatory affair: Affairs that have developed from the desire of governments to protect public health, by controlling the safety and efficacy of products in areas including pharmaceuticals, veterinary medicines, medical devices, pesticides, agrochemicals, cosmetics and complementary medicines, through R&D and clinical trials.

Risk assessment: Examination or assessment of likelihood of possible dangers or risks in a biological material to characterize the nature and magnitude of health risks to human and ecological receptors (e.g., birds, fish, and wildlife).

Screening homology: Screening and identification of those structures that are most likely to bind to a drug target, typically protein receptor or enzyme.

Specification: The detailed description of an invention in the patent document. It includes figures, diagrams, complete description, title, claims, etc.

Stakeholders: A person, a group, or an organization that has direct or indirect share in an organization. It can either affect or get affected by the organization's actions, objectives, and policies.

Statute: An established law or rule. It is an act passed by the legislative body.

Subsidies: Financial benefit given by the government industry or non-government institution to prevent the decline of that industry.

Trans-boundary movement: International trade and germplasm transfer.

Tribunals: Bodies outside the court's hierarchy, but having administrative and judicial functions like the Patent Office.

Wild weeds: Any plant that grows wildly and profusely, especially the one that grows among cultivated plants, depriving them of space, food, etc.

WIPO: The World Intellectual Property Organization, an intergovernmental organisation responsible for the promotion of intellectual right protection throughout the world. It has its headquarters in Geneva, Switzerland.

Xenotransplantation: The term used to describe the transfer of living cells, tissues and organs from nonhuman animals into humans for medical purposes.

Related Web Sites

http://plantauthority.gov.in/ (Protection of Plant Variety and Farmers Right Authority, India)
http://www.upov.int/ (International Union for the Protection of New Varieties of Plant (UPOV))
http://www.ipindia.nic.in/ (Intellectual Property India)
http://www.gian.org/ (Gujarat Grassroots Innovations Augmentation Network)
http://www.wisegeek.com/what-is-patent-litigation.htm (Patent Litigation)
http://www.indianlawcds.com/latest/Current%20Statutes_2005.htm (Patent Amendment Laws)
http://copyright.gov.in/ (Indian Copyright office)
http://www.education.nic.in/CprAct.pdf (Indian Copyright Act, 1957)
http://www.lawzonline.com/ (Indian Bare Acts, Rules & Regulations)
http://www.ipindia.nic.in/ipr/design/design_act (Design Act)
http://www.ipindia.nic.in/girindia/ (GI)
http://www.wto.org/ (World Trade Organization)
http://www.wipo.int/ (World Intellectual Property Organization)
http://www.iprsonline.org/ (India's Plant Variety Protection and Farmers' Rights Act)
http://agricoop.nic.in/ (The Protection of Plant Varieties and Farmer's Right Act, 2001)
http://indiapatents.blogspot.com/2009/06/patent-classification-system.html (Patent Classification Systems)
http://www.kipo.ke.wipo.net/ (Budapest Treaty)
http://www.law.cornell.edu/lii/contact (Legal Information Institute)
http://www.jpo.go.jp/tetuzuki_e/faqs.htm (Japanese Patent Office)
http://www.ipo.org/ (Intellectual Property Owners Association)
http://caselaw.findlaw.com/ (United States Court of Appeals, Federal Circuit)

References

Anuradha, R.V., Regulatory and governance issues relating to genetically modified crops and food: An Indian case study by Independent Consultant, New Delhi, India.

Chakrabarty, A. M., "Patenting of life forms: From a concept to reality", in *Who Owns Life?* Prometheus Books, Amherst, NY, 2002.

Chakrabarty, A. M., "Genetics research and the judicial decision", *Notizie Di Politeia*, 18, 2002, 99–102.

Degrass, G., Alexandrova, N. and Ripandell, D., "Databases on biotechnology and biosafety of GMOs," *Environmental and Biosafety Research*, 3, 2000, 145–160.

Frumkin, M., "The origin of patents", *Journal of the Patent Office Society*, , XXVII(3), 1945, 143.

Gartland, W.J., "Government Guidelines, National Institute of Health", Bethesda, MD, 20205.

Hulme, E.W., "The history of the patent system under the prerogative and at common law", *Law Quarterly Review*, 46, 1896, 141–154.

Johar, A. and Narnaulia, S., "Patenting life in the American, European and Indian way", *Journal of Intellectual Property Rights*, 15, 2010, 55–65.

Malviya, R., *et al.*, "Biotechnology innovations patent: A review", *International Journal of Pharmaceutical Sciences Review and Research*, 3(2), 2010, 131–133.

Pushpa, B., "The social, moral, ethical, legal and political implications of today's biological technologies", *Biotechnology Journal*, 2006, 34–36.

Senan, S., Haridas, M. G., Prajapati, J. B.,"Patenting of microorganisms in India: a point to ponder", *Current Science*, 100(2), 2011, 159–162.

Stobbs, G.A., *Software Patents*, Aspen Publishers, 2000, p. 3.

"An Introduction to Biological Weapons, their Prohibition, and the Relationship to Biosafety" (April, 2002), Paper originally distributed as a Third World Network Briefing Paper in April 2002 at the Intergovernmental Committee for the Cartagena Protocol (ICCP-3) Meeting, The Hague, Netherlands.

"Biosafety and the Environment: An introduction to Cartagena Protocol on Biosafety", United Nations Environment Programme, DEC/Information Unit for Conventions, International Environment House, Geneva, 11–13, chemin des Anémones, CH-1219, Châtelaine, Switzerland.

"Guidance Document for the Risk Assessment of Genetically Modified Plants and Derived Food and Feed" (2003). Prepared for the scientific steering Committee by the Joint Working Group on Novel Foods and GMOs composed of members of the scientific committees on plants, food and animal nutrition.

Index

A

Advantages of patent laws, 9
Allergenicity assessment methods, 178
Animal-derived food allergens, 176
Application for grant of patent, 7
Asgrow Seed Co. vs Winterboer, 216
Atomic energy act, 91
Author's right, 16

B

Bag labels, 104
Biodiversity and IPR, 121
Bioethical issues, 184
  in gene therapy, 186
  in plants, animals, microbes, 184
Bioethics advisory committees, 190
Bioethics and its scope, 182
Bioethics guidelines, 193
Bioethics, 182, 188
Bioinformatics patenting, 122
Biological data, 203
Biological spillage, 210
Biological weapons, 194
Biosafety database, 203
Biosafety guidelines, 160
Biosafety in gene therapy, 171
Biosafety levels, 130
Biosafety management, 164
Biosafety, 129
Branches or theories of bioethics, 183
Broadcasting rights, 16
Bt Brinjal, 218
Bt Cotton, 220
Budapest treaty, 38

C

CAC, 152
Capacity building, 133
Cartagena protocol, 132
Case studies, 214
CBD, 135
CERA, 136
Classification of patents in India, 47
Compulsory license, 90, 111
Concerns and challenges of GMO, 141
Concerns related to animal biotechnology research 141
Concerns related to transgenic plant biotechnology, 142
Consumer acceptance, 189
Containment methods, 206
Convention on biological diversity, 152
Convention on human rights and biomedicine, 192
Conventions and treaties, 27
Copyright infringement, 18
Copyright©, 14

D

Databases, 202
Defender's defence, 97
Delta Pineland Co. vs the Sinker's Corporation, 217
Design act 2000, 10
Design patent, 49
Diamond vs Chakraborty, 214
Different approaches to ethics, 183
Dimminaco A.G., 215

DLC, 154
Doha round, 32
Duties of patent holder, 86

E

Ecological safety assessment, 172
Environmental issues, 188
Equitable assignment, 87
Essentialities of plant protection, 106
Ethical issues in human cloning, 186
EuropaBio, 191
European Patent Organization (EPO), 41
Evolution of patent laws, 21
Evolution of patents in microorganisms, 53

F

FAO, 135, 151
Farmers movement and its NGO, 200
Filing patent application, 76
Food allergens derived from plant origin, 176
Food allergy, 176
Food and safety standard bill, 162

G

GEAC, 154
Gene campaign, 199
Gene flow, 143
Gene patenting, 124, 125
Genetically engineered products, 167
Golden rice, 221
Good laboratory practices, 206
Grant of patents, 74

H

Harward College vs Canada, 216
Health and safety issues, 189
History of Indian Patent System, 22

I

IBSC, 154
ICGEB, 135
Indian biosafety framework, 136
Infringement of copyright, 97
Infringement of design, 99
Infringement of patent rights and offences, 92
Infringement of trademark rights, 98
Infringement, 112
Injunction, 96
Intellectual property appellate board, 74
Intellectual property rights, 1
International regulatory bodies, 151
Invention, 62
ISB, 136

L

License, 88
Limitations of patent rights, 90

M

Major consequences of gene flow, 145
Managing biological waste, 211
Material Transfer Agreements (MTA), 104
MEC, 154
Movement and import of GMOs, 169
Myriad's case on gene patenting, 217

N

National regulatory bodies, 153
Neem patent, 215
New patent regime, 126
Non-governmental organizations (NGOs), 197
Non-patentable inventions, 66

O

OECD, 135, 151
Ownership of patent, 84

P

Patent act 1970, 23
Patent agent, 99
Patent authorities, 72
Patent cooperation treaty, 37

Patent growth, 119
Patent holder, 85
Patent laws, 54, 116
Patent management, 118
Patent office, 70
Patent on plants, 102
Patent specification, 80
Patentability in microorganism-related inventions, 69
Patentable ingredients of biotechnology, 59
Patentable inventions, 63
Patenting biological products, 57
Performer's right, 16
Plant breeder's right, 103
Plant patent, 49
Plant variety protection and farmer's right act, 106
Pleiotropic effect, 173
Practices for biosafety level 1, 207
Prevention of food adulteration act, 1954, 161
Products developed from RDT and their biosafety issues, 169
  bovine growth hormone, 170
  human growth hormone, 170
  recombinant insulin, 169
  recombinant tryptophan, 170

R

RCGM, 154
Registration of plant variety, 109
Regulatory measures for biosafety, 159
Regulatory systems, 150
Restoration of patents, 92
RFSTE, 199
Risk assessment, 130
  for planned introduction of GMO, 131
  for the release of transgenic crops, 131
  of food and additives obtained from GMO, 132
  of RDT products, 168
  risk groups and biosafety levels, 130

S

SBCC, 154
Seed policy 2002, 162
Socioeconomic issues, 188
Sociolegal issues, 188
Special patents, 50
sui generis system (India), 105
Surrendering of patent, 91

T

Technology use agreements, 104
The biosafety clearing-house, 134
The codex alimentarius commission, 135
The international plant protection convention, 134
Trade secret, 12, 103
Trademarks™, 11
Transfer of patent rights, 87
Transgenic animals, 187
TRIPs, 33
Turmeric patent, 215

U

UPOV convention, 113
USPTO, 39
Utility patent, 49

V

Various aspects of assessment and evaluation on GMO to ascertain biosafety, 146

W

Word Intellectual Property Organization (WIPO), 48
WTO treaties, 32
WTO, 135, 151